Scotland and the Easter Rising

Scotland and the Easter Rising

Fresh perspectives on 1916

edited by

KIRSTY LUSK and WILLY MALEY

with an Afterword by

OWEN DUDLEY EDWARDS

Luath Press Limited

EDINBURGH

www.luath.co.uk

First published 2016
Reprinted 2016

ISBN: 978-1-910745-36-6

The authors' right to be identified as author of this book
under the Copyright, Designs and Patents Act 1988 has been asserted.

The paper used in this book is recyclable. It is made from low chlorine pulps
produced in a low energy, low emission manner from renewable forests.

Printed and bound by Bell & Bain Ltd., Glasgow.

Typeset in 11 point Sabon by Main Point Books, Edinburgh

This book is dedicated to the memory and the mind of Ian Bell, who passed into history as this collection was going to press, and whose last words of the piece he wrote for this volume may stand as an epitaph of sorts: 'But silence, as my grandmother knew, falls away in time. Then you must speak for yourself.' We are left to contend with his silence now, to learn from his words and wisdom, and to speak for ourselves.

Contents

KIRSTY LUSK AND WILLY MALEY

*Not only was the Easter Rising an attempt at declaring Irish
independence from Britain, it was also a statement of equality and
equal suffrage for women and the first attempt to assert a Socialist
Republic.*

ALLAN ARMSTRONG

*The words of James Connolly proved to be remarkably prophetic. In
'Labour and the Proposed Partition of Ireland' Connolly warned there
would be 'a carnival of reaction both North and South', if the uk state
was able to impose such a settlement.*

RICHARD BARLOW

*For the Scottish Gael Sorley MacLean, the ghostly attendance of
Connolly is affirmed through his absence and the 'red rusty stain'
forms a nexus of some of the poet's great themes: wartime heroism,
Marxism, and the fate of the Gaelic world.*

IAN BELL

*I don't remember his name being mentioned during the long argument
that preceded Scotland's independence referendum in September
2014... The fact remains that when it mattered most his birthplace
excluded Connolly yet again.*

It seemed important to him that she knew that Connolly was a socialist, not an Irish nationalist. – In this city we know nothing about our real identity, he said passionately, – it's all imposed on us.

The Irish past summons us provided we keep it as tutor not as jailer. The Scottish future can remain one of ideals provided we blunt their agency for hurt.

Acknowledgements

The editors wish to thank the following for their invaluable help with this book: Dermot Bolger, Pat Bourne, Stephen Coyle, Owen Dudley Edwards, Ellen Howley and Gavin MacDougall. A collection like this depends above all on the quality of its contributions, so we also wish to thank our contributors for the range and richness of their submissions and for the passion and enthusiasm they showed for the project. The editors wish to extend a special and heartfelt thanks to Lotte Mitchell Reford and Jennie Renton at Luath, whose heroic efforts in getting this book into print provided the perfect finish to what was a collective effort from the start. Their voices are a vital part of this volume too.

Timeline

1792   Thomas Muir speaks to convention of Scottish societies
        sympathetic to the French Revolution, reading an address from
        the United Irishmen, is soon arrested and eventually sentenced to
        transportation.

1820   Weaver Andrew Hardie is executed at the culmination of the 1820
        Glasgow Rising.

1845–9 Potato blight causes Famine in Ireland and prompts mass emigration
        around the world, including Scotland. Between 1841 and 1851, the
        Irish population decreased by 20% with over 80,000 Irish people
        coming to Scotland over this ten-year period. By 1851 7.2% of
        Scotland's population was Irish-born.

1848   Fifteen thousand Chartist radicals gather at Calton Hill to protest
        the arrest of two of their leaders.

1865   Greenock Irish National Association founded.

1868   June: James Connolly born to Irish parents in Edinburgh.

1882   James Connolly joins the British army, lying about his age. He
        deserts seven years later in 1889, and marries Lillie Reynolds.

1888   Scottish Labour party founded by RB Cunninghame Graham and
        Keir Hardie.

1889   July: Charles Stewart Parnell makes his first political visit to Scotland
        and is made a Freeman of Edinburgh. Parnell makes a public speech
        on Calton Hill.

1890   James Connolly joins the Scottish Socialist Federation.

1891   October: Constitutional nationalism suffers a severe setback with the
        death of Charles Stewart Parnell, after corrosive split.

1892   May: Margaret Skinnider born to Irish parents in Coatbridge.

        November: James Connolly joins Scottish Labour Party.

1893   Nora Connolly, second child to James and Lillie Connolly, is born in
        Edinburgh.

1894–5 James Connolly stands twice for elections to Edinburgh Council. He
        is unsuccessful on both occasions.

1895   First Gaelic League branch outside of Ireland is formed in Glasgow.
        The Pádraig Pearse branch remains active in 2016.

1896	May: James Connolly moves to Dublin with his wife Lillie and takes a job as a secretary of the Dublin Socialist Club.
1902	June: Patrick Pearse visits Glasgow to give an Irish Language lecture on 8 June. It is his second visit to the city, the first being in 1899.
1903	Sean Mac Diarmada, one of the seven signatories of the Proclamation of the Irish Republic, moves to Edinburgh for work. He returns to Ireland before the end of the year. Mac Diarmada would go on to become the contact point for Glasgow Volunteers prior to the Rising.
1905	November: abstentionist nationalist party, Sinn Féin (We Ourselves), is established.
1912	April: *Third Home Rule Bill* introduced to Parliament which would establish an Irish parliament to deal with Irish affairs. The bill is due to come into effect in 1914.
	May: James Connolly proposes the establishment of an Irish Labour Party at the annual trade union conference. The motion passes 49 votes to 19.
	September: Over 500,000 Irish Ulster Unionists sign the Ulster Covenant pledging to block any attempts to implement Home Rule. Anybody who could prove they were born in Ulster could sign: around 2000 signatures from England and Wales.
1913	January: Ulster Volunteer Force (UVF) established to prevent the introduction of Home Rule.
	August: Organised by Jim Larkin, founder of the Irish Transport and General Workers' Union (ITGWU), and James Connolly, thousands of workers across Dublin go on strike for improved conditions and better pay. This event, known as the Dublin Lockout, lasts five months until January 1914.
	September: James Connolly, in prison for his part in the Dublin Lockout, goes on hunger strike.
	November: Connolly, along with Jack White and Jim Larkin, establishes the Irish Citizen Army (ICA) to protect striking workers.
	11 November: First meeting of the Irish Volunteers, formed in response to the UVF in order to protect the Irish people.
1914	April: Cumann na nBan (The Women's League) founded as a volunteer force for women to work with the Irish Volunteers.
	July: 900 rifles are landed at Howth by the *Asgard*. Nora and Ina Connolly participate in their dispersal. Later that day, the King's

Own Scottish Borderers shoot four civilians on Bachelor's Walk.

August: Britain declares war on Germany. Scotland sends 690,000 men to the front. Home Rule Bill is postponed for the duration of World War 1.

September: The 1914 Home Rule Act is passed. With the outbreak of wwi it is postponed for minimum of 12 months. As war continues beyond 1915, the Act does not come into force and is eventually replaced with Government of Ireland Act in 1920.

1915   February: Scottish politician John Campbell Hamilton-Gordon, 1st Marquess of Aberdeen and Temair, resigns from his second term as Lord Lieutenant of Ireland.

May–September: Irish Republican Brotherhood (IRB), a republican organisation established in 1858 to fight for Irish Independence, establish a military council. Believing, with the outbreak of war, that 'England's difficulty is Ireland's opportunity', they begin planning a Rebellion.

December: Having joined the recently formed Glasgow branch of Cumann na nBan, Margaret Skinnider travels to Ireland smuggling bomb-making equipment under her hat, at the invitation of Countess Markievicz. Irish Volunteers from Glasgow are regularly smuggling weapons and explosives to Countess Markievicz and Sean Mac Diarmada in preparation for action.

1916   January: James Connolly joins IRB military council, adding the forces of the ICA to the planned Easter Rising.

February: Conscription is introduced in Scotland. When members of the Glasgow Irish Volunteers are conscripted, they travel instead to Ireland and join the Kimmage Garrison.

April: John Maclean is imprisoned in Edinburgh Castle for sedition, where he expresses support for the Rising.

18 April: Patrick Pearse visits the Kimmage Camp to give talk to Volunteers including the Glasgow participants in the Rising. The Kimmage Garrison is 56 men strong.

21 April: The Aud arrives at Tralee Bay carrying 20,000 German rifles for the Rebellion but goes unmet by leaders of the Rising.

22 April: The Aud is captured by British forces. Sir Roger Casement is arrested.
Eoin MacNeill, commander-in-chief of the Irish Volunteers, issues call to forces not go out on Easter Sunday as planned.

23 April (Easter Sunday): Meeting of the Military Council to discuss

the situation. The Rising is put on hold until the following day.

24 April (Easter Monday): The Rising begins at noon. James Connolly commands military operations from the Headquarters at the General Post Office (GPO) throughout the week. A skilled markswoman, Margaret Skinnider takes position as a despatch rider and sniper at the Royal College of Surgeons on Stephen's Green. The *Dundee Evening Telegraph* wrote: 'Revolt in Ireland – Indications that it is spreading'.

26 April: Skinnider is shot three times attempting to set fire to houses in the nearby Harcourt Street. After the surrender Skinnider is brought to St Vincent's hospital where she remains for several weeks. Despite being questioned by police, she is released on medical grounds and gains a permit to return to Scotland.

27 April: Connolly is severely wounded.

28 April: Charles Carrigan, an Irish Volunteer from Glasgow, is shot in Moore Street leading the charge with The O'Rahilly. It is his 34th birthday.

29 April: Leaders surrender to British army.

3 May: Glasgow Volunteer John McGallogly is court-martialed alongside Willie Pearse and sentenced to death. His sentence is repealed to life imprisonment.

3–12 May: Leaders of the Rebellion are executed by firing squad at Kilmainham Gaol over a nine-day period. This includes James Connolly who, due to his injuries, has to be tied to a chair for his execution on May 12. He is the last leader to be executed by firing squad.

June: James Connolly's older brother, John, dies in Edinburgh and is buried with full British military honours.

August: Sir Roger Casement executed in London for treason. Sir Arthur Conan Doyle is amongst those who plead for clemency on his behalf.

Two hundred Irish revolutionaries are brought to Barlinnie Prison in Glasgow. They only remain a short period of time before being moved to Frongoch in Wales. Part of the reason is the sympathy shown to them by the Irish community and Scottish suffragettes.

December: Margaret Skinnider travels to New York, joining Nora Connolly.

1917 Margaret Skinnider tours America speaking about the Rising and gathering support for the Republican cause. Her autobiography,

Doing My Bit for Ireland, is published in New York. Before the end of the year, she returns to Dublin, taking up a teaching post.

1918   Nora Connolly O'Brien writes *The Unbroken Tradition*, her account of the events of Easter Week, while staying in New York with Margaret Skinnider.

November: End of World War I.

December: Sinn Féin wins landslide victory in Westminster elections. Members do not take up seats in Parliament. Countess Constance Markievicz is elected first female MP.

1919   January: Sinn Féin establish an Irish government (Dáil Éßireann) in Dublin. Two days later an isolated attack on a member of the armed police force, the Royal Irish Constabulary (RIC), sparks a series of violent events and guerrilla warfare which lasts three years and is known as the Irish War of Independence. During this time, Sinn Féin membership in Scotland rose to around 30,000. Margaret Skinnider is particularly active in the War throughout 1920/21.

Emergence of Irish Soviets and revolutionizing of large parts of the country.

1921   July: A ceasefire is declared.

December: After weeks of talks and negotiations, the Anglo-Irish Treaty is signed by Michael Collins and Arthur Griffith. It allows for the establishment of an Irish Free State, although the King would remain Head of State. It also firmly establishes the border between Northern and Southern Ireland. Opinion is polarised in Ireland.

1922   June: Due to fierce opposition to the terms of the Treaty, Civil War erupts in Ireland. During this time Margaret Skinnider works as Paymaster General for the Provisional Irish Republican Army until her arrest on 26 December for possession of a revolver and her subsequent imprisonment. Nora Connolly, James Connolly's daughter, takes over Skinnider's position as Paymaster General until her arrest in 1923.

December: Southern Ireland becomes the Irish Free State.

1923   February: Margaret Skinnider goes on hunger strike in opposition to the signing of the Anglo-Irish treaty.

May: Civil war ends as Anti-Treaty forces are significantly diminished.

1925   Margaret Skinnider is denied her military pension on grounds that it only applied to male soldiers.

1933	The Connolly House in Dublin is attacked repeatedly, and attackers offered illicit sanction by the Church and main political parties.
1934	April: Scottish National Party (SNP) founded with merger of the National Party of Scotland and the Scottish Party.
1936	Communists and Socialists including James Connolly's son Roddy and Scottish MP Willie Gallacher are assaulted at the Easter Parade on 20th anniversary of the Rising.
1938	Skinnider is finally awarded her military pension.
1949	April: As the Republic of Ireland Act 1948 comes into effect, Ireland becomes a fully independent nation.
1968	June: Plaque to commemorate James Connolly's birthplace is erected in the Cowgate, Edinburgh. Official state commemoration also included naming a train station in Dublin after him.
1971	October: Margaret Skinnider dies in Dublin. She is buried beside famous revolutionary Countess Markievicz in Glasnevin cemetery, Dublin.
1999	12 May: First meeting of the devolved Scottish Parliament takes place.
	December: After years of unrest and violence in Northern Ireland, the Good Friday Agreement is signed, signalling a degree of peace in the North.
2014	September: Scotland holds referendum on Independence which is rejected 55% to 45%.
2015	May: SNP win 56 out of a potential 59 seats in an historic result in the UK General Election.
2016	April: Centenary of the Easter Rising. Glasgow City Council is planning a memorial of the Irish Famine.

Introduction: Remembering the Rising

Kirsty Lusk and Willy Maley

Scotland and the Easter Rising is a title that will raise a few eyebrows as well as some hackles. The Rising is a defining moment in Irish history, and much of the focus in the centenary year will be on how it laid the foundations of a nation in the form of the Irish Republic. But the events of 1916 are also of enormous importance for Scotland, for the Irish in Scotland, and for Irish-Scottish relations. Edinburgh-born James Connolly was one of the leaders of the Rising, and one of the seven signatories of the Proclamation of the Irish Republic on Easter Monday, 24 April 1916. Connolly and his socialist politics were shaped in Scotland. Yet Connolly's Scottish birth and upbringing is often reduced or overlooked in accounts of the Rising, as is his early stint in the British Army, because these are awkward facts that complicate the motivations behind the Easter Rising. With conscription in effect in Scotland and the First World War at its height, the Rising and Connolly's involvement in it were figured in Scottish newspapers as acts of betrayal. Ironically, Connolly's father moved to Edinburgh from the 'Scotstown' area of Ballybay, County Monaghan. Connolly's motivation, background, politics and Scottish connections have yet to be thoroughly explored, or widely acknowledged, perhaps because they threaten to challenge official histories of the Rising. The part played by the diaspora is exemplified by Connolly's presence at the heart of the Rising.

We are still coming to terms with the complexity of Irish-Scottish relations and Scotland's role in the making of modern Ireland. That relationship was characterised by Connolly's Clydeside contemporary, John Maclean, in the title of one of his pamphlets as *The Irish Tragedy: Scotland's Disgrace* (1920). Maclean was responding to a moment of crisis and danger, when Scottish troops were being used to suppress Irish aspirations to independence. Links between the two countries are more nuanced, less negative, than the parcelling out of 'tragedy' and 'disgrace' would suggest. Indeed both Connolly and Maclean can be seen as architects of a Celtic communism committed to forging more positive and progressive bonds between these neighbour nations than the forced marriage of union and empire, with its legacy of sectarianism and its policy of divide and rule – 'Scots steel tempered wi' Irish fire', in the words of Hugh MacDiarmid. The Irish-Scottish relationship has too often been viewed through an Anglo-Irish or Anglo-Scottish lens, with the dominant partner in the Union dictating the terms of debate. It is time to reconfigure that debate in Irish-Scottish terms.

The purpose of this book is to draw attention to the Scottish dimension of the Easter Rising, and to explore that dimension from a variety of perspectives. Connolly is obviously the most significant figure connecting Scotland with events in Ireland in 1916, but he is not the sole focus for *Scotland and the Easter Rising*. Another leader of the Rising, Sean Mac Diarmada, worked as a gardener in Edinburgh in 1904. The role of Irish revolutionary groups on Clydeside in the lead-up to and during the Rising is a neglected subject, as is Scottish support for the Irish Citizen Army and the attitude of the revolutionary left, including John Maclean, to the Rising.

Not only was the Easter Rising an attempt at declaring Irish independence from Britain, it was also a statement of equality and equal suffrage for women and the first attempt to assert a Socialist Republic. Women like Coatbridge-born Margaret Skinnider, author of *Doing My Bit For Ireland* (1917), played a key role in the events of Easter 1916. Born of Irish parents, Skinnider declares at the outset of her memoir of the Rising, in which she was actively engaged, 'Scotland is my home but Ireland is my country'. The suffragettes' struggle for women's rights also impinged on the struggle for independence. Skinnider observed that women:

> had the same right to risk our lives as the men; that in the constitution of the Irish Republic, women were on an equality to men. For the first time in history, indeed, a constitution had been written that incorporated the principle of equal suffrage.

Skinnider also mentions the support of the Scottish suffragettes for the Irishmen held in prison in Glasgow after 1916 and suggests that it was this sympathy, along with that of the Irish in Glasgow, that led to them being moved elsewhere.

Had Scotland voted Yes in 2014, it would have secured its independence in 2016, the centenary of the Easter Rising, led by a socialist republican from Edinburgh. Irish and Scottish histories have long been entwined and determined by relations with England and the British state. As that grip loosens there is the prospect once more of radical change and new connections and conversations. This book brings together a range of historians, writers and relatives of participants in order to explore Scotland's role in the Rising and the legacy of 1916 in Scotland today. The essays and interventions gathered here are variously critical, cultural and creative; they are never cosy, comfortable or complacent. History is an open book, not a closed door. The story of the Rising is still being told, and in these pages the reader will find much to ponder, much to discuss, and much to disagree with. This collection challenges official histories of Easter 1916 by reflecting the alternative narratives that were at work within the Rising itself and presenting different perspectives on the Scottish dimension. It is also a collection that reflects on the complexity of Irish-Scottish connections today. These articles are complementary and contradictory, clashing and conciliatory, as they look from influence to legacy, from active participation to cultural commemoration, from Ireland to Scotland and back. The questions of independence and equality raised by Easter 1916 remain relevant today, which is why remembering the Rising, in all its richness and diversity, is vital not just for the Irish in Scotland but also for Scottish civic society as a whole.

The roads towards Scottish and Irish independence have been long and are still to reach their destinations. Scotland and Ireland have a shared history of strife and played a marked role in each other's increasing closeness to independence – as evidenced throughout this book. While the differences between their respective journeys to that goal in the past 100 years have often been figured in terms of their relationship with violence – setting the armed uprising and execution of its leaders by the military in 1916 against the constitutional referendum in Scotland in 2014 – this perspective overlooks the ways in which Ireland and Scotland are connected, their national struggles entwined in a palimpsest where influence and alteration and reaction have been key aspects. It also distracts from the remarkable similarities in the increasing national movement in Ireland of the early 20th century and Scotland in the 21st century. The roots of both can be found in not just nationalist feeling but also a driving urge to change social conditions through self-determination; in increasing gender equality; in youth engagement with politics; in the importance of the media, literature, theatre, speeches and music. In this book there are essays that respond to all these key aspects, the writers bringing their own experiences and understandings to bear on what remains a complex but critical historical event. Opening the debate and raising awareness of these different voices, there is perhaps the first step towards reconciliation, because without open discussion that will never be possible.

To Shake the Union: The 1916 Rising, Scotland and the World Today

Allan Armstrong

ON THE 50TH anniversary of the 1916 Rising, Charles Duff, a former member of British intelligence, who had resigned in 1937 because of Foreign Office support for Franco in Spain, wrote a book entitled *Six Days to Shake an Empire*. The inspiration for this title came from the American socialist journalist John Reed's *Ten Days that Shook the World*. Written in 1919, this book had anticipated a global revolutionary transformation following the 1917 Revolution, triggered by the Bolshevik seizure of power in Petrograd in October.

By 1966, in the last year of Duff's life, and with the benefit of hindsight, he could clearly see the ongoing break-up of the British Empire. This was recognised even by Conservative Prime Minister, Harold Macmillan in his 1960 'Wind of Change' speech. However, in contrast to the thoroughly shaken British Empire, Reed's new international revolutionary order, predicted in 1919, had not come to pass.

Yet no book has been published to argue that the 1916 Rising was 'Six Days that Shook the Union' – the Union in question being the United Kingdom of Great Britain and Ireland. For Reed had his sights set upon the whole world; whilst Duff limited his analysis to the 'dissolution of the British Empire into the British Commonwealth of Nations.' Only Ireland was 'finally accepted in 1949 as being a "foreign country"', which, in its 'rather detached role... was not in the least concerned whether others followed suit or not.'

Duff was making a fairly accurate assessment of the conservative foreign policy of Sean Lemass' Fianna Fail government in the 1960s (with the US gaining more influence at the expense of the Vatican). Meanwhile, north of the border, Terence O'Neill's Ulster Unionist government made no attempt to challenge the UK's own conservative foreign policy. This was also drawing the UK ever closer to the USA, as post-Second World War British governments increasingly accepted their now subordinate position in the global order. Furthermore, Irish partition was by then such an established part of the political and social landscape that even O'Neill felt he could tentatively pursue a 'good neighbour' policy and invite Lemass to Stormont in 1965.

Thus, Duff wrote his book before the tensions brought about in Northern Ireland by the 50th anniversary of the 1916 Rising. His book was also completed before Gwynfor Evans took the Carmarthen seat for Plaid Cymru in the 1966 by-election and fully a year before Winnie Ewing took the Hamilton seat for the SNP in the 1967 by-election. If the days marking the future of the British Empire were clearly numbered by 1966, the future of the Union still seemed secure.

Today, it is widely recognised that it was the 'failed' 1916 Rising, which catapulted Sinn Féin to its electoral triumph in the 1918 Westminster General Election. Sinn Féin won 73 out of 105 Irish seats. Over the next five years, the Irish Revolution was to prise 26 counties away from Westminster control, and to establish an Irish Free State recognised by the League of Nations. This Irish Revolution was very much seen as a threat to the Union.

In order to roll back this Irish Revolution, the UK state refused to recognise Sinn Féin's electoral mandate, imprisoned members of the new Dáil, and launched a ferocious military campaign to suppress any exercise of Irish self-determination. This challenge was only eventually contained through the bloody enforcement of Partition and by providing support to the Free State forces in the Irish Civil War between 1922 and 1923. The essentials of the new British imposed partitionist settlement still remained in place in 1966. The words of a certain James Connolly proved to be remarkably prophetic. In 'Labour and the Proposed Partition of Ireland' (*Irish Worker*, 14 March 1914) Connolly warned there would be 'a carnival of reaction both North and South' if the UK state was able to impose such a settlement.

However, roll forward to 2016, and the Union is being shaken once more. The Scottish referendum campaign, from 2012 to 2014, brought about its own democratic revolution. 97% of those eligible registered to vote; and 85% actually voted, the highest participation rate ever recorded in electoral politics within the UK. The campaign extended from city housing schemes, long abandoned by official party politicians, to small town and village community centres throughout Scotland.

Nearly every official media outlet was on the unionist No side, including the BBC, which fell into a default defence of the word signified by its first initial. The mainstream parties, Conservative, Lib-Dem and Labour, all put aside their differences and united in Better Together to defend the Union.

The unionists were countered by Yes supporters resorting to independent media and online communication. Beyond the official SNP Yes campaign could be found the Radical Independence Campaign, Women for Independence, Asians for Independence, and even English People for Scottish Independence. The new Scottish nation being sought was not ethnic but civic, open to all who choose to live here.

Yet, as in 1916 Ireland, the Scottish campaign to exercise national self-determination was 'defeated'. There was only a 45% Yes vote on 18 September 2014. Nevertheless, such has been the impact of Scotland's democratic revolution that, as in 1918 Ireland, this 'defeat' led to an unprecedented nationalist electoral victory. The SNP took 56 out of 59 Scottish seats in the May 2015 Westminster General Election. Despite some unionist attempts to make a separate 'Ulster' out of the Shetlands and Orkney, even there it was a close-run thing.

So, once again, a panicked UK state, British government and the mainstream unionist parties, drawing on their long historical experience, have all been making attempts to roll back democratic revolution and to imprison it within the conservative and reactionary institutions of the UK state, particularly Westminster.

First came Lord Smith's enquiry to sideline the empty federalist promises made by Gordon Brown during the referendum campaign. Then came Cameron's official Con/Lib-Dem coalition response, which was to further dilute even Lord Smith's proposals. Now, in the aftermath of the May General Election, the new aim is to 'house train' the SNP's 56 MPS.

The likely consequences of such pressures can best be understood when the political and social differences between 1918 Sinn Féin and post-2015 SNP are taken into account. Although Sinn Féin sought the creation of a new Irish ruling class, drawn not from the old Ascendancy, but from the small farmers and Irish professional classes, by 1918, Sinn Féin had become openly republican and was strongly anti-British imperialist.

Today's SNP leadership also represents a wannabe ruling class, seeking to win over Scottish business leaders, local corporate managers, as well as state and private professionals to its project. But their challenge is not so radical as Sinn Féin's in 1918. The SNP government's 'Independence-Lite' proposals accept the British monarchy, and hence the long reach of the UK state's Crown Powers. They also accept Scottish military subordination to the British High Command and membership of NATO, and hence continued participation in US/British imperial wars.

Politically, the SNP more resembles the pre-First World War Irish Parliamentary Party (IPP). Whilst the IPP included sentimental supporters of Irish independence, in practical terms, it sought Irish Home Rule, or what today might be termed 'Devo Max'. It accepted the continued existence of the imperial parliament at Westminster and looked for an enhanced Irish role within the British Empire.

On paper, the IPP offered no challenge either to the continuation of

Westminster or the British Empire. However, a British ruling class, facing mounting economic and military (especially naval) challenges to their global supremacy, was not willing to experiment with constitutional change and come to some new accommodation with the IPP. Instead conservative unionism depended on reactionary landlords and empire-dependent business owners, particularly in the Clyde/Laggan/Mersey triangle. As a consequence, a policy of intransigence was pursued. A civil war was planned to prevent the implementation of the Third Irish Home Rule Bill in 1913–14. Significant sections of the British ruling class welcomed the First World War to avoid this prospect.

Today the SNP leadership confronts a British ruling class more tied to the City of London. Having, with some difficulty, managed their retreat from the formal Empire (as witnessed by Charles Duff in 1966), the City is very dependent on the informal 'empire' of global finance. Above all else, the City wants to retain its leading role in this arena. To do this, it needs the unquestioned backing of the UK state, something all the unionist parties have ensured. However, under the current ruthless global corporate order, any state that is unable to hold its territory together will soon be thrown to the dogs. Add to this the uncertainties brought about by the 2008 Financial Crash and it is easy to see why all the mainstream unionist parties are opposed to any potentially destabilising constitutional experimentation. And that goes not just for 'Independence-Lite', but for 'Devo Max' too.

Up against this, there is a limit to what can be done by 56 SNP MPs in Westminster. This is why Scotland's democratic revolution has also been a challenge to the SNP leadership. Issues have been raised which can not be satisfied through conservative constitutionalist politics, or mild social democratic but still neo-liberal economics. This is why the SNP leadership has put a lot of effort into hoovering up all those Yes voters, and as new party members, and has tried to convert them into cheerleaders for their 56 MPs at Westminster and 64 MSPs at Holyrood.

The SNP leadership is very wary of the radicalising potential of the movement for Scottish self-determination, based on the republican principle of the 'sovereignty of the people'. This is why they have gone back to their earlier support for the liberal reform of the existing UK constitution, based on the principle of the sovereignty of the 'Crown-in-Parliament'. Thwarted by Miliband's rejection of SNP overtures before the 2015 General Election, they are struggling to find liberal unionist allies at Westminster for their 'Devo Max' proposals.

Of course, it was mainly the horrors of the First World War that led to the drift of support from the constitutional nationalist IPP in 1914 to the now republican and anti-imperialist Sinn Féin by 1918. In this respect Scotland today's gradual democratic revolution has been in stark contrast to Ireland's 1916 Rising. The SNP government produced no Scottish equivalent of the 1916 *Proclamation of the Irish Republic,* but published its *White Paper,* based on its 'Independence-Lite' proposals to be negotiated with Westminster. Instead of convening a constituent assembly to embody the sovereignty of the people, a Yes vote would have led to negotiations with Westminster. Selected unionist MSPs would have been brought into the SNP's 'Team Scotland'. The road to a new Scottish Free State was to be opened without Ireland's initial republican challenge, or its subsequent counter-revolutionary clampdown.

Nobody would wish a world war to bring about the radicalisation of the struggle for national self-determination. Therefore, the issue facing us today is whether the political conditions exist which could not only shake but break the Union.

A key component of the 1916 republican coalition was James Connolly's Irish Citizen Army (ICA). This had been born in the economic, social and political maelstrom brought about by the 1913 Dublin Lockout. In this immediate pre-war period, whilst Connolly still lived in Belfast, he promoted autonomous women's organisation in the Irish Textile Workers Union alongside Winifred Carney (as part of the ICA, she was to join Connolly in Dublin's General Post office in 1916). He was also a supporter of women's suffrage, another radical movement of the time.

Furthermore, in the context of the pre-war campaign to win Irish Home Rule, Connolly was central to the development of the new Irish Labour Party (ILP). The ILP was to campaign for independent working-class interests in any new Dublin Home Rule parliament. And, along with the majority of socialists in the Second International, Connolly opposed the ever-growing warmongering of competing imperial states, especially the UK and Germany. Nevertheless, the First World War still went ahead.

Today, people are more aware of the horrors brought about by world wars. Despite the British government's attempts to promote First World War commemorations to ease the way for more military interventions, the memory of such wars and the debacle of post-2003 Iraq make it harder for the ruling class to whip up jingoism. There is also considerably greater support today for social and national movements based in countries suffering brutal imperial repression, such as Palestine.

Women's suffrage was not won in the UK before the First World War. Yet who would have thought, even a decade ago, that Ireland (or 26 counties of it, anyhow) would vote for gay marriage. This has provided a new cross-border challenge to reaction in Northern Ireland, with the potential to cross the

Catholic/Irish and Protestant/'Ulster'-British divide in a way other political, economic and social movements have found it difficult to achieve.

Therefore, a political space is opening up in which we can look again at the 1916 *Proclamation of the Irish Republic*. However, just as James Connolly would have argued, this would not be some nationalist endpoint, but a contribution to a renewed international struggle. This was closer to John Reed's vision than to Charles Duff's. The Union should not only be shaken but broken, showing that Another Ireland, Another Scotland and Another World Are Possible.

The Shirt that was on Connolly: Sorley MacLean and the Easter Rising

Richard Barlow

Anns na làithean dona seo	In these evil days
is seann leòn Uladh 'na ghaoid	when the old wound of Ulster is a disease
lionnrachaidh 'n cridhe na h-Eòrpa	suppurating in the heart of Europe
agus an cridhe gach Gàidheil	and in the heart of every Gael,
dhan aithne gur h-e th' ann an Gàidheal,	who knows he is a Gael
cha d' rinn mise ach gum facas	I have done nothing but see
ann an Àrd-Mhusaeum na h-Èireann	in the National Museum of Ireland
spot mheirgeach ruadh na fala	the rusty red spot of blood,
's i caran salach air an lèinidh	rather dirty, on the shirt
a bha aon uair air a' churaidh	that was once on the hero
as docha leamsa dhiubh uile	who is dearest to me of them all
a sheas ri peilear no ri bèigneid	who stood against bullet or bayonet
no ri tancan no ri eachraidh	or tanks or cavalry
no ri spreaghadh nam bom èitigh:	or the bursting of frightful bombs:
an lèine bh' air Ó Conghaile	the shirt that was on Connolly
anns an Àrd-Phost-Oifis Èirinn	in the General Post Office of Ireland
's e 'g ullachadh na h-ìobairt	while he was preparing the sacrifice
a chuir suas e fhèin air sèithear	that put himself up on a chair
as naoimhe na 'n Lia Fàil	that is holier than the Lia Fail
th' air Cnoc na Teamhrach an Èirinn.	that is on the Hill of Tara in Ireland.
Tha an curaidh mòr fhathast	The great hero
'na shuidhe air an t-sèithear,	is still sitting on the chair
a' cur a' chatha sa Phost-Oifis	fighting the battle in the Post Office
's a' glanadh shràidean an Dùn Èideann.	and cleaning streets in Edinburgh.

(MacLean, 270-1)

SORLEY MACLEAN / SOMHAIRLE MACGILL-EAIN'S 'National Museum of Ireland / Ard-Mhusaeum na h-Éireann' brings together contrasts of presence and absence, past and present, nationalism and socialism, bardic utterance and private reflection, all with a deft economy. MacLean's poem was written in 1971 – at the height of the conflict in the north of Ireland – a year in which the poet 'takes part in the first Cuairt nam Bàrd' ('poets' tour'), visiting a series of locations in Ireland in the company of Colonel Eoghan Ó Néill, and receives a standing ovation at Trinity College, Dublin' (MacLean, xlix). MacLean's visit, combined with the 'evil days' of the so-called 'Troubles' in the North, leads to a contemplation in the poem of earlier Irish history, and the festering laceration of Ulster is connected with Connolly's wounding in the Dublin General Post Office (GPO) in 1916 (see also the 'tormenting wounds / cràdhte, fo chreuchdaibh' in the poem 'Séamas Ó Conghaile' / 'James Connolly', MacLean, 442-3).[1] But how can the 'old wound of Ulster / seann leòn Uladh' be in the 'heart of Europe / cridhe na h-Eòrpa'? Despite its north-western position in (or rather off) Europe, Ulster is the 'heart' of the continent for MacLean because the fate of the Gaels or what Joyce called the 'Celtic World' (Joyce, 124) are absolutely central to MacLean's concerns.

As is well known, Connolly was badly injured by a bullet during the British assault on the GPO, a location where he was commanding military operations during the Rising (MacLean's attention to wartime bodily injury may have a biographical connection – he was seriously wounded by a mine at the Second Battle of El Alamein in 1942).[2] However, the 'rusty red... rather dirty' bloodstain on Connolly's shirt exhibited in 'National Museum of Ireland' contrasts with the strange imagery of orderliness and cleansing at the poem's close: '[t]he great hero is still... cleaning streets in Edinburgh / [t]ha an curaidh mòr fhathast... a' glanadh shràidean an Dùn Èideann' (Connolly grew up in Edinburgh's Cowgate, the son of Irish immigrants). Furthermore, the sacred terms used in the poem – 'sacrifice', 'holier' – effectively frame the Rising in orthodox Pearse fashion, as a noble, sanctifying ritual. Perhaps this should not be that surprising, since even the Marxist Connolly eventually began to conceive of the Rising in these terms. [3] Connolly's shirt becomes, for MacLean, a quasi-religious icon, an object to be venerated. Compare 'Calbharaigh' / 'Calvary', where the poet rejects Christianity in favour of contemplating a 'foul-smelling backland in Glasgow... where life rots as it grows / air cùil ghrod an Glaschu / far bheil an lobhadh fàis' and on 'a room in Edinburgh... where the diseased infant writhes and wallows till death / air seòmar an Dùn Èideann... far a bheil an naoidhean creuchdach / ri aonagraich gu bhàs'. In both poems larger or distant themes are linked to more immediate or local concerns, and, crucially, back to Scotland (here again we have MacLean presenting social and political issues with a vocabulary of disease, injury, and death).

Of course, Connolly is a heroic figure to MacLean not simply because of the Edinburgh/Scotland connection but also through the linkages of class-consciousness and anti-colonial sentiment. The poem also suggests that MacLean regards Connolly as a fellow Gael (although Pearse was the Irish language advocate of that era, not Connolly). Mainly, MacLean's admiration is a result of Connolly's Marxism and the action he took in the April of 1916. As Raymond Ross notes, 'throughout MacLean's poetry... we are confronted with images of, and references to, heroic figures whose moral or political passion is evident through action' (Ross, 97). 'Names like Lenin, Connolly, John Maclean etc. are more to me than the names of any poets' MacLean once stated (MacLean, qtd in Ross, 94). MacLean's radicalism stemmed from the history of his island and his people:

> [h]is great-grandfather was the only one of his family who had not been evicted to Canada or Australia during the Raasay clearance of 1852–4, and two of his paternal uncles had been friends and fellow-workers of John Maclean, who MacLean once described as 'the last word in honesty and courage... a terrific man' (Black, xxix).

As Raymond Ross writes, '[m]uch of MacLean's subject matter, embodying as it does a Marxist outlook, is political' (Ross, 92).

'National Museum of Ireland' also demonstrates MacLean's heavy emotional investment in Gaeldom as a whole. The attention paid to Irish and Scottish connections here and elsewhere in his work comes from MacLean's sense of being a poetic spokesman of a specific people and community. The lines 'every Gael... who knows he is a Gael / gach Gàidheal... dhan aithne gur h-e th' ann an Gàidheal' and the movement from the Dublin GPO to the streets of Edinburgh are part of this. Elsewhere, as Christopher Whyte has written, MacLean 'envisages a kind of utopia, where the divisions between Scots and Irish are negated' (Whyte, 73)[4] and his 'utterance' has 'a public, bardic strain' (Whyte, 157). Similarly, Seamus Heaney has written of hearing MacLean reading his poems in Gaelic:

> this had the force of revelation: the mesmeric, heightened tone; the weathered voice coming in close from a far place; the swarm of the vowels; the surrender to the otherness of the poem; above all the sense of bardic dignity (Heaney, 2).[5]

And yet, as Whyte has written, the ending of 'National Museum of Ireland' 'suggests that the miracle it embodies is dependent on the poem's individual consciousness' (Whyte, 74). The poem is an unusual synthesis of a declarative public statement and a personal, lyrical epiphany. All of this is achieved with a Modernist frugality and the kinds of 'juxtaposition and paradox' (Thomson, 268) utilised in the *Dàin do Eimhir*.

MacLean's 'National Museum of Ireland' is also an amalgam of a form of nationalism (if we can consider Irish and Scottish Gaeldom as a kind of 'nation' – at the very least the poem is an expression of a sort of communalism based on linguistic links and shared experiences of English colonialism) and of socialism, a synthesis not dissimilar to the Rising itself. The Rising can be considered, to some extent, as a synthesis of socialism and nationalism given that it relied on the merging of Connolly's Irish Citizen Army with the Irish Volunteers and Cumann na mBan. Furthermore, the poem displays in miniature the central concerns and influences of the Scottish Literary Renaissance (SLR), of which MacLean's earlier poetry was a crucial part: an interest in national (or Gaelic) identity and national revival as well as Irish intellectual, cultural, and political connections. There was a strong Irish influence on the SLR as whole, especially on Hugh MacDiarmid, who:

> welcomed Irish immigration into Scotland, as sustaining 'the ancient Gaelic commonwealth,' while by 1930 the creation of Clann Albann, 'a paramilitary nationalist organization,' suggested that the Scottish Celticists were bent on following the Irish example to a disturbing conclusion... Hugh MacDiarmid presented a strongly re-masculinised Scotland in the shape of *A Drunk Man Looks at the Thistle* (1926), while praise for the Irish example remained commonplace, MacDiarmid himself commenting that 'Scottish anti-Irishness is a profound mistake'. (Pittock, 84-5)

The linguistic experimentation of MacDiarmid owes a great deal to Joyce, while MacLean owes a debt to Yeats, especially in his *Dàin do Eimhir* sequence. The SLR was also implicitly and explicitly politically engaged, especially with nationalist/revivalist politics but also with socialism (this is in comparison to the English Modernism of Woolf, Eliot, and Lawrence, which tended to be politically reactionary, often overtly).

Alongside the juxtapositions of nationalism and socialism and the personal and the public, there is a strange tension in the poem 'National Museum of Ireland' between absence and presence. The shade of James Connolly somehow becomes more material, more bodily despite his death, the haunting lack at the poem's centre. As Emma Dymock has noted, 'MacLean's poetry is inhabited by many ghosts' (Dymock in MacLean, xli). Similarly, in 'Hallaig' MacLean 'suggests that, given the power of his individual imagination, the deported villagers can continue to be present, on a mystical, magical level' (Whyte, 74). At the end of the first stanza of 'National Museum of Ireland' the Lia Fail, a symbol of power and sovereignty, is somehow magically still residing at Tara. [6] Like the presentation of history in *Finnegans Wake*, ancient and modern collide here and Connolly is supernaturally 'fighting the battle' in the present tense ('a' cur a' chatha'). Brendan Devlin has made the following remarks on MacLean's conception of history (with a dash of essentialist culturalism):

[t]hat the poet should turn so naturally and unaffectedly to an event of almost three centuries earlier is an aspect of the Gaelic mind which often seems puzzling to the Anglo-Saxon (Devlin, 84).[7]

For many Irish writers the Easter Rising becomes subsumed into larger artistic preoccupations or themes: for Yeats it is linked to the issue of personal responsibility, and to his musings on the transformation of transient things into permanent forms. For Joyce, the event forms part of the cyclical histories of rising and falling people and societies in *Finnegans Wake*. For the Scottish Gael Sorley MacLean, the ghostly attendance of Connolly is affirmed through his absence and the 'red rusty stain' forms a nexus of some of the poet's great themes: wartime heroism, Marxism, and the fate of the Gaelic world.

Bibliography

Black, Ronald (Ed.). *An Tuil – Anthology of 20th Century Scottish Gaelic Verse*. Edinburgh: Polygon, 1999.

Devlin, Brendan. 'In Spite of Sea and Centuries: An Irish Gael Looks at the Poetry of Sorley MacLean' in Ross, Raymond J and Hendry, Joy. *Sorley MacLean – Critical Essays*. Edinburgh: Scottish Academic Press, 1986, pp. 81–9.

Eagleton, Terry. *Heathcliff and the Great Hunger*. London and New York: Verso, 1995.

Foster, RF *Modern Ireland 1600–1972*. New York: Penguin, 1988.

Heaney, Seamus. 'Introduction' in Ross, Raymond J and Hendry, Joy. *Sorley MacLean – Critical Essays*. Edinburgh: Scottish Academic Press, 1986, pp. 1–7.

Joyce, James. *Occasional, Critical, and Political Writings*. Oxford: Oxford University Press, 2000.

MacLean, Sorley / MacGill-Eain, Somhairle. *Caoir Gheal Leumraich / White Leaping Flame – Collected Poems*. Edited by Christopher Whyte and Emma Dymock. Edinburgh: Polygon, 2011.

McGarry, Fearghal. *The Rising – Ireland: Easter 1916*. Oxford: Oxford University Press, 2010.

Pittock, Murray. *Celtic Identity and the British Image*. Manchester: Manchester University Press, 1999.

Ross, Raymond J 'Marx, MacDiarmid and MacLean' in Ross, Raymond J and Hendry, Joy. *Sorley MacLean – Critical Essays*. Edinburgh: Scottish Academic Press, 1986, pp. 91–107.

Thomson, Derick. *Introduction to Gaelic Poetry*. Edinburgh: Edinburgh University Press, 1989.

Townshend, Charles. *Easter 1916 – The Irish Rebellion*. Chicago: Ivan R Dee, 2005.

Whyte, Christopher. *Modern Scottish Poetry*. Edinburgh: Edinburgh University Press, 2004.

Connolly and Independence

Ian Bell

THE SPEECHES, AS I remember, were not enthralling. Perhaps that was just me. A 12-year-old's patience for solemn perorations is finite and Edinburgh's Cowgate, that smear of high blackened walls and greasy cobbles, was never a byword for momentous occasions. My memories of a Saturday in June 1968 are of boredom, a badge, and nagging bemusement.

We were in the Cowgate for the sake of someone famous to whom, it turned out, some of us were related. His name and dates were on the plaque they had unveiled. His profile was on the neat bronze and green enamel lapel badge the trades council handed out for a souvenir. That was one part of the puzzle: since when did we know famous people?

Memory's footnote says we didn't really know this James Connolly. Or rather, we had come to know something of him, as a family, just a handful of years before the gentleman from the embassy and the colleague from the Irish Congress of Trades Unions – I couldn't have said which was which – appeared in the Cowgate's dank canyon to commemorate the centenary of the birth.

What did we know? That Connolly was famous, chiefly, for getting himself killed. His reasons were as obscure as the rhetoric on a summer Saturday was prolix. It would not have eased a 12-year-old's puzzlement much to hear that most people in the city of Edinburgh, and in Scotland, shared his ignorance. The great man had suffered the usual fate: he was famous elsewhere.

Beyond a handful, no one in his birth country knew much about him. One part of what they did know was held to be distasteful. In Edinburgh, in Scotland, it was customary – is still customary – to remember the famous figure, if at all, for his less flamboyant deeds. The archaeologists of the labour movement's pre-history would give him his due. Scholars would grant him an honoured place within the Marxist tradition. All well and good.

If you grew up where I grew up, meanwhile, Connolly's life was a folk tale. Just a couple of generations before my birth, for him and others we could name, for old people I knew, existence had been beyond imagining. Livestock had been better treated. The fact that Connolly had achieved literacy was a victory. That kind of story, reliably 'inspirational', was worth telling. The other one, the one with guns, green uniforms, proclamation and executions,

37

was beyond bounds.

It had taken a 15-year campaign to win the plaque by the Cowgate arch. Edinburgh's council had declined the opportunity to send a representative to its unveiling. For the city of his birth and mine, the man who waged war against an empire was best ignored, the better to be forgotten. He was, for Scotland, 'difficult'. Born at 107 Cowgate he might have been, but Connolly was someone else's hero. The Irish – and some were never reticent about saying it – could have him.

None of this counts as revelation. A figure of international significance has been neglected by the country of his birth. Native sectarianism (as we call it) and republican violence; caricatures of nationalism and a labour movement's supposed internationalism; finally the Marxism, rebuking all who followed: contradictions enough to be going on with. Connolly has been too damned difficult. Odd bedfellows have conspired to agree that, what with one thing and another – and with one thing above all – he has been impossible to accommodate.

This is more than neglect. For Scotland, it amounts to willed amnesia. It allows bizarre disjunctions. Fine books and credible figures pile up praise for a thinker, a national hero, the 'hero of the working man'. Mention his name in Edinburgh and ugly noises won't stay beyond the woodwork for long. So history, that property held in common, is erased. The people, to whom properly history belongs, are dispossessed.

The first version of the Connolly plaque was levered from its grimy wall almost as soon as it was unveiled. Loyalists made a wee symbolic gesture of their own. It was, to be fair, a gesture well understood by anyone who took an interest in the matter. Years later, when I was working as a night porter in an Edinburgh hospital, a colleague boasted that he had been in on the (slightly pissed) nocturnal jape. Honour had been satisfied, so he reckoned. He was a staunch trade unionist.

By the middle of the 1960s something of the truth had been prised out of granny, finally. She had kept most of it to herself for most of half a century. There was no mystery in that, not for her. In her book, there were things of which you did not speak. In working class Edinburgh, for long years, an uncle who had taken up arms against the British state was certainly one of those things.

As a child in 1916 she had been chased home from school by street Arabs when news of the execution came. Her own father had been victimised by the council and sacked for his socialistic shenanigans. Yet that father, his brother's mentor in socialism and organised labour, had been granted a British Army veteran's funeral after he died in that same May. Emotions were liable to be confused. Understanding, if sought, was not expressed.

In time, Katie Connolly had married a Protestant. She knew enough about love-in-poverty, but she also knew how Knox's city looked on these unions, and on the Irish. More reticence. A Fenian uncle – Fenian for shorthand – who had died for his treason was reason enough for utter silence. By the '60s, nevertheless, that discretion, that suppression, was becoming hard to maintain.

My father had come across the C Desmond Greaves biography of Connolly in a public library not long after it was published in 1961. Dad had begun, as granny might have thought, to pry a little. As 1966 and the 50th anniversary of the Rising approached, meanwhile, people with questions were turning up at Craigmillar Castle Avenue. By the time Ireland began to prepare its state events to mark the half-century, granny was on the invitation lists and in the reviewing stands. She was rediscovering family and memories. She brought us back a set of commemorative stamps.

There is a photograph from '66. It shows granny in her best hat giving a tall, distinguished looking man what was once known as an old-fashioned look. Perhaps it was something Eamon de Valera, octogenarian president of the republic, had said. Elsewhere in the line there is a fierce looking white-haired little woman who looks as though the photographer has caught her – it would be no surprise – in mid-denunciation. Our supply of famous unknowns had doubled.

Nora was granny's cousin, second child to James. She was also Senator Nora Connolly O'Brien, author, Sorbonne graduate, former correspondent with Trotsky, unbending republican and inveterate activist. She was, further, the garrulous, chain-smoking, sometimes comical and always hard-bitten Nora. After '66, she became an annual visitor. Her cousin, my grandmother, had kept her knowledge of James Connolly to herself for half a century. Nora lived for her father's memory. You could make something of those facts.

You could explain it away as a tale of two countries and two long-parted cousins. Ireland's history, you could further say, was Ireland's business, not ours. When Nora was visiting Scotland in the 1970s, in any case, the Troubles had made a lot of people (though not her) a little circumspect. The emblematic fact remains that granny had spent her life saying nothing about James Connolly; Nora talked of little else.

Yet one issue could induce reticence in the senator, too. Memory mattered more to her than anyone I have ever met, but the uses to which memory are put mattered too. Sitting by Scottish firesides, joking with grandad (whom she adored), scattering ash as she stabbed the air, Nora hated to admit that her father had been born in Edinburgh.

Given half a chance, she preferred the old myth of a birthplace on a Monaghan farm. She would not even concede – never in my hearing, at any rate – that she herself had been born in Edinburgh, in a Lothian Street tenement. It was of profound importance to Nora that her father, Ireland's hero, had been born on Irish soil.

No doubt she remembered some of the jibes he had once endured because of his Edinburgh accent. No doubt there were old bruises. But in this her socialism succumbed to ancient fictions. Some notion of authenticity and nationality lingered to the last. For her, where Connolly's venerated memory was concerned, neither the well-established, irritating facts nor the internationalist rhetoric mattered.

Another little metaphor. In this piece of history, they accumulate. So Scotland chooses to forget James Connolly while Ireland holds him in the vice of approved memory. So a niece stays silent while a daughter prefers to misremember. So two women are born in Scotland to an Irishness, refused or embraced, that sets confused echoes sounding down the years. Then there's the Scot, Connolly himself, who approaches his death knowing that no comrade in Scotland, Britain, America, or Europe will remember what is fundamental to him: he's Irish.

I don't remember his name being mentioned during the long argument that preceded Scotland's independence referendum in September 2014. You could call that odd, given all he wrote, said and did, but only if you know nothing about the Scots, their complications, and their complicated attitudes towards an independent Ireland. The fact remains that when it mattered most his birthplace excluded Connolly yet again. And Edinburgh, city of 'snobs, flunkeys, mashers, lawyers, students, middle-class pensioners and dividend hunters', voted No overwhelmingly.

Was Ireland's republic ever an example to those who voted Yes? Sometimes, in general terms, in the agreed, bland, consensual terms of modern European nationhood. Anything else, like Connolly himself, was too damned difficult, liable to start a fight, and better avoided. Stalwarts of the Labour Party in Scotland, otherwise capable of admiring the man to bits, certainly found nothing to say about him when they were damning atavistic nationalism and advertising their credentials as socialists and internationalists.

Equally, the Yes campaign made nothing of his name. Many of the younger activists had never heard of him, of course. The Scottish National Party is meanwhile leery, for tangled historical reasons of its own, of Irish examples in general and James Connolly in particular. The willed amnesia inflicted where he is concerned is part of a wider forgetting, in any case, in these family matters. Scotland and Ireland resemble a pair of cousins with a habit of misremembering old truths.

When we had our vote a misrepresented nationalism collided with a Labour Party defending (so it said) an internationalist ideal. I do not maintain that Connolly reconciled socialism and nationalism just by getting himself killed. By the end, there were plenty of contradictions he left unresolved. Nevertheless, the neglect of his memory is also the neglect of certain other memories. In September 2014, Scotland was the poorer for forgetting.

Once upon a time in Europe, a pair of ideals, socialism and nationalism, were not everywhere inimical, or regarded as such. Once upon a time, James Connolly seemed to assert that internationalism without an acknowledgement of national identity is a forlorn, empty gesture. In the 21st century, in any case, class politics has ceased to be a simple (or simplistic) refutation of nationalism. Connolly's argument, unfinished as it may be, can no longer be dismissed as an atavistic spasm.

Back in 1968, even the idea that Scotland would ever contemplate independence would have sounded like one of the dafter jokes. Few spoke seriously of such a thing. James Connolly was just another shunned idealist, another of those lost leaders who had wasted his time and his life on foolish causes. Silence at home was his reward. But silence, as my grandmother knew, falls away in time. Then you must speak for yourself.

A Terrible Beauty

Alan Bissett

AULD ALFRED'S PUT Hi Ho Silver Linin on the jukebox an it's a classic an at, usually gets me on ma feet for a wee shimmy aboot. No the fuckin day but. Heid's loupin. Knew ah shoulday nipped it eftir tannin pint number six last night – naw, Gordon Cage Esquire hadtay bring the voddy aff the bench. Never mind the grape an the grain whit aboot the grain and the fuckin tattie! Nae government warnins aboot that.

No fae that shower.

Even the sunshine ootside's a pain in the cunt – *too* bright man like a Sunny D advert or sumhin. John's wipin the bar an keeps lookin up at me aw worried, zif ma heid's a big rotten pumpkin aboot tay faw aff ma shooders. He points at the telly. Cage, he goes.

Erray is the fat cunt. Eck. Geen it the whole The Scottish People cerry-oan, then dane that smug smirk ay his. Ah'll fuckin Scottish People ye.

We are the People.

Been in the toon centre? John goes, eyebrow gon up like at.

Aye man, ah goes. Place is crawlin wi them. Uncalled for.

Watch them scatter the morra, he goes. Way hame greetin.

Ah just grunts. The morra? The morra John? The morra Scotland could be independent and *me* and *you* and *him* – ah points at auld Alfred sittin in the corner wi his dug, starin intay space, pint gawn flat in frontay him – there's *nane* ay us'll be fuckin British. Too late the morra bud.

Ah'll eywis be British, John goes, zif at's at, zif he's the authority oan the matter and no the fuckin constitutional lawyers.

Whit aboot you, auld yin? Ah shouts ower an Alfred wakes fae his dwam like ahv scaled a drink oan him.

Whit's that Cage?

Scotland votes Yes the day we'll still be British?

He coughs an shuffles aboot oan his seat. Can hear the rusty cogs in his brain turnin. Proberly a while since he's hadtay hink aboot sumhin other than the gee-gees or the Bears or Hi Ho Silver fuckin Linin. Even his wee dug looks up at me, like he's geen the matter some thought.

We'll still live on the island Britain but, he goes. We'll still be British in that respect.

John snorts, then glances at me.

Just statin the fact, goes Alfred, rubbin his dug's neck.

Dinnay geez it, ah says. He's forgettin sumhin. We might be *oan* Britain, Alfred, but we'll no be *in* Britain, know whit ah'm sayin?

He just shrugs. Unaware ay basic fuckin realities. Then sumhin occurs tae me. Turns roon oan ma stool so ah'm facin him full-oan.

Ye voted the day, Alfred?

Ah did, aye. Course ah did son.

He lifts his pint tay his lips an looks up at the telly. News has moved ontay David Cameron's big spam face. He's anither cunt, but still prefer him tay El Presidente Eck.

And?

Alfred sets his pint back doon an there's foam on his lips.

And whit?

Ah looks at John ziftay say fuck's wi him? John just smiles an shakes his heid but sumhin aboot this makes me hink he knows sumhin ah dinnay. Turns back tay Alfred. It's clickin intay place noo, sure it is.

And how did ye vote?

The auld boy disnay even blink, just frowns like fuckin De Niro or some cunt.

Ah voted Yes.

Err it is. Right, ah goes, tryin no tay gie him the satisfaction ay showin him how riled ahm are aboot this, aboot him betrayin Queen an country like this, him wi the cheek tay sit in a Rangers bar wi Her Majesty's face above it an Sandy Jardine's signed jersey fae 1978 behind it, an a framed Davie fuckin Cooper testimonial programme mounted on wannay its waws, and a Union Jack flyin ootside, naw. Ah'm no geen the auld cunt the pleasure. But if he wants tay believe in fairy stories aboot a land ay milk an honey eftir we've voted for Eck's mad sche-

Ah voted No, goes John, an even though ah'm well aware he's bein a sook, ah'm still relieved ah'm no oan ma Jack Jones.

Each tay their ain, is aw Alfred gets fae me.

Exactly son, he goes. It's a democracy.

Ah take a swig fae the Irn Bru that's gontay work on ma hangover – although it's only at the erectin scaffoldin stage – an dinnay add the obvious: it'll no be a fuckin democracy wance the SNP have got their feet under the table ay an independent Scotland. They'll no fuckin stoap til we're aw salutin statues ay Eck an learnin Gaelic, an them that refuse'll be rounded up intay Hampden Park an gored wi fuckin bayonets.

Nazi cunts.

Then he comes oot wi it. Comes right oot wi at and ah havetay leave. Ah havetay actually get aff ma seat, feenish ma Irn Bru an get ootay there afore it becomes an international incident or sumhin. He goes:

It's got nuhin tae dae wi the Rangers son.

Dunno whit makes me needtay dae it but ah needs tay dae it. Gets on the subway at Govan an heads intay the toon. Let's see whit this aw looks like *heid oan*. Like if ye're feartay spiders they get a big tarantula tay sit oan yer haun, whitsit cawed – aversion therapy. Aye ah've got an aversion awright. Let's see whit these cunts have done tay Glesga. *Oor* Glesga. Second city ay the fuckin Empire an at, wrecked by scroungin Paddys wance upon a time, noo blighted by Nationalist bigots.

The subways nice an cool eftir the brightness ootside the boozer, an ma hangover hauds its wheesht. Even the train rattlin aboot's kinday nice an ah starts tay feel a bit snoozy.

Ma faither usedtay take me tae the gemmes oan this train. Me sittin oan ma hauns lookin roon at aw the Bears. Big men. Real men. Rangers men. Could feel it even then. The songs startin, the feet stampin an me bein feart at first – wha widnay be? – but then ah looks up at ma Da an he's smilin an his fit's poundin tay an he's geen it

> Follow, follow, we will follow Rangers.
> Up the Falls, Derry's Walls, we will follow on.
> Dundee, Hamilton, fuck the Pope and the Vatican.
> If you go to Dublin we will follow on!

an ah hadtay join in. Couldnay help it. Some ay the guys seen me singin along, gettin hauf the words wrang, they starts clappin an cheerin but. The wee man! Gon yersel! Minds wantin tay feel that forever.

Hame.

Accepted.

Yer ain kind.

When he wis in the hoaspital at the end, coughin the blood oot his lungs, it wis aw we had left tay talk aboot. Truth be telt, he wis a bitter man. Ah'd be sittin err nextay his bed haudin his haun but, an he'd croak oot Whit wis the Rangers Celtic score son?

We won Da. Two nil.

An he'd roll ower, totsey smile on his face, for a few seconds feelin nae pain.

At Hillheid twa teenage lassies wi Yes badges get oan. Wee saltires paintit

oan their cheeks. They're laughin awa. Cannay be much aulder than ma
Chelsea. She's at her mithers. Wish she was wi me the night, so we can stey
up an watch the vote comin in, watch Eck gettin his big fat dreams crushed
under a resoundin NAW, then have a boogie roond the room tay Taylor Swift
or Wan Direction or whitever it is she's intay the noo. Mibbe even let her have
a wee drinkay wine.

Fine wine! Heh.

Ah looks at the lassies: their hair aw done up for the day, their trainers
aw shiny new, the daft hope spillin oot their faces every time they laugh. Feel
sorry for them. They dunno ony better, dae they.

The fuckin parents but.

Soon as I gets oot at Buchanan Steet ah feels it: it's in the air. Hingin there
like a smell. The city reeks ay Yes. It's like they've fuckin tane ower awready,
aw streamin intay George Square. Boys in Scotland tops. Auld yins wi tartan
ower their shooders. Student types flyin Lion Rampants. Wifies wi Saltires
oan their mugs like in that stupit Mel Gibson film. Thoosands ay them.

Ah strides past Queen Street, heid nippin again, an even the Gaelic sign
ootside the station bugs ma tits. *Glahschu*. Wha even caws it that but. It's
Glesga, ya choobs. *Gles. Ga.*

Sun's hammerin doon an ah stauns there in the middle ay George Square,
takin it aw in – the flags wavin an the bagpipers giein it laldy. Then some
fucker starts playin Loch Lomond on their phone an it spreads through the
square. Whit, we at a fuckin weddin? An they're *smilin* aw dippit like. Whit
they smilin aboot? They've nae idea if they've even won or no. There's a
memorial in this square tay British soldiers wha died for these cunts FREE-
DUM an dae they even care? Pissin on the memory, that's whit this is. Gled
ye're no here tay see it, faither, the city that ye loved so much gawn aff its
Berwick-upon-Tweed. It's like the centre ay the plughole an the rest ay Britain
– aw that pride an history an defiance – is just swirlin doon intay it an they're
aw celebratin as it drains awa.

That's when ah sees them.

Twa cunts wi Celtic taps oan. Airms roond each other grinnin as they sing
along tay Loch Lomond. Proberly fullay Buckfast. Or drugs. Chancers like
that we'd end up chuckin money at in an independent Scotland. Wannay
them's haudin up an Irish tricolour, the ither yin wavin a flag wi the face ay
some auld Fenian oan it. JAMES CONNOLLY it says oan the flag above the
cunt's face. EASTER RISING 1916 it says aneath it.

Nuhin tae dae wi the Rangers, Alfred, aye?

Grievance-hunters like the SNP are a natural fit for that shower but. They
can greet the gither aboot the evil Brits an rip the pish oot the Forces. Oor

Boys wha stood up against Hitler an even noo spread peace throughoot the world. A rage like ah've never felt afore siezes me. The disrespect. The en-fuckin-titlement. Oan the verge ay tears an for some reason ah just want ma faither tae haud ma haun and tell me everyhin's gonnay be awright, like when ah wis a bairn an we watched a film an the goodie's takin a poundin aff the villains, an he'd see that ah looked feart an he'd say Dinnay worry Gordon son, the gid guys eywis win.

But aw Da, is it true is it true is it true?

Ah'm a bawhair awa fae chargin right ower tae the pairay them, grabbin they fuckin flags aff them an stuffin them doon their mouths, pointin tay the war memorial and screamin That's whit heroes look like, ya ungrateful Mick bastarts! But then ah hears it, small an still ahind me

Da?

Turns roon an there she is: Chelsea. Scotland flag paintit oan her face. Starin at me. Whit ye daein here, Da?

It's like the world doesnay even make sense onymair. Like everyhin that held it the gither has dissolved intay chaos an terror.

Naw, hen. No you tae.

Whit d'ye mean, Da?

It's her mither. Has tae be. Saft-minded an saft-hertit, eywis wis.

Whit's she said tae ye, Chelsea. Ye cannay listen tay her, ah mean like she means well hen, but yer Ma she's... she doesnay understaun aboot –

Da, says Chelsea. This is the best experience ay ma life. Look at it. Scotland's wakin up, Da. *Scotland's wakin up!*

Every word's like a tattooist needle on ma skin. Ma mooth's went dry. Ma hangover's poundin poundin poundin wi the rhythm ay Loch fuckin Lomond, the Gaelic bit that makes everybody link airms an jump up an doon an it's just me an Chelsea staunin still in the middle ay this madness, like we're meetin for the first time. Ah seizes oan sumhin.

See this pair, ah goes, pointin ower at the Taigs, aff their face an fawin aboot. See whit side ye're on here, hen?

She looks ower at them but it doesnay seemtay bother her. Da it doesnay mean ah don't love the Rangers, but it's no aboot that. It's aboot *Scotland*. Dae ye no get it?

It's her that doesnay get it. They've goat tae her. Their brainwashin.

Oh ma lassie, c'mere. Opens ma airms an she comes intay them, but there's a stiffness aboot the wey she hugs me. No like when she wis a wean, when she'd jump up at me an ah'd swing her in the air roon an roon an her giggles floatit through the room an ah'd never felt so much love, like ma hert wis burstin wi it, an nuhin wid ever be bad again.

Ah'd better go Da. Gontay a victory perty wi Danielle an Jodie. See ye the morra but?

Aye hen.

Wannay her pals takes her haun an pulls her intay the crowd, beamin, her wee fingers wavin at me. Same wey they did when she disappeared intay her Primary One class that day.

Dinnay worry Da. Everyhin's gonnay be awright!

Pushes on through the square, haulin folk oot ma road. Ma heid feels like it's aboot a fit wide. Nae cunt better start. There's a few Rangers tops crowded ootside the cooncil buildins, wi some ither folk wavin Union Jacks. Thank fuck. It's like an oasis ay sanity in the distance. Heads ower tay them. Polisman sees me approachin an hauds up his hauns, but ah'm like – ah'm wannay them, officer. No wantin nay trouble. Polis cunt takes a couple ay seconds tae appraise me then lets me in. Straight awa ah feel mair relaxed. Notice a couple ay they Britain First cunts that sell their shite ootside Ibrox. Nae time for they fascist fuckers, gie the club a bad name an at, but among aw this even they feel like a port in a storm. Couple ay them look at me an nod.

Awright Cage!

Turns roon an it's Eric Sharp. Season ticket holder. Sometimes meet up wi him eftir the gemmes. Welder. Gid cunt.

Whit ye make ay aw this? he goes. Actin like they fuckin own the place an at.

Ah just grunts and tells him aboot Auld Alfred's patter in the pub earlier.

Aw that's a shame, ah like that auld boay. Suppose some folk are just getting caught up in the hype but. See the Jungle Jims?

Aye, ah goes. Pathetic. Ah mean, whit point they tryin tae make wearin Celtic taps the day, ih?

They'll piggyback oan anyhin, goes Eric. Liverpool fans must've chucked them.

Aye, well they wantay make it sectarian, we'll make it fuckin sectarian.

Chelsea. Ma wee lassie. That's whit these nationalist cunts've done – divided the nation. Turned faimly against faimly, neebor against neebor.

Eric's like Ah saw wannay they SNP cunts oan the telly earlier, geen it aw this Festival ay Democracy pish. Carnival atmosphere. Thought haw pal, caw it for whit it is. It's a rebellion. An uprisin.

No that these polis cunts are bothered, ah goes, gesturin tay the boays in blue scannin us – *us!* – for trouble.

Haw, shouts Eric. PC Plod! Twa thoosand folk that wey an yese are bothered about 20 ay us!

Police Scotland but, ah minds him. SNP creation. Salmond's fuckin stormtroopers.

Then Eric lowers his voice an leans in. Hing is, Cage. Reckon *they're* gonnay clear this square the morra? Naw, mate. It's gonnay be left tae the People. As per.

Ah hear ye, mate. Ah hear ye loud an fuckin clear.

Better text Chelsea the night an tell her tae make sure she's no here the morra. She might be wannay thaim noo but ah couldnay forgive masel if onyhin happened tay her. Just couldnay.

Aye, ah says tae Eric, lookin oot at the forest ay Saltires, aw ay them oblivious tay the war memorial staunin proud an true in their midst. Britain. Earth's greatest democracy. A beacon ay light in a world ay darkness.

These Nationalist cunts've learnt fuck all fae the Taigs. They want an uprisin? Aye well, we'll show them whit happens. Fuckin shair we will.

Who Fears to Speak?

Joseph M Bradley

Remembering

THE EASTER UPRISING of 1916 stands as a dramatic and outstanding event representing a partial-culmination of centuries of conflict between and within the islands of Great Britain and Ireland. The insurgency was also important in terms of contemporary European history and a marker for a range of future anti-imperialist endeavours around the globe. The particular flame set alight in 1916 also preceded subsequent events in a national struggle with a variety of economic, social, ethnic, cultural, political, military and moral constituents.

In numerous cemeteries in Ireland you can see a sprinkling of graves of people killed during past centuries as a result of Ireland's historical anti-imperialist struggle. In addition, many larger graveyards have Republican plots, explicit reminders of those who have participated in active, sometimes military, service campaigns against the perceived forces of British occupation, division and domination. In Belfast's Milltown Cemetery, many from County Antrim are particularly remembered in a seamless line drawn between those fighting 'the cause' in the distant past and those who have been killed or have died in more recent decades. Such memorials fear not to speak of the fight for liberty on the part of the United Irishmen 1798, Robert Emmet 1803, the Fenians 1867, the IRB of Easter 1916, or struggles of more recent times.

Colonialism in Ireland

Scots have had a decisive role in the Irish-British past and present national, ethnic and religious conflict. After all, it was in the main from Scotland in the 17th century that tens of thousands of Protestants were planted in Ireland's conquered Ulster Province under terms that allowed them, for the benefit of the British Crown, Government and Military, to acquire land and power and to forthwith dominate and control the remaining native Irish Catholics in religious, cultural, economic, military and political terms. Native Irish Catholics 'were driven off their land and forced to starve or emigrate [many to the western part of the Province where land was poorer and often hilly]'.[8]

Historian ATQ Stewart believes that 'the core of the Ulster problem is the problem of the Scots'.[9] Graham Walker concurs that 'the problem of the Scots is central to any analysis of Ulster or Irish history'.[10] Further, Ronald Kowalski notes 'Scots soldiers came to play a prominent and at times savage role in the army of Empire'.[11] The planted English and Scottish communities in Ulster also gave birth to Orangeism, an ideological, political, cultural and religious force that has profoundly impacted on Irish-British history and which has amongst its identities today, the memory and celebration of Ireland's colonial conquest. Many Ulster-Scots (Scotch-Irish) settlers also went on to have a significant impact on the expansion of Empire in North America while others returned several generations later to Scotland. As soldiers, administrators, planters and colonial elite, Scots were at the forefront in building and sustaining the British Empire.

The Relevance of Historical Knowledge and Understanding

As William Faulkner said: 'The past isn't dead and buried. In fact, it isn't even past'. It is in such a context it can be recognised that in recent decades Scots soldiers have played a prominent role in Ireland's/Britain's northern 'Troubles'. The Royal Scots and Black Watch were at the heart of events which led to the enforcement of an impromptu curfew on Belfast's Lower Falls Road in 1970 when four civilians were killed by the British Army, at least 78 civilians and 18 soldiers wounded and 337 people arrested. This critical event is popularly thought to have altered many Catholic and Irish nationalist minds regarding the potential role of the British Army in protecting their homes in the face of Loyalist attacks and as defenders of peace rather than as major contributors and originators to re-emerging issues which were to lead to around 3,000 deaths over the next 25 years.

Not long after the Falls Curfew two sergeants from the Argyll and Sutherland Highlanders were found guilty of stabbing to death two Catholic men on a farm at Newtonbutler in County Fermanagh. The Black Watch was regarded by many Irish nationalists as amongst the most oppressive in the British Army. During the Troubles, while on frontline duties in the fight against militant Irish Republicanism the regiment was accused of killing 12 innocent civilians during 11 tours of duty. In 2015 *The Herald* newspaper noted that dissident militant republicans (working against the Peace Process) had exploded a device in County Down near the headquarters of MI5 'within a sprawling complex, which houses Scottish soldiers as well as the secret service': this report reflecting the continued presence of Scottish/British soldiers within barracks in the north of Ireland even during a significantly demilitarised 'peaceful' period in the north of Ireland.[12]

In 1914, nearer the events of the Easter Uprising, in preparing for rebellion Irish nationalists attempted to import arms. As the guns passed along the banks of the River Liffey at Bachelors Walk Dublin, a few hundred yards from the GPO, scuffles and stone throwing led to the King's Own Scottish Borderers firing on the crowd, killing three and wounding, including by bayoneting, more than 30. Scottish soldiers in the British Army were involved in suppressing the Rebellion of 1916 and experienced action in the subsequent years of the Irish War of Independence, when the Lanarkshire and Aberdeen areas alone provided almost 10% of all Black and Tans during the post 1916 phase of the Irish struggle for liberation. Although latterly Scottish soldiers have killed and been killed elsewhere, notably in Afghanistan and Iraq, none have killed or been killed in Ireland since the 1990s Peace Process began.

Like many countries Scotland/Britain continue to be significantly military societies. This is evident in the ongoing recruitment campaigns through the popular media and in schools in an effort to replenish the ranks of the state's armed forces. Though less explicitly contributing to recruitment and a romanticising of soldiering, playing a part in recent years has been the popularity of theatre production Black Watch, a play intensely promoted by the Scottish Government and the country's popular media. Likewise celebrations and commemorations around Armed Forces Day, televised Royal Wootton Bassett barracks funeral ceremonies and hundreds of events focused on wearing and displaying the red poppy to remember, amongst other things, Britain's war dead. For the Scottish Black Watch regiment alone the wearing of a poppy can signify action in World Wars I and II, battles in Egypt, Portugal, Spain, Waterloo, Crimea, the Boer War, France, Korea, Burma, Kenya, Syria and Mesopotamia (the area in and around modern Iraq). Critically with cause for disquiet among many members of the Irish diaspora in Scotland, such commemorations include football games. When these have involved Celtic football supporters, a significant number have protested and objected. The discourse of glorifying the British military forms part of what one observer notes as 'the official Golden Thread mythology'.[13]

However, critically missing from this 'Golden Thread', which forms part of the spoken narrative in the Black Watch play, is Ireland. In this context, a broader inspection shows a dominant overarching narrative historically offered on the part of the British Government, military and media that this 'Irish' conflict represented a war between Catholics and Protestants: and more frequently using modern terminology, a war described as being against extremist Irish republican terrorism. Such narratives can often disguise the reality of Scots/British soldiers in Ireland and how this presence has been frequently disrupted, often violently, by Irish rebellions and uprisings. Rarely has the conflict been understood as one in which millions of deaths, Protestant, Catholic, Irish, British, civilians and soldiers of a variety of types, have ensued as a result of the British conquest, colonisation and partition of the island of Ireland. A significant aim of the insurgents of 1916 was to bring this historical conflict to an end.

This overarching ideological production that obliterates knowledge and understanding of the conflict between and within these islands constitutes a master narrative that reflects an indolent representation of important strands of British/Scottish-Irish relations. This can also function to 'forget' Scotland's significant contribution to military, political, cultural, religious and economic discord regarding its past imperialist activities and their deep and profound, often ongoing consequences. In 2012 Scotland's First Minister Alex Salmond was upbraided by former northern-Irish SDLP MP Seamus Mallon when he attempted to draw a parallel between Ireland's anti-colonial liberation struggle and perceived 'bullying' visited upon Scotland on the part of an overly centralised UK London Government. *The Scotsman* newspaper reported that Mallon suggested 'Mr Salmond should brush up on his history', saying many Scots were members of the Black and Tans, the notorious British militia that gained a reputation for violence in Ireland after the Great War. Mr Mallon said:

> Scotland was part of the bullying that took place in Ireland. People from Scotland were the cornerstone of the plantation of Ulster. I think Alex is a very able performer, but his knowledge of history is a little weak. As recently as 15 years ago, you had Scottish regiments here, enforcing the writ of Britain so, I think I could recommend a good history of Ireland for him.[14]

The use of a false historical analogy is an infinitesimal demonstration as to why very few celebrations (and one reason why this book stands alone) will take place in Scotland and throughout Britain with regards the Easter Uprising of 1916: one of the first significant battles on the part of native peoples against Britain's Empire, later followed by similar uprisings in Africa and Asia. Knowledge and understanding of Ireland, even large scale Irish immigration to Scotland, is virtually absent from the Scottish education system. It might be argued that the Irish have almost become invisible in most aspects of modern Scottish society. Generally, apart from a few exceptions, the Irish or indeed Catholic experience in Scotland is comparatively absent from research, novels, histories and stories in Scottish literature and beyond. Above all else, in terms of an absence of remembrance and observance, the

Irish Uprising was 'against' British imperialism, hardly a matter for most Scots, English and Welsh, or the British state, to celebrate.

Liberation

Few in Scotland have heard of Irish-born Padraic Pearse and English-born Tom Clarke, two of the seven signatories to the historic Easter Proclamation, and seven who form half of the 14 executed by British Army firing squads in its immediate wake. Few in Scotland might also have heard of the numerous second and third generation Irish that fought in the GPO with Glasgow/Lanarkshire, Liverpudlian and London accents, or indeed, any past Irish revolutionaries. Apart that is possibly of the names of people such as Protestant Republican Wolfe Tone (mainly due to the popular music group named after him) and Catholic Republican Sean South (because Celtic football supporters have sung a song about him for more than half a century), two rebels from different eras to that of 1916. The only person who it might be claimed is known by some left-leaning politically minded people in Scotland is James Connolly: more often with respect to his political ideas, activities and writings and not as a result of his 'nationalist' activities in 1916.

As a socialist revolutionary Connolly's writings and his status as a leading and symbolic left-wing activist and visionary of the late 19th and early 20th century make him familiar to some in Scotland. His name is also known because of recent past Republican demonstrations organised by the Irish political, mainly diasporic body in Edinburgh, the James Connolly Society. However, these marches did not attract attention in Scotland for their challenging ideological perspectives, in memory of a man to be remembered, and were rarely represented in the popular media as a protest against perceived British militarism during the recent Troubles in Ireland. They are mainly recollected for their capacity to attract ('cause trouble') attacks on the part of various bodies of Scottish Loyalists in support of Britain in Ireland, and the media's representation of such events as part of a narrative of 'sectarianism' in Scotland. However, for a small number of politically aware or political activists Connolly remains a symbol of their left-wing politics.

For many decades Connolly's name has been revered and remembered amongst the politically minded within the multi-generational Irish diaspora in Scotland – especially the many thousands introduced by the popular Irish ballad group the Wolfe Tones to his deeds and his execution whilst sitting wounded on a chair. Indeed, as an Edinburgh born Irishman a special kinship is often felt towards Connolly (and in recent years Coatbridge born Margaret Skinnider) on the part of such people.

Regardless of perspectives on military actions, whether for or against war styled violence, unrestrained, controlled or contextual, it is not difficult to recognise how the men and women of 1916 saw few other viable options when they became the most recent Irish generation to attempt to liberate their land. The British were viewed by such Irish nationalists as battle hardened oppressors, masters on all cultural and political fronts of staggering levels of propaganda. Not only in Ireland, but in recent decades British soldiers had been in action in China, Afghanistan, India and South Africa, and of course 1916 took place with World War 1 in the background. According to Ewen MacAskill and Ian Cobain, compared to Britain, 'No other country, even those with similarly militaristic traditions, has been engaged [in warfare] continuously over such a long span', since at least the First World War and almost certainly since Scotland and England went into Union in the 17th century.[15] During its history, British forces or forces with a British mandate have invaded, had some control over or fought conflicts in 171 of the world's 193 current UN member states – nine out of ten of all countries. Facing such might it is not difficult to see that a dominant part of the nationalist narrative around Easter 1916 is that those who 'struck a blow for Irish liberation' knew they could not win by military means. This was an action in which a great sacrifice was required as a springboard to future freedom.

Men like James Connolly and subsequently Tom Barry in the War of Independence had themselves been former members of the British Army, possibly attracted by the sense of habitus; gaining employment, a wage, adding spice to a perceived dreary lifestyle, family and local community tradition or compelled by some other reason. Others like Michael Collins, who took part in the 1916 Insurgency and was a significant leader during the War of Independence showed an astute realism and capacity to engage in war against a vastly superior enemy. For others that took part in the Rising itself, like Padraic Pearse, who reportedly didn't fire a shot and was a deeply spiritual man, Joseph Mary Plunkett of similar mould, and many others involved in 1916 and the struggle thereafter, becoming a soldier was a choice made as a result of a range of circumstances – indeed, for many, their reluctant soldiering meant there were few other choices given their analysis of being in an occupied and enslaved country.

It should also be remembered that although in Irish nationalist eyes their country had been historically subjugated, raped, pillaged, occupied and colonised, the British soldiers they fought against in 1916 and thereafter were fellow human beings. Many if not most of them had perceived limited choices when it came to employment and even wartime conscription. Many had been under-educated, bred and shaped in a military society; a state where conquering other countries was seen as normal and a right. Many were undoubtedly men who showed remarkable bravery during the First World War – bravery for some undoubtedly even in the fight against the Republican forces of Irish liberation during 1916. In a spiritual sense, Christians believe that God does not judge soldiers on the basis of the colour of their uniform, but in terms of their motivations and morality, their sense of right and wrong no matter how that has been constructed – if and why they killed and what they sought by doing so. The sense of 'duty' in terms of British soldiering cannot likewise be discounted, the feeling that it is the right thing to do – that is, going to fight for your country in a war represented by Government and a compliant media and propaganda filled uncritical population as war in pursuit of right against wrong.

Arguably, a significant proportion of humanity is led blindingly into war after war, century after century. All wars contain elements of 'terrorism', a word often used today by governments, military and media to say, 'they're wrong, we're right', 'they fight a dirty and unfair war; we fight a clean justified one'.

People can be as genuinely pacifist, tactically pacifist, mildly militant or as militant as they wish or are shaped to be by political, religious, social and cultural influences. In Ireland, whatever the conclusion, many men and women have 'sacrificed' their lives to acquire Irish liberation from a perceived imperialist neighbour – a colonising power that has been the root cause of deep, profound and widespread violence, suffering, famine, desolation, degradation, discrimination and division. In a fundamental sense, such thinking goes a long way to explaining why the men who were executed in the wake of the 1916 Rebellion are so widely admired, by people in Ireland, among the diaspora and amongst many others. For such anti-imperialists, their names are to be remembered with deep and unending pride: Éamonn Ceannt, Tom Clarke, James Connolly, Seán Mac Diarmada, Thomas MacDonagh, Padraic Pearse, Joseph Mary Plunkett, Roger Casement, Con Colbert, Edward Daly, Seán Heuston, Thomas Kent, John MacBride, Michael Mallin, Michael O'Hanrahan and William Pearse. In Dublin's Garden of Remembrance where significantly a wreath was laid by the British Queen Elizabeth in 2014, the names of these patriots are remembered alongside many others that as the memorial garden on Parnell Square says, 'died for Irish freedom'.

'They will never understand why I am here': The irony of Connolly's Scottish connections

Ray Burnett

Once to every man and nation comes the moment to decide...
(James Russell Lowell, quoted by James Connolly,
The Workers' Republic, 13 November 1915)

Introduction

ON THE AFTERNOON of Tuesday 9 May, 1916, shortly before his execution, James Connolly was permitted a visit by his wife, Lillie, and their daughter, Nora. When asked by her father, 'Have you seen any socialist papers?' Nora replied that she had not. Connolly's response was one of perceptive, if resigned, anticipation: 'They will never understand why I am here. They will all forget I am an Irishman.'[16] Connolly's brief but prophetic comment was all too accurate. The reaction to his involvement in the Easter Rising within the leadership of the socialist and labour movement in Scotland was one of disbelief, disavowal or disdain. Any muted expression of support was confined to scattered pockets of the rank-and-file.[17]

From the present perspective of post-referendum Scotland there is a striking relevance in this pronounced absence of 'understanding' within Scotland's organised left. And there is a deep irony when the significance and potential of Connolly's own seminal insights on the building of a radical national-popular bloc are set against the indifference and antipathy of his two closest Scottish left associates – John Leslie and John Carstairs Matheson.

Background

The 'auld toon' Connolly was born into in 1868 had been the heart of subaltern, insurrectionary Edinburgh, the locus of a communal memory, history and legacy of struggle in which its Scots and immigrant Irish residents shared a sense of common cause.[18] Only 20 years before, the Cowgate had been the place where 'a number of clubs regularly assemble to discuss and to mature their seditious and treasonable plots'.[19] Those named after Emmet, John Mitchel, etc. commemorated the Irish tradition; the Wallace, Burns, Muir, Baird and Hardie, etc. of the majority were dedicated to the independent, resistance and revolutionary tradition of Scotland.

The Carrubber's Close of his childhood had housed the secret arsenal of the capital's 'physical force Chartists' on the north side of the High Street where the everyday conversation of the residents was of 'arming and street-fighting'. From the close he would have looked directly over to the 'Political Martyrs' monument dedicated to the memory of the United Scotsmen leaders of the 1790s, led by Thomas Muir whose reading of an address from the United Irishmen had resulted in arrest and transportation. Beyond was the Calton Hill, the radicals' assembly place, where in July 1848 some 15,000 had gathered to protest at the arrest of two of their leaders for declarations made earlier on the hill in support of insurrectionary events in France and Ireland.[20]

The Old Town and Southside of his early life was also the terrain of a vigorous subaltern culture, a legacy that had promoted and sustained a distinctively Scottish identity and perspective throughout the post-Union decades. It was, in Hamish Henderson's phrase, a tradition that always had 'something of the rebel underground about it' in the irrepressible Scots of its everyday discourse, poetry, music and song, the bawdy and the street broadsides, the pulsating, dissident repertoire of subversive song, from the 'rebel' Jacobite to the 'viva la' Jacobin.[21]

John Leslie

This distinct sense of Scottish identity and perspective was acknowledged in the 1880s when England's embryonic socialist movement began to spread out from metropolitan London to the provincial outposts. Henry Hyndman of the Social Democratic Foundation and William Morris of the breakaway Socialist League, the two leading figures, both commented on it.[22] Awareness, however, did not mean approval. The movement Connolly was inducted into in 1889 may have been located in Scotland but the incorporating process of Britification had taken place.[23] Instead of augmenting a developing Scottish left, he was recruited into an outlying branch of London's provincial left, the subaltern 'Celtic fringe' offshoots of organisations that were firmly metropolitan and wholly Anglocentric. Their publications and promotions were prolific and frequent, but the content, policies and ideas were firmly rooted in the history and cultural backdrop of England and an all-pervasive dominant Englishness. The titles tell it all, from Hyndman's *England for All* to Blatchford's *Merrie England*.[24]

Ironically, John Leslie, the dedicated activist, often deemed his 'mentor', who initiated the young Connolly into this movement had also been born in 'auld toon' Edinburgh to Irish parents. Resolutely Scots in speech, with a liking for poetry and song and the outdoors, Leslie also composed several of his own poems and songs in Scots. A regular contributor to *Justice*, the SDF paper, in 1894 he introduced its Irish readership to the importance of *The Irish Felon* and the ideas of James Fintan Lalor, writings that are generally thought to have substantially influenced Connolly. Given his birth in the Canongate, his upbringing in Blackfriars Street and his evident grasp of history, poetry and song, it is hard to believe that Leslie would not have been aware of Edinburgh's own memory of *The Irish Felon,* a short-lived weekly with an avid readership in the Cowgate. Nor, especially if his attested youthful involvement with the Fenian movement is valid, that he was not aware of the city's insurrectionary tradition back through 1848 to its roots in the 1790s. And while Leslie went on to approve of Connolly's efforts to build a socialist movement rooted in the distinctive history and culture of Ireland, there is no sign of an awareness or appreciation of the potential for a similar initiative in the Scotland to which he devoted all his energies.

Connolly, on the other hand, from the earliest of his public and private observations, showed a sensitive awareness of the importance of place, culture and identity for any analysis of the praxis of class and power. In his own early contributions to *Justice*, he demonstrated an intuitive capacity to flesh out how the latter manifested itself in the distinctive social nuances in the profile of the populations of Edinburgh and Leith. Through his subsequent 'R. Ascal' column in the local Edinburgh *Labour Chronicle,* he also revealed an equally attuned ability to draw on the icons of Scottish history and the touchstones of cultural distinctiveness that his readership readily identified with, to humorously deflate the self-importance of Scotland's Liberal hegemony. This is graphically illustrated in an article based on mock defiance of his editor's stricture to write only on local matters, where Connolly invited reflection on a recent gathering of the ruling party:

> At the great Liberal Meeting at Cardiff, the audience closed the proceedings by singing 'Auld Lang Syne'. This world is a vale of tears and suffering. If I had been allowed to even mention this meeting, how I might have delighted the readers of this paper by conjuring up before their mind's eye the truly humorous spectacle of 10,000 Welshmen, in the throes of a desperate struggle with the intricacies of the Scottish dialect, trying to sing 'Auld Lang Syne' and look cheerful. Such are the humiliations we have to undergo at the hands of the Liberal Government.
>
> Oh, for the heroism of Wallace, the genius of Bruce, or wild sweeping sword of M'Gonagall, to avenge this outrage on 'oor guid Scotch tongue.'[25]

A few months later, in May 1896, Connolly and his family left Edinburgh for Dublin. The application of his fertile creative mind to the grounding of his socialist critique of the ruling order would now develop in a different national context. A series of major articles soon followed. The first appeared in Belfast's *Shan Van Vocht* in late 1896, the remaining three in Keir Hardie's *Labour Leader* in Glasgow. Ironically it was in the socialist press of the country he had left behind, towards the end of a sustained critical survey of the social, economic, cultural and political history of Ireland that he concluded:

> The interests of labour all the world over are identical, it is true, but it is also true that each country had better work out its own salvation on the lines most congenial to its own people.[26]

Partly in terms of content, and entirely in terms of method, Connolly's explicitly 'land and labour' approach to the lessons of the past had direct relevance to Scotland. With John Leslie or any of his other early Edinburgh associates, the exhortation to develop a socialist analysis organically rooted in the particularity of Scotland's past found no takers. With the Scottish associate who was to emerge as his close contact and confidant in the next phase of his life, it was an exhortation that would be vigorously rejected.

John Carstairs Matheson

After his 1896 departure, it was John Carstairs Matheson who emerged as Connolly's closest associate within the left in Scotland and until spring 1914 they maintained a close correspondence. A Gaelic-speaking Falkirk schoolteacher of Highland extraction, Matheson regularly gave his greetings in Gaelic phrases, deployed the occasional Gaelic word or Scots phrase. He placed their personal contact within a wider discourse on the Celt and the Saxon, as a liaison of the 'sea-divided Gael'. While Connolly readily responded within this mutually felt framework of ethnic and cultural difference, it was usually in a light-hearted humorous fashion as in his 1903 expression of fraternal support to Matheson in the context of an internal dispute with 'Sassenach' comrades within the SDF:

> Brother, as you go down into the valley of tribulation, among Sassenachs, and other unclean animals, my heart is surely troubled on your account. I bethink me of Wallace and many a Highland wight whose fate may be yours...[27]

Ironically in terms of their private correspondence, if not their public positions or writings, it was the ever-serious Matheson who made the most insightful comment as to how embedded the lack of understanding of the national question was within the English left. Observing how, for some people, 'general principle is a positive curse', only serving as a means to 'save them the bother of thinking, and of studying facts', he reflected on how an ascendant Englishness perceived the lesser nations:

> And as a matter of fact with the average Englishmen, 'internationalism' is nationalism, or Anglo-Saxondom in its sublimest expression. For the nationalism of the Englishman does not consist of thinking of himself and his fellow-countrymen as a nation, but as the ideal types and patterns of glorified humanity. And that feeling exists among English socialists as much as among Primrose Leaguers. Hence the naive surprise that an Englishman manifests when a member of another nation prefers his own ways to his.[28]

The double irony in Matheson's position lies not only in his forceful outlining of this analysis to Connolly in the light of things to come and their very divergent positions in relation to the outbreak of war and its implication. More immediately, it relates to Matheson's stance in 1908 in relation to his own approach to events in Scotland. Having written to Connolly castigating 'the English internationalist' for an application of internationalism to the Irish which meant:

> we shall use the same methods of argument, propaganda and organisation towards Irishmen as are used with Englishmen, no matter how different the former may be in the matter of psychological background created by different economic, social and historic conditions and no matter how ignorant we, the attempted organisers, may be, of the said psychological background.[29]

Matheson concluded:

> Upon my soul, James, I think of all the denizens of the British Isles, we Celts are the only realists on board – the only men who face facts.[30]

However, when faced with 'the facts' of the critical conjunctural moment in Scotland of political and social events surrounding the 1906–11 Liberal governments, it was Matheson himself who preferred abstracted principle to complex and shifting reality. Dismissively informing Connolly of *Forward*, the new paper of the 'Scotch ILP', he castigated Tom Johnston, its editor, for 'treating landlordism and capitalism as problems capable of separate solutions' and supporting the fresh outbreak of crofter agitation and Hebridean land raids:

> (By the way James, you have probably met the crofter-fishermen type – and if so can you imagine more essentially and congenitally individualistic?).[31]

In his own paper *The Socialist*, Matheson was even more scathing. He was aware of this Highland clamour for land from his own family background. But he had given up 'atavistic emotions' in his teens in order to promote 'full class interests' and now:

> I strongly protest against the association of Socialism in Scotland with a backward agrarian movement, and with wildcat schemes for the repatriation of the... rocks of the Hebrides and West Highlands.[32]

And as a new expression of inter-linked cultural, political and social nationalism emerged, in no small part associating itself with radical national developments in Ireland, it was Matheson who resolutely refused to '*examine it and act rationally and logically*'; the very failing he had condemned the English left for in relation to Ireland through the 'prejudice raised by their [own] interpretation of internationalism'. Matheson's prejudice, clearly fortified by the prevailing educational orthodoxies was that Scotland's distinct cultural and political identity had effectively ceased in 1707. And from this perspective, as he conceded to Connolly:

> Some of these Comun nan Albannach, Gaelic Scotch nationalists have got on my top... Anyhow I am in the position of maintaining that while the nationality of Ireland is a thing that cannot be ignored, the attempts to engender the nationalist idea in Scotland is a reactionary piece of damn foolishness.[33]

As with Leslie, even more so with Matheson, it is one of the greatest ironies in Connolly's relationship to Scotland that the activist, organiser, writer, historian and educationalist most aptly placed to promote, assimilate and apply the innovative ideas of Connolly to Scotland's distinct social, cultural and political history as a means of building an organically rooted and distinct Scottish left was so resolutely opposed and in subservience to the very myopia he so lucidly detected in the dominant Britified and Anglocentric alternative.

Conclusion

In the final months of 1915 Connolly wrote a series of articles for *The Workers' Republic* looking back over the history of Ireland's revolutionary tradition to prepare the ground within the movement for an armed uprising. 'In 1848' he reflected, in the issue of 13 November 1915, 'the real revolutionary sentiment was in the hearts of the people'. For the most part, however, the leaders were wanting 'in the essential ability to translate sentiment into action'. Lacking audacity, they were 'unable to take that leap in the dark which all men must take who plunge into insurrection.'[34] In the light of what lay ahead there is a certain sense of the wheel having turned full circle in this focus on the significance of the events of 1848. For this was an unconscious evocation of the 'seditious plots' of the clubs in the Cowgate, the secret arsenal of Carrubber's Close, the insurrectionary memory inscribed on the streets and closes of the Edinburgh of his childhood.

In Scotland in 1915, while not expressing an anti-war position *tout court*, Tom Johnston's *Forward* had been systematically exposing the myth of national, 'we're all in this together', unity. Under the banner of fighting 'The Huns at Home', he exposed evictions by Highland landlords of tenants with sons killed or serving in the army, reported the war-profits in coal, wheat and armaments of industrialists, landowners and farmers and the rack-renting landlords in cities. Johnston also delved deeply into Scottish history to make a scathing serialised indictment of *Our Noble Scots Families*. It was all an exemplary intuitive exercise in how to aggregate a radical national-popular bloc of common cause and shared class interest. Ironically, given the failure of the left in Scotland to realise the potential in the approach elaborated on by Connolly since his early years in Edinburgh it lacked the political agency of a distinct Scottish left to take it forward.

The fact that it was his two closest socialist associates within Scotland, first Leslie, then Matheson, who did not have perceptiveness or vision to draw on what was so lucidly laid before them is one of the enduring ironies in the story of Connolly's relationship to Scotland and its legacy. Connolly had concluded his reflections on 1848 with a line from James Russell Lowell: 'Once to every man and nation comes the moment to decide...' After the Rising, when Connolly had made his own personal decision and news of his execution broke, Leslie was in reproachful despair, Matheson was silent. Scotland's sole open expression of understanding, approval and implicit acclaim of Connolly's decisive seizing of the moment came not from the voices of labour but from Ruaraidh Erskine of Marr, the founder and editor of the radical independence and nationalist *Scottish Review*.[35] In the Scotland of 1916 that was the greatest irony of all.

Anti-imperialist Insurrection

Stuart Christie

I HAVE NO idea how many anarchists, Scottish or otherwise, were involved in the anti-imperialist insurrection in and around Dublin on Easter Monday 1916; what I do know, however, is that a substantial number of the workers' militia known as the Irish Citizen Army (ICA) were inspired by the syndicalist, Industrial Unionist and libertarian socialist ideas promulgated by labour union leaders James Connolly and James Larkin. These socialist republicans may have shared the barricades with the Volunteers of the Irish Republican Brotherhood (IRB) that day, but they did not share their ideology. They were fighting a class war *for* national liberation, not for a sectarian, middle class nationalism. As Connolly warned the ICA just before the rising:

> if we should win, hold on to your rifles because the Volunteers may have a different goal. Remember, we're out not only for political liberty but for economic liberty as well.

There was no 'may' about it.

My family link with the Irish War of Independence/Civil War may sound like the germ of a Ken Loach pitch for *The Wind That Shakes the Barley*: two cousins from rural 19th century Ireland, both devout Catholics – who may never have met – thrown by events and circumstances into an armed social and political conflict in which a terrible irony was born.

John Ring, my maternal grampa, was, technically, English. Born in Salford in 1878, his parents had recently arrived as immigrants in an attempt to escape the poverty and misery of rural life in their hometown of Abbeyleix, Queen's County (now Laoise), Ireland.

Grampa, a dyed-in-the-wool Anglophile, made up for his nationalist relatives by swearing unswerving loyalty to the British Crown during what was, possibly, its most expansionist imperialist phase. I remember Mum telling me that the only time she saw him cry was on hearing the news of the death of King George VI. In 1892, aged 14 (falsifying his age), he signed up in Dumfries with the 3rd Reserve Battalion of the King's Own Scottish Borderers. He went on to fight in the north-east of India around the Khyber

Pass, and in South Africa, and received the Queen's Medal with clasp and King's Medal with clasp for his part in the South Africa Campaign, 1900–02. Discharged in January 1913, he had served 21 years, having completed his military service as Colour Sergeant.

When the World War broke out he was recalled to Maryhill Barracks, Glasgow, as a reservist to join the 5th Battalion of the Highland Light Infantry (HLI), in which he served as Regimental Sergeant Major for a further nine years, training troops for 'The Big Picnic' and other imperialist military disasters such as Gallipoli, Loos, Mesopotamia (Baghdad), the invasion of Russia at Archangel, and Ireland – a campaign he never mentioned.

It has often played on my mind that the men he trained included Churchill's Auxilliaries and 'Special Constables' of the Royal Irish Constabulary Reserve Force, the hated and hateful 'Black and Tans'.

One of Grampa's cousin's, however, Michael Joseph 'Joe' Ring – perhaps the most famous of the Rings – was from the other end of the spectrum. Born in Galway in 1891, Joe's parents settled in Westport, Co. Mayo, in the late 1890s, and when the Irish Republican Botherhood formed the 'Volunteers' in Westport in 1915 – in response to Carson's Unionist militia Ulster Volunteer Force (UVF) – Joe was among the first to join. Aged 23, he was appointed Commander of the Volunteers in Westport, and took part in the Easter Rising of the following year, having formed his own guerrilla flying column, the first of its kind in the conflict.

On 9 May 1916, when the Easter rebellion was finally put down in the West of Ireland, Joe was arrested under the Defence of the Realm Act and interned in Frongoch POW camp in South Wales along with Michael Collins, Arthur Griffith and 1,800 others. Released under the general amnesty of Christmas 1916, Joe returned to Westport where he set about reorganising the local Volunteers and radicalising and training the youth movement, Fianna Eirann, their prospective recruits in the coming War of Independence.

The opening shots of the war in the west of Ireland were fired on the night of 29 March 1919 with the murder of John C Milling, the Westport Residential Magistrate who had tried and sentenced Joe the previous March to six months' jail in Sligo for 'unlawful assembly and drilling'. Martial law was declared in Westport and the military drafted in while the Royal Irish Constabulary (RIC) detained the principal suspects, including Joe, but despite intense investigation and brutal interrogation, no one was ever charged with the killing.

With the formation of the West Mayo Brigade of the IRA in September 1920, under Tom Derrig, Joe Ring was appointed OC of the Westport district battalion area. A few months later, in November 1920, the arrival in the area of the 'Black and Tans' – the hated British paramilitary police units recruited from prisoners and ex-servicemen, many of them Scots and possibly trained by my Grampa who, according to my aunt, served in Ireland at the time – ratcheted up local tensions considerably.

It didn't take long until the local military authorities identified Joe as an Active Service Unit (ASU) leader. Edward O'Malley, in his book *Memories of a Mayoman*, refers to an incident in which Joe read out the following dispatch:

The Crown Forces at Westport Quay have a life-size photograph of you. If captured, you will be shot, and your body dragged through the streets of Westport. This information comes direct from Military headquarters.

Joe's notoriety increased following a number of gunfights with the RIC and ambushes of Black and Tan/RIC military convoys, the most important being an engagement at Carrowkennedy on 2 June 1921. In reprisal, his house in Drumindoo outside Westport was burnt to the ground and a £2,000 reward posted for information leading to his capture.

Following the truce of July 1921 he was asked to assist in setting up the Irish Civic Guard, the Gardai, in which he held, from their inception in February 1922, the nominal rank of Chief Superintendent.

In May 1922, after the signing of the Anglo-Irish Treaty and the formation of the Irish Provisional Government, Joe Ring was involved in putting down what became known as the Kildare Mutiny, a confrontation between the new Gardai's old RIC officers – those who had collaborated with Michael Collins, the IRA's Chief of Staff – and the new recruits of old republicans.

By this time the civil war between the supporters and opponents of the Irish Free State as a British Commonwealth Dominion was in full swing; Joe Ring was appointed a Brigadier-General in the Irish (Free State) National Army. Tasked with putting down the 'Irregular' (anti-Treaty republicans) rebellion in Connaught, he was given a cross-channel ferry, the *Minerva* fitted out as a troop carrier, and given command of a sea-borne landing in Clew Bay to capture the towns of Rosmoney and Westport, the headquarters of the Irregular forces in the province, while Major-General Mac Eoin attacked from the landward side. Both towns were taken without loss of life and 103 Free State troops interned on Rosmoney Island were released.

Seven weeks later Brigadier Joe Ring was dead, killed on 14 September 1922 in an ambush by anti-Treaty Irregulars at Tubbercurry, on the outskirts of Bonnyconlan, Ballina, a skirmish that became known as 'The Battle of the Ox Mountains'. It was less than a month after the death of Michael Collins, also the victim of an Irregular ambush. When the news of Joe's death broke in Westport on market day, all the shops and businesses in the town were immediately closed, while the blinds and curtains of private homes were drawn in a mark of popular respect.

The well-known Kerry author, Padraig O Siochfhradha, wrote the following appreciation of Joe's contribution to the Irish war of Independence in the *Mayo News* the week after his funeral, which ended:

> The marching tread of his fighting column will never again re-echo in the night through his native hills, and the red grouse squat in the purple heather undisturbed. Woods and stream and western sea are hushed in sorrow. A chivalrous heart is stilled, a brave and generous soul gone. Mayo, you dare not claim a braver soul than Ring.

By May 1923, nine months after Joe Ring's death, the Civil War in Ireland was over, leaving the nationalist 'Free Staters' – representing the industrial, commercial and landed interests of the 26 counties and British capitalism – victorious. They quickly moved to neutralise their class enemies and crush the growing unrest and dissent among agricultural workers and smallholders in the rural districts and the strike actions and factory occupations by workers' movements, strike committees and pickets in the towns and cities. By the spring and Summer of 1923, as Labour historian Emmet O'Conner observed, the Free State was routinely deploying thousands of its paramilitary Special Infantry Corps – former IRA and IRB Volunteers – in 'response to factory seizures' and the 'disruption of essential services'.

Despite the heroic attempts by Connolly, Larkin and their comrades of the ICA on Easter Monday 1916 to break the alliances between the financial circles of Ireland and the British Empire and establish a genuinely worker-friendly democratic socialist Republic, by 1923 the links between those countries' ruling elites remained unbroken and the hopes and dreams of the men and women who sacrificed their lives for a new Ireland had been hopelessly corrupted, and their ideals abused and manipulated out of all realistic shape. It is difficult to accept that some complicity for that unfortunate outcome, albeit in a minor way, lies with my family.

Commemorating Connolly in 1986

Helen Clark

Sing a Rebel Song
The Story of James Connolly
Born Edinburgh 1868 Executed Dublin 1916
City Art Centre, Market Street, Edinburgh –
8 November to 6 December 1986

Come workers sing a rebel song, a song of love and hate
Of love unto the lowly and hatred to the great
The great who trod our fathers down, who steal our children's bread
Whose hand of greed is stretched to rob the living and the dead.

Written by Connolly in 1903 in Edinburgh and set to music by Gerald Crawford of the Socialist Labour Party.

Introduction

In 1985 the newly elected Labour Group of the then Edinburgh District Council approved a motion for the City of Edinburgh Museums to stage an exhibition in 1986 to mark the 70th anniversary of James Connolly's execution. The only public reference in Edinburgh to Connolly at this time was a plaque in the Cowgate. In 1968, after a long campaign, the Edinburgh and District Trades' Council presented to the city a plaque to commemorate Connolly's birth. It was mounted on a wall in the Cowgate, a few yards from his birthplace. Five days later, it was stolen and replaced by the plaque which can be seen today. The exhibition hoped to make amends for the neglect by the city of his birth by generating a greater interest in Connolly's life and work. It was visited by 9,736 visitors.

Preparation

The exhibition was planned for the late autumn of 1986 in the City Art Centre. The proposed format was of panels of text and photographs and display cases of objects related to Connolly's life and the causes for which he campaigned. A great deal of display material had to be sourced and borrowed from Ireland and I was lucky enough to make a 3-day trip to Dublin in September 1986.

During this visit I met with Padraig Ó Snodaigh at the National Museum of Ireland, Francis Devine of the Irish Transport and the General Workers Union and the Bakery and Food Workers' Amalgamated Union to look at objects, banners and sculptures that we could borrow for display. In addition to objects, we needed images to illustrate the display panels. I was shown a large number of interesting photographs by John O'Dowd, Secretary of the Irish Labour History Society, Pat Johnson at the Dublin Civic Museum, and Peter McMahon of the National Library of Ireland. Ken Hannigan from the Public Records Office of Ireland lent me some copies of documents from a recent exhibition held there. At Kilmainham Jail I met Pat Cooke and identified more photos and took photographs of the stone breaking yard and the plaque to those executed there in 1916. On my return loans were organised and copies of images ordered. I also contacted Tom Wylie at the Ulster Museum to locate images relating to Connolly's time in Belfast.

Loans

A large number of items were borrowed from Ireland and Padraig O'Snodaigh from the National Museum very kindly agreed to co-ordinate the uplift and return of all the loans from the different Trade Unions.

From the National Museum of Ireland we borrowed the following objects:

A Sketch of Connolly by Sean O'Sullivan
Connolly's hat and bloodstained vest worn during the rising
Book used to conceal bullets
Irish Citizen Army Special Mobilisation Order signed by Connolly
Irish Citizen Army recruiting leaflet
Copy of the surrender signed by Pearse, MacDonagh and Connolly
Membership cards of the Irish Transport and General Workers Union
Easter Greeting postcard with Connolly's portrait 1917
Copy of a pass signed by Connolly
Postcard facsimile of the surrender order
An anti-recruitment poster 1914
Handbill 'Reasons to join the Irish Citizen Army'
Irish Citizen Army membership card 1914
One complete Irish Citizen Army uniform
Votes for Women badge worn by Hannah Sheehy-Skeffington
Labour Party Banner, 'Workers Honour Connolly every day with a fighting Labour Movement'
Tramwaymen's Strike Leaflet

The Bakery and Food Workers Amalgamated Union lent a stunning carved wooden bust of Connolly. The Federated Workers' Union of Ireland lent their banner with a portrait of James Larkin addressing the crowds during the 1913 Lock Out. Finally the Irish Transport and General Workers' Union lent their Belfast Banner bearing Connolly's portrait, the Dublin No. 19 Branch Banner and a James Connolly Birthday Celebration Programme dated 5 June 1909.

The exhibition was further supplemented by pamphlets and booklets from the Edinburgh City Libraries.

The Exhibition

Sing a Rebel Song consisted of display cases of objects and 19 panels with quotes, text and photos. Each panel had a quote from Connolly at the top.

Introduction

Sing a Rebel Song – The Story of James Connolly, born Edinburgh 1868 – executed Dublin 1916

'The cause of Labour is the cause of Ireland the cause of Ireland is the Cause of Labour. They cannot be dissevered' (*The Workers' Republic*, 8 April 1919).

1 **Early Years – Edinburgh 1868–1882**
'Irish History has ever been written by the Master Class – in the interests of the Master Class' (*Labour in Irish History*, 1901).

2 **The Army 1882–1889**
'Here then is the conquest. National liberty, personal liberty, social security all gone; the country ruled by foreigners; the Irish race landless, homeless, living by sufferance upon the mercy of their masters' (*The Reconquest of Ireland*, 1915).

3 **Edinburgh – the Socialist Revival**
'Our demands most moderate are – we only want the earth!'
'Be Moderate' (A song by James Connolly, 1907).

4 **Edinburgh – Local Leader 1894–1986**
'The landlord who grinds his peasants on a Connemara estate and the landlord who rack-rents them in a Cowgate slum, are brethren in fact and deed' (Election Address, St. Giles Ward, 1894).

5 Dublin – The Workers' Republic 1896–1903

'If you remove the English army tomorrow and hoist the green flag over Dublin Castle, unless you set about the organisation of the Socialist Republic your efforts would be in vain. England would still rule you' (*Shan Van Vocht*, January 1897).

6 America 1903–1910

'To me, therefore, the Socialist of another country is a fellow patriot, as the capitalist of my own country is a natural enemy' (*Forward*, 15 August 1915).

7 Return to Ireland 1910

'Socialism will mean in Ireland the common ownership by the Irish people of the land and everything else necessary to feed, clothe, house and maintain life in Ireland' (*Irish Nation*, 23 January 1909).

8 Belfast Organiser 1911–1912

'We are out for Ireland for the Irish' (*The Workers' Republic*, 8 April 1916).

9 Sectarianism and Strife 1912

'Yes, ruling by fooling is a great British art with great Irish fools to practise on' (*The Irish Worker*, September 1914).

10 Women

'Her life is darkened from the outset by poverty and the drudgery to which poverty is born, and the starvation of the intellect follows as an inevitable result upon the too early drudgery of the body. Of what use to such sufferers can be the re-establishment of any form of Irish State if it does not embody the emancipation of womanhood?' (*The Re-conquest of Ireland*, 1915).

11 Belfast – linen slaves 1912–1913

'How can a person or class be free when its means of life is in the grasp of another?'
(*Labour, Nationality and Religion*, 1910).

12 The Lockout 1913

'The great "lockout" in 1913–14 was an apprenticeship in brutality, a hardening of the Irish employing class' (*The Workers' Republic*, 18 December 1915).

13 Arming for Independence
'We believe in constitutional action in normal times; we believe in revolutionary action in exceptional times' (*The Workers' Republic*, 4 December 1915).

14 Imperialist War
'All these horrors in Flanders or the Gallipoli Peninsula, are all items in the price Ireland pays for being part of the British Empire' (*The Workers' Republic*, 20 November 1915).

15 The Road to Revolution
'Christmas Week, 1796–Christmas Week 1915 – still hesitating' (*The Workers' Republic*, 25 December 1915).

16 The Easter Rising
'We succeeded in proving that Irishmen are ready to die endeavouring to win for Ireland those national rights which the British Government has been asking them to die to win for Belgium [...] I personally thank God that I have lived to see the day when thousands of Irish men and boys, and hundreds of Irish women and girls, were ready to affirm the truth, and to attest it with their lives if need be' (Court Martial Statement, 9 May 1916).

17 Execution
'Apostles of Freedom were ever idolised when dead, but crucified when alive' (*The Workers' Republic*, 13 August 1898).

18 The Legacy
'We found the workers disorganised, and we proceeded to organise them. We taught them to use their organisation for their own moral and material advancement and as a result have endued them with a higher sense of dignity of manhood and womanhood' (*The Irish Worker*, 28 February 1915).

The exhibition was accompanied by a video 'James Connolly on behalf of the Provisional Government', an RTE Production made in 1966. The script was written by Owen Dudley Edwards and the contributors were Sidney Gifford, Archie Heron, Cathal O'Shannon, Mary Connolly Richards, John Docherty, Nora Connolly O'Brien, Elizabeth Gurley Flynn, William McMullen, Ina Connolly Heron, Roddy Connolly, Sean O'Ceallaigh and Frank Fahy.

The Opening

Owen Dudley Edwards opened *Sing a Rebel Song* on 7 November 1986. He referred to another Connolly song, 'We only Want the Earth' and went on to say that it would not be asking the earth of Edinburgh for the city to create a proper and permanent memorial to one of its most extraordinary sons. Padraig O'Snodaigh addressed the gathering saying that the Irish were a little envious of Edinburgh as Connolly's birthplace, though they were delighted to aid in his repatriation with material for the exhibition. The Gaelic poet Aonghas MacNeacail read Sorley MacLean's poem 'Ard-Mhusaeum na hÉireann' ('The National Museum of Ireland') in Gaelic and English. MacLean was inspired to write his tribute to 'the hero who is dearest to me of them all' on seeing Connolly's blood-stained vest in Dublin. This gave poignancy to the occasion as the vest was displayed in the exhibition. The event was enlivened by a performance by 'Left Turns' of Connolly's own 'Rebel Song' written in 1903.

Response

Sing a Rebel Song attracted 9,736 visitors between 8 November and 6 December 1986. It was well received with some great reviews in the press. Hamish Henderson wrote:

> the exhibition is to be greatly welcomed. Without doubt, this great working class hero was one of the most extraordinary and gifted men ever born in Edinburgh – it is about time this was recognised.'

Ian Bell wrote:

> *Sing a Rebel Song* goes some way towards making amends for 70 years of wilful blindness on Edinburgh's part.

An early day motion was put to the House of Commons by Tony Benn, Ron Brown, Martin Flannery, Eric Heffer, James Lamond and Gavin Strang:

> That this House congratulates Edinburgh's Lord Provost and his Council for recognising one of the City's most famous sons, James Connolly, a Socialist who emigrated to Ireland and played an important part organising Catholic and Protestant workers in the struggle against Green and Orange Toryism in the early years of this century.

Not all visits however were welcome; some young men stormed in, and wanted to know the name of the person who set up the exhibition so they could 'fill them in'. On a similar note, in the People's Story Museum we have a panel with a photo of James and Lillie Connolly with their daughters Mona and Nora. This photo was slashed with a knife in about 1992.

The Travelling Exhibition

Although we returned the objects on loan to the lenders in December 1986, the exhibition panels were designed so they could travel. The panels from *Sing a Rebel Song* were lent to the Museum of Labour History in Liverpool in April 1988. Like us, the museum borrowed objects from the National Museum of Ireland. Desmond Greaves of the Connolly Association opened the exhibition. The exhibition was also displayed in Dublin to accompany the production of the book in May 1989.

The exhibition panels have also been lent to many Edinburgh based groups over the last 25 years.

The Book

A temporary exhibition is by definition temporary. A more lasting legacy was needed and Irish History Workshop proposed a book of the exhibition, which would contribute to a greater understanding of Connolly's life and works. Council staff wrote, compiled and designed the book, *Sing a Rebel Song*, and Irish History Workshop paid for the majority of the printing costs. In 1989 2.000 copies were printed and all of these have been sold.

The Behans: Rebels of a Century

Maria-Daniella Dick

*Any young fella with a drop of Irish blood in him had joined the
Rebellion in 1916. That was the call, and they rallied to it. Yes, they
considered it worthwhile.*[36]

A REBEL FAMILY steeped in revolutionary republican and socialist politics, the
history of the Behans keeps time with a history of the radical 20th century.
Kathleen Kearney was born in 1889; a self-described Fenian since birth, she
was to become 'the mother of all the Behans', as the title of her autobiography,
told to her son Brian, goes. Kathleen was the mother of seven children by two
husbands. Her first husband Jack Furlong having died, leaving her a young
widow with a small child, Rory, and pregnant with Sean, she later married
Stephen Behan in 1922, with whom she would have Brendan, Seamus,
Brian, Dominic and Carmel. Although through both marriages she would be
explicitly interlinked with the national cause, Kathleen had a 'rebel spirit'
by birth;[37] her brother was Peadar Kearney – the composer of 'The Soldier's
Song' and 'Labour's Call', an addition to 'The Red Flag' invoking James
Connolly – who was part of the Supreme Council of the Irish Republican
Brotherhood and would later participate in the Rising.

Kathleen Kearney was introduced to Jack Furlong at a dance in aid of
Cumman na mBan. Her brother and husband were active in Easter Week,
'[t]he men of my family and my husband... all in Jacob's biscuit factory in
Wexford Street [Bishop Street]: Jacob's Garrison we called it'.[38] Kathleen
herself was a courier in the Rising, carrying her first message to Padraig Pearse
and James Connolly in the GPO. Her memories of the Rising emphasise the
human aspect of its leaders:[39]

> I took my dispatch to the leaders of the Rebellion, and I must say they
> didn't look like the heroes they really were. Connolly was a little fat man
> with a great big moustache; Pearse was wall-eyed, God bless the mark!
> I had met him before at a ceilidh... He didn't speak much to the likes of
> me – too busy.[40]

As Kathleen noted, however, support for the Rising had been slow in coming, partly because many families, including her own, had men fighting in the British Army during the First World War. Kathleen's mother-in-law Mary Ann Furlong, known as Granny Furlong – 'a remarkable woman, a rebel all her life',[41] and a Catholic socialist with a picture of Lenin on her wall – sewed uniforms in her basement for Easter Week. Nearing the age of 80, she determined to travel to England to help the cause and ran an IRA safe house there: '[h]er ambition,' as Ulick O'Connor succinctly puts it, 'was to blow up the English'.[42] She would be jailed, along with her daughters Evelyn and Emily, after a bomb went off in her house. Their fame preceded that of their now more famous relations; as Dominic Behan notes, '[w]ith a granny and two aunts doing time for the cause I was a popular figure in the young Republican circles of south-west Dublin where my brother was at that time virtually unknown'.[43] That brother, Brendan, was born of Kathleen's second marriage, to Stephan Behan. Having been widowed when Jack Furlong died in the 1918 influenza epidemic, she went for help to Countess Markievicz, who found her a job in the home of Maud Gonne MacBride on St Stephen's Green. Kathleen met Behan in 1919 and married him in 1922; Brendan Behan was born in 1923 and his father first saw him when his mother held him up to a cell window outside Kilmainham Jail, where Stephan was a republican prisoner.

Brendan, who had been 'rocked in the cradle to the air of "The Red Flag"' was marked as a prodigy from childhood;[44] his mother recalls being asked by his teacher, Sister Monica, 'Mrs Behan, are you aware you are raising a genius?'.[45] He also followed in the family traditions, becoming a member of Fianna Éireann at the age of eight and graduating to the IRA as a teenager, first as a courier and then as a member. Dominic called Brendan 'a Republican in the Frank Ryan stamp'[46] and after an attempt to join the International Brigade was thwarted by his mother, Brendan travelled to England, ostensibly to see his Granny Furlong but actually to run explosives, where he was arrested in Liverpool. Brendan immortalised his subsequent history in *Borstal Boy* and *Confessions of an Irish Rebel*, such that it became part of the legend of the Behans, yet from the ages of 16 to 22 he spent the majority of his life between three prison sentences.[47] During his second imprisonment, for shooting at a detective in Glasnevin Cemetery during the anniversary commemoration of the Rising, Brendan wrote to a fellow IRA prisoner Jim Savage quoting James Connolly:

Brendan Behan 3501 HM Prison Liverpool 193199-441. Rearrested Mountjoy Prison. Attempted murder (amongst other things) of Broy Harriers 5 April '42. 'The great only appear so because we are on our knees. Let us rise.' J Connolly.[48]

Although the imprisonments would furnish him with material for his plays *The Quare Fellow* (1954) and *The Hostage* (1958) along with the autobiographical memoirs, Brendan Behan was freed at the age of 23 and was to die at the age of 41. He lived the life of his convictions, and his politics, and the legacy of the Rising, were to inform his life until the end. In 1956, he wrote a Letter to the Editor of *The New Statesman and Nation* on the subject of Stephen Rynne's *All Ireland*, which had been reviewed in those pages, in which he described himself as 'a Dublin man of working-class Connolly and Larkin Socialistic origin'.[49] When offered a newspaper column for the *Irish Press*, he defended it against the *Independent* because the latter had called for the execution of James Connolly.[50] In his memoir of Brendan, entitled *My Brother Brendan*, Dominic counters claims that he had become politically disillusioned towards the end of his life:

> People have said things about him which are just not true. For example, that he died politically disillusioned. Rubbish! The tape I quote towards the end of the book will disprove that, not to mention that Hugh McDiarmuid [sic], the great Scots poet, was at lunch with Barbara Niven and I when Barbara told me how Brendan had just given her ten pounds for the *Worker* that same morning. It was in the summer of 1963.[51]

In addition to Connolly, there would be another Irish-Scottish connection for the Behans. If they had been connected through republican and socialist politics to one Scotsman, they were also to take those politics to Scotland. Brendan and Dominic knew MacDiarmid because Dominic had lived with him for three years when he moved to Glasgow, where he met Josephine Quinn, who also came from a socialist family and whom he was to later marry in London. Brian and Dominic had also become writers; a fact that led to a tension with Brendan, who asked '[w]hat does Dominic think; that geniuses are born in litters?'.[52] He did, however, later attend the premiere of Dominic's *Posterity Be Damned!*, the play that features 'The Patriot Game' as its theme, and Dominic would become storied in his own right for it and other works, including 'McAlpine's Fusiliers' and 'Connolly Was There'. Dominic and Josephine lived initially in England, where he was writing for the BBC, but he returned to Scotland and was active in socialist politics in Glasgow. In 1988, a group of writers and activists contributed to an anthology entitled *Workers City: The Real Glasgow Stands Up*, conceived as a rejection of the official nomination of Glasgow as European City of Culture in 1990; Dominic was among the contributors, with a piece entitled 'Call Me Comrade' and a poem, 'Babylon'.[53] In 'Call me Comrade', he recalls taking the campaign for national self-determination to London along with Freddie Anderson, a fellow Irishman, writer and socialist who had made his home in Glasgow, and Matt McGinn, the folk singer-songwriter of Irish descent who was born in the Calton. The piece ends with the poem, which is prefaced by a discussion of his influences as a writer, cited as from 'the dialectical poets of Ireland and Scotland, mainly MacNeice, MacDiarmid, Hamish Henderson and Sydney Goodsir Smith'.[54] Dominic Behan died in Glasgow in 1989; his ashes were scattered on the Royal Canal in Dublin. Brendan Behan died in 1964; he is buried in Glasnevin Cemetery. Kathleen Behan survived Brendan, and died in 1984 at the age of ninety-four. In her memoir, she tells her son Brian that the rebel leaders were 'like holy men. They died like saints',[55] their deaths turning the tide of public opinion towards the War of Independence:

> The very announcement of the death list was really the end for the British in Ireland, even though we did not know it then. Really, you know, the people couldn't stand it, and when they heard that James Connolly was strapped to a wheelchair and then shot, it maddened them [...] They had kept faith with the Republican ideal, and in an act of madness went out again to affirm that Irishmen would not be part of the Empire. Our rebels were defeated, but in the manner of their going they snatched victory from the jaws of defeat.[56]

After Easter

Des Dillon

Outside of Kilmainham

I count the living beads of a holy rosary
down the strands of my DNA,
The sorrowful mystery of Newgrange, Tara and Patrick.
Plantation, potatoes, sharks in the coffin ship's wake.
Liberty. Rising. James Connolly tied to a chair.
Sinn Féin rebels whispering partition. Civil War.
Celtic sixty-seven. First communion. Bernadette Devlin.
Bloody Sunday, Provos, Brits, Thatcher, Brighton.

I've been tied by rosary beads to a chair.
Destined to be boxer, poet, sinner, raconteur.
Down the gun barrel of time, over seven seas
Famine voices sing Ave, Ave, Ave Maria.
A great crowd has choked in my chest
I gasp, *God's curse on you England you beast.*

Garden of remembrance, Falls Road (for Jinky)

Sunlit names on black marble, gold:
volunteers O'Carroll, McCartney, McKelvey, Malone,
ghost me to Columba high Woodwork desks,
last Monday in January nineteen seventy-two,
rain blurred windows and the room filling
with the steam of youth. Our famine stained accents
blethering of Buckfast and girls till Duffy howled;
Did yous cunts not see what happened in Derry?

Thirteen dead. Fuckin Brits done it!
And Duffy summoned up ancestral wrath.
Boys! Boys! Register! Our Irish names rung
like bells – over black rosaries for Bloody Sunday –
Ahearn! Here sir. Breen! Here sir. Callaghan!
Here sir. Duffy. There sir. Pardon? There sir.

Uprising

This Other culture, though they bring no soldiers now,
still put gunpowder in my mouth,
bullets in my nose and ears and their tomorrow
on my eyes – then paint my skin with failure.
But the old ways are in me still, resisting
the colonisation of my soul. Mark my words,
the Troubles have not breathed their last with you.
We won't bring armoured cars nor tanks nor guns.

We will be as shoals of fish or birds of the air
joyful in our medium, carefree in direction,
wheeling and revolving, gathering, gathering, gathering.
In splinters of light we will shift, disperse
and be teeming over and around and through
all of your history, lighting your deeds as we go.

Never Goanna Dance

You say I've never danced with you cos sober
feet ain't got no rhythm. But listen, you don't
only dance with your feet on the dance floor.
I have been dancing sean-nos unnoticed
through sickness and health, heel and toe over
these few square feet of Scotland. Unseen,
I have stamped out reels and jigs, shuffled
airs and laments over old friends gone,

floated through unbearable joy, spun
and tip tapped in the garden through swallows
and blackbirds, howling dogs in the flowers,
cats' choirs in shivering cherry blossoms.
I have danced, darling. And I'm never
gonna dance again, the way I've danced with you.

Sean-nós dance is an older style of traditional solo Irish dance. It is a casual dance form,
as opposed to the more formal competition-oriented form, of Irish stepdance.

Wedding # 1 The Meal

The bride, in white and curls falling and the groom,
a smile to charm nuns and bankers, are seated.
In the *craic*, colourful hats and clamour, starters
are laid and I see a hundred Irelands on the plates.
In a green sea of calm jelly Eire
presents its fragile altar of dreadful peace:
a slice of Orange laid there; out of place
accepted as part yet not part – bittersweet

where would we be without it? On the Orange
a Red Hand of Ulster strawberry ironically unaware,
of its Sacred Heart possibilities. Radiant spirit.
Golden waves of melon lap the plate:
winding shores of Tir Na Nog where tides
rise over terror and float us all ashore.

Wedding # 2 The Dance

She's the Queen of all things Irish.
A white topped wave skirting shores
where ages and generations clap and sway
but things beneath and deep remain the same.
Irish Jive! She's this way, he's that, holding
the beat of one-two-three-spin;
holy trinity; hands in sacred grip.
Everybody join in! One two three spin.

In red later, she watches from the top table
the little Irish dancers padding lightly
over a heavy tradition of love and guns.
We've travelled far and weary us Irish.
On this Holy day, no-one's thinking
of the dry eyed bigot in the corner drinking.

Wedding # 3 The Party

Four tall girls dance near the stage edge.
It could be the world's edge; the final precipice.
Or they could be four green future fields.
You'll be alright, alright. Like the complicated Celtic
circles embroidered on the breast of your dresses you'll burst
from this dance floor through reels and jigs and shining eyes.
Out and out and conquer far lands,
space even, because that girl is jumping heights

that leave us gasping at our own ability to leave
potato and bog and swing along on a song,
on the right road or the wrong, toward the stars.
'What is the stars?' I ask Joxer, 'What is the stars?'
That is the question. And what is the moon too?
And this wedding – what does it mean? What does it do?

Wedding # 4 The Parting Glass

We've come to Marion's wedding from prison ships
universities Armalites Carmelites abbeys and schemes
the shuffling diaspora of migration and famine and fear.
Always moving out, pushing up
On building sites and mines, motorways and roads
steelworks, railways and drunken jail cells, corners
in asylums, parks, ghettos and slums we sang
our songs till the walls were damp with tears –

Now our children and our children's children
Will climb the steps we have built for them
with poems and tears and laughter and guns.
May they always, always sing our songs.
In the *craic*, colourful hats and clamour,
and someone singing Athenry. We have come a long way.

Margaret Skinnider and Me

Peter Geoghegan

ARRIVING IN SCOTLAND in 2004, I knew almost nothing of the Irish history of the place. Drawn by a stipend from Edinburgh for a PhD, I was largely ignorant of the links between my native and my, somewhat reluctantly, adopted land. I had read about the potato pickers but mine, I assured myself, was a modern tale of migration, unhindered by the baggage of the past (ha!). Ireland was an hour and a budget flight away, not an active part of my life in Scotland. But the longer I spent here the harder such blindly subjective narratives became to sustain. When I abandoned Edinburgh for Glasgow a few years later the 'where are you from?' questions became more frequent, more inflected. Some wanted to claim my Irishness, to invite me to watch Celtic matches and sing rebel songs; others wanted to traduce it, to find out what foot I kicked with. The history of the Irish in Scotland, I finally understood, has always shaded my life here. And this history would colour my experiences of Scotland's constitutional upheaval in summer 2014, and its relationship with Ireland's own tumultuous departure from the United Kingdom almost a century earlier.

When I moved to Glasgow I rented a flat on Mingarry Street, not far from the Botanic Gardens. On nearby Kersland Street a young Coatbridge schoolteacher named Margaret Skinnider had lodged in the months leading up to 1916. Skinnider, who was born in 1892 and would go on to become the only woman injured in active service in the Easter Rising, chose the West End deliberately as it was then, as now, a 'part of the city not under suspicion – there were not many Irish people living in the place.'

Skinnider, with family from Emyvale in County Monaghan, became an integral part of the local branch of Cumann na mBan, a women's organization founded in Dublin in 1914 that would play a key role in the struggle for independence. Soon she was smuggling weapons to Dublin, sailing for Ireland ahead of the rebellion with 'detonators for bombs and the wires [...] under my coat.' That line comes from Skinnider's own account of the Rising, published just a year after the event in the United States. The folksy title – *Doing My Bit for Ireland* – betrays something of its rheumy-eyed style, but the book is not without charm. Literary magazine *The Dial* remarked approvingly that

Skinnider's text 'makes the Irish revolutionaries live for us, especially their executed leaders, so that the Irish question presents itself as an essentially human problem, and the rights of small nations changes from a battle cry to a demand for constructive thought.'

Even by the standards of Easter 1916, Skinnider was a *sui generis* rebel. She learned to shoot in Scotland – such was her proficiency that Fianna youth came to watch the bespectacled 'Glasgow boy' take aim. She began Easter week in Rathmines, in the bohemian digs of Constance Markievicz, 'the Countess' before proceeding to the frontline. Around 2am on the Thursday morning, Skinnider was shot three times while attempting to burn down properties on Harcourt Street ('My disappointment at not being able to bomb the Shelbourne Hotel was what made me unhappy,' she wrote.) After treatment at the Royal College of Surgeons and then St. Vincent's Hospital, Skinnider was arrested amid the embers of the Rising and brought to Bridewell Police Station.

Skinnider eventually made it back to Scotland, and then on to the United States where *Doing My Bit for Ireland* formed a small part of a much wider campaign to appeal to Irish Americans for support in the burgeoning War of Independence. The dead men of the Rising – all the female fatalities were civilians – were already on the road to martyrdom.

Skinnider, unlike many of her contemporaries, was no reactionary Irish nationalist. In 1914, she attended protests outside Perth Prison. Suffragettes incarcerated inside were suffering appalling force-feeding. She would later take part in a hunger strike herself in Mountjoy, in February 1923, in opposition to the signing of the Treaty.

Margaret Skinnider never appeared in the history books that I devoured as a lank-haired teenager in Longford. I had never heard her name until I started going to Coatbridge in 2014, ahead of the independence referendum. I was drawn to 'Little Ireland' and its unselfconscious Irishness, its GAA teams and Irish dancing schools. One bright summer's afternoon, a few weeks before the referendum, I visited the headquarters of the local chapter of Cairde na hÉireann, the largest Irish republican organisation in Scotland. The green, white and gold of the Irish Tricolour hung above a small storefront. Metal bars ran across the windows. Margaret Skinnider's name appeared over the door.

As I stood squinting into the narrow, dark shop front, a tall, broad-shouldered young man with short hair and acne scars arrived to let me in. Inside was like a republican Belfast version of the shortbread and tartan tourist traps on Edinburgh's Royal Mile. James Connolly and Bobby Sands smiled down from t-shirt racks. Palestinian flags and copies of the Proclamation of the Irish Republic and the Sinn Féin newspaper *An Phoblacht* were all on sale. There were H Blocks pins and books about De Valera and Michael Collins in the communal library. A republican flute band was based in the centre but much of the energy went into running a food bank – in 2013, unemployment in North Lanarkshire was 20% above the Scottish average.

In 1919, Sinn Féin had three branches in the town. In the 1950 general election the tiny Irish Anti-Partition League ran a candidate in the town. The violence in Northern Ireland never spilled over into armed sectarian conflict in Scotland, but the Troubles did resonate across the Sea of Moyle. Tensions were not confined to Old Firm clashes. A group called the Young Scottish Loyalists had a paid up membership of 1,500 in 1982. A few years earlier, the first republican band in Coatbridge, the James Connolly Republican Flute Band, was established.

Cairde na hÉireann – 'friends of Ireland' – was set up after the Northern Irish peace process, around the turn of the millennium, 'because of the needs for a political organisation given the end of the armed struggled and the need to unite Ireland politically' said Franny McAdam, a Coatbridge taxi driver and Cairde na hÉireann's national organiser. Out of a Scottish membership of 600, some 70 are in Coatbridge. In the back room of the Skinnider Centre, sun-bleached photographs of marchers in Belfast with 1980s haircuts were stuck to the walls. Every year Coatbridge holds the biggest republican march in Scotland.

Why, I asked, did so many people in a Scottish town take such a passionate interest in the place where their grandparents and even great grandparents were born? McAdam looked a bit surprised at the question, but answered nonetheless.

'Scotland never embraced the Irish. It actively stopped the Irish from voting. I know people who dropped the 'O' off their name just to get jobs. If the Scottish had embraced the Irish we would probably feel more Scottish.'

For most of the 20th century, Irish Catholics were generally wary of Scottish nationalism. While there were no Saltires or Yes stickers in the Skinnider Centre, there was no doubting where the referendum loyalties lay. 'I believe the Scottish people have the right to self-determination as well as the Irish people,' said McAdam. 'Obviously as republicans we would like to see the break-up of the Union.'

A couple of weeks later I returned to Coatbridge. This time I was visiting the local Orange Hall, a squat, two-storey building a short walk from the generously named Sunnyside Station. A featureless grey façade mirrored the overcast sky. There was a streaky mark on the only window that looked onto the street.

'That's just an egg,' said Jim McDonald, local Orangeman and my guide for the day as he opened the heavy wooden front door and led me into the reception. A homemade poster beside the fruit machine advertised the following week's 'Red, White and Blue Sash Bash'. The Orange Hall was busy. In the large function hall a dozen or so elderly women sat eating sandwiches and drinking tea from glass cups. Their weekly bingo session was due to start shortly. I gave a loud, smiling 'Hello'. Almost everyone waved back.

Unbidden, McDonald gave me a tour of the walls of the hall. There were prints of King Billy on his steed and faded framed photographs of the Queen flanked by the Duke of Edinburgh and a yellowish Queen Mother. There were pictures, too, of lines of Orangemen in black suits and white gloves standing to attention.

'That's the Loyal Sons of Ulster,' McDonald pointed up at a semi-circle of broad-shouldered, middle-aged men. They looked mostly plump and contented. Established in 1906, the Loyal Sons are one of more than ten lodges affiliated to Coatbridge Orange Hall. All the founder members were Ulstermen. McDonald was descended from Irish stock, too. The absence of Protestants from the local St Patrick's Day festival was a source of grievance. Earlier, as we walked up from the train station past rows of council flats, he had complained that Catholics received preferential access to housing.

McDonald led me to a small meeting room on the second floor of the Orange Hall. On a table inside was a sheaf of papers, including a photocopy of a clipping from the *Airdrie and Coatbridge Advertiser* dated September 1912. Above a notice about a boy scouts' parade was a slightly larger classified ad. 'Copies of the Solemn League and Covenant can be signed at the Conservative Club on Church Street', it declared in serif font. 'Support Loyal Ulster'. Irish Protestant anti-Home Rulers drew up the 'Ulster Covenant', the name consciously echoing the 17th century Presbyterian Covenanters that fermented rebellion across the Lowlands and beyond. On Ulster Day, 28 September 1912, around half a million signed the Covenant. Only those who were natives of Ulster were eligible to put their names to the declaration. Addresses of relatives or friends had to be proffered as proof. In Coatbridge alone, 860 men and 96 women put their names to the Covenant. McDonald's paternal grandfather, a bricklayer called James, gave an address on Sandy Row, a famously loyalist south Belfast neighbourhood, although he had been born and raised in Scotland, not Ulster. ('He cheated a bit,' his grandson said.) McDonald followed this grandfather – and later his own father – into the Orange Order.

We climbed up a short ladder into the hall's dusty, narrow attic to admire the Lodge's flags and standards. There was a bright Orange banner with a figure of King Billy, sword raised, and another with a Bible scene, Christ surrounded by children. A cushioned red box about a foot wide lay on the ground. This would hold the Bible at the front of an Orange procession. It was covered in protective plastic with 'LOL No 8' scribbled in pen across it. A padlock barred the way to a separate, smaller room where the band's instruments were kept. They would be needed that weekend. Most of the Coatbridge lodges were participating in the massive Edinburgh parade calling for a No vote. Orangemen from across the UK were coming to join. McDonald's friend Dawson Bailie, former Grand Master of the Belfast Lodge, was travelling over.

Ireland was foremost in McDonald's mind ahead of the referendum. 'If it was a Yes vote what would happen in Northern Ireland? Would Sinn Féin want a vote to separate in Ireland, too?'

Margaret Skinnider spent the vast majority of her adult life in Dublin. Despite her affinity for Monaghan, she seems to have been a city girl at heart. In many ways her post-1916 life was even more remarkable than her footnote in that historic Easter week. After initially being denied a military pension because the Army Pensions Act was adjudged to be 'only applicable to soldiers as generally understood in the masculine sense' she returned to teaching. Skinnider became a moving spirit in the Irish National Teachers' Organisation (INTO), agitating in particular for wage parity for female teachers. Despite her war wounds, she lived to 79. In 1971, Skinnider was buried in the republican plot at Glasnevin cemetery. My mother's parents, who lived most of their married life just behind the graveyard, are also there. Next time I visit them, I'll look out for Margaret Skinnider's gravestone, too.

A Beautiful Thing Wronged

Pearse Hutchinson

AT THE FOOT of the altar in a church in Italy, I saw, just after Easter 1988, four tall vases filled with Easter lilies. I couldn't help thinking that was more than I'd seen in the streets of Dublin in the whole of Easter Week.

When I was growing up, and for a long time after that, the whole city was ablaze, every Easter, with those lilies. Elegant bits of oval paper, pinned to lapels. Intense green, deep orange, pure white. The coat without one was the exception.

It made the city more beautiful, it made the people more beautiful. A lovelier emblem can seldom have been invented. We wore it in honour of the brave people who went out in 1916 to fight for the freedom of Ireland. To risk their lives for that hope.

They believed that Ireland has as much right to independence as England (or Italy, or Brittany, or Catalonia). A simple belief – though now apparently too difficult to grasp for some of 'the best brains in the country', as Fine Gael used to advertise themselves.

My father was born in Seville Place, [Dublin], the son of a carpenter. When he was five, the family was flooded out; my grandfather couldn't find work here. He found a job in Glasgow, where my father grew up. He became a printer, rising in due course to the dizzy height of managing director of a firm called Millars (I asked Hugh MacDiarmid about it once, he remembered the firm well). My father was treasurer of Sinn Féin in Glasgow. During the War of Independence he was offered the choice of resigning the job or resigning from Sinn Féin – and all other pro-Irish activities. He refused to do either, was sacked, deported, interned in Frongoch, imprisoned in Mountjoy.

My mother's parents – one from near Convoy, one from near Moville – met, both aged 16, sitting on butter-boxes in the steerage of the Derry boat; both going to Glasgow, one to be a messenger-boy, the other 'into service'. He prospered ('a well-doin' mon'), they married. My mother was born in the Cowcaddens (worse than the Gorbals) before prosperity struck. She met my father in Sinn Féin.

She was a friend of Constance Markievicz, whom she always talked about as Madam. One Sunday the two of them were collecting for Sinn Féin outside a largely Catholic church in Glasgow. Mass over, the pious poured out, and put the two heretics to flight – incited thereto by the Irish-born West Briton in the pulpit. (The West Britons, the wealthy in spirit, we have always with us). Running for their lives, Constance and Cathleen Sara were hauled onto the back-platform of a tram by a big Highland conductress, who pushed them inside, urged the driver to get going, and fended off the loyalist harpies.

Cathleen and Harry took the losing side in the Civil War. So, like many another, he couldn't get work in his native city. They went back to Scotland, she went back to teaching and kept lodgers. I was born there in 1927. When de Valera got into power in 1932, she wrote to him asking him to get my father a job in Dublin, so they could bring up their only son in 'holy Catholic Ireland'. Considering their sacrifices for the cause, he complied: with a job in the Labour Exchange for two pounds a week (was that good even then?). In the '40s, Harry was rewarded with a better job, in the Stationery Office, at 12 pounds a week. My mother kept lodgers, and sometimes worked on the Sweep.

Growing up, these were among the household names: Madam' Markievicz, Madam' Despard, the Honourable Albinia Broderick, Senator Margaret Pearse (who got me into St. Enda's, the last to be enrolled before it closed). Mrs. Pearse, Father Dominic, Father Albert. These were on Mammy's lips (are there any Mammies left or are they all Mummies now?: West Britain *Abu*). The names Daddy kept harking back to were: Keir Hardie, Willie Gallacher, Voroshilov, Herbert Spencer, Connolly, Larkin.

Since the setting-up of the state there has been no greater tragedy than this: the sundering of the separatist and socialist.

Dan Breen said on TV, not long before he died: 'We got our freedom too late. We should have got it in '98'.

He also said, in the same interview: 'They talk about a God of mercy. No God of mercy could allow the pain I'm suffering now.' He was dying of cancer.

I was forced to learn Irish at school (the Gaelic League via the Easter Rising). I was forced to study other subjects. I liked languages, so I didn't get biffed for Irish, or English or Latin. I did get six on either hand, not with a leather but with, much worse, the leg of a chair, for not being able to sing in tune. It didn't make me hate music.

At 15, I discovered sex; at 17, booze. I rather liked both. My mother, a passionate thwarted woman, claimed to disapprove of both. This led to constant wrangles.

Brought up to be both a Republican and a catholic, I opted out, fairly early on, of Holy Rome. (The great saint from Bergamo came too late for me). Opting out of Irish Catholic Puritanism, I for a few years in my 20s, identified

Irish Nationalism with it – a stupid and simplistic mistake (not unlike the simplified, and from the mammonite viewpoint highly convenient, version of 'revisionist' history peddled at us for too long now by politicos and media-pundits).

We live in an age of euphemism, lies, misnomers: 'Northern Ireland', 'The Province', 'Europe', 'the special relationship', 'the Gulf'. There was even a radio lecture-series called 'The Long Relationship' (frequently acrimonious). When did you last hear a 'respectable' Irish politician risk the word Imperialism?

Anthony Coughlan said on the radio in 1987 that the 1916 Rising and the Proclamation 'were the title-deeds of this state'. I believe he was right – as were Gerry Adams and John Stalker when they spoke, in their different ways, of 'unfinished business'. Are Irish 'liberals' against all imperialism except English? Against no murders except the IRA's?

The Proclamation spoke of 'welfare'. How many of those multi-national money-lenders, none of whom will ever die on a trolley, know what the word means?

Who stopped us wearing a beautiful emblem? Was it really the Stickies and the Pinnies? Or bourgeois shoneens?[57]

I want to wear an Easter Lily in honour of Pearse and Connolly and all their comrades; of my father and mother and all the other sacrifices; of all the suffering generations – Black and Basque and Irish.

Perhaps when we're all 'neat and clean and civilised', and misruled incurably from Brussels, room may be found in a glass case for an Easter Lily captioned: 'captured off Rockall from the last of the terrorists.'

It's a lonely thing to wear a beautiful thing wronged.

Home Rule, Sinn Féin and the Irish Republican Movement in Greenock[58]

Shaun Kavanagh

AS A PORT town, Greenock was a node of international trade and a channel of movement and migration. In the whole of Britain, by 1871 only London had more Irish migrants per head of population than Greenock. A significant hub of the Irish diaspora, then, Greenock was at the heart of operations for Irish Republicanism in Scotland. Due to its close proximity to Ireland, Greenock was a strategic locale that continued to be significant for the shipment of munitions and explosives. Moreover, Greenock offered convenient cover for 'rebels' on the run during the Irish War of Independence. While the more affluent members of the Greenock-Irish enclave chose not to deviate from constitutional (principally Liberal) means, others in the Greenock-Irish community were drawn beyond the 'respectable' parliamentary ways to support Ireland's cause through physical force nationalism. Republican forms of politics, previously overshadowed by the Land League and the Home Rule movement, gained new prominence. This chapter will explore the context for support for Irish republicanism through the lens of the Irish diaspora in Greenock. Attention will be given to the disparities between the constitutional Home Rule movement and the revolutionary fervour of the Irish Republican Brotherhood and Sinn Féin.

I

In the autumn of 1865 the *Greenock Advertiser* reported statements from several witnesses who observed a brigade of Fenians 'going through a skirmish drill, under the command of an officer' behind the paper mill at Beith Dam, at the present-day 'Cut'. The newspaper informed its readers that 'the local brotherhood is 900 strong... it is time that something should be done to put a stop to this dangerous folly.'[59] As a result of the press interest, it was reported that a number of Fenians had left for Ireland, 'where we sincerely hope they will not return to annoy us'.[60] Such reports were indicative of the 'Fenian Panic' that intensified during the mid-19th century in Scotland.[61] A combination of various organisations of physical force Irish nationalism, the

Fenian movement remained the most expressive outlet of Irish separatism in Scotland in the 19th century. By the 1870s however, the majority of the Greenock-Irish community had embraced the legal and confident Land League, and later, the Home Rule movement.

The constitutional nationalist movement in Greenock began with the founding of the Greenock Irish National Association in 1865. Although there was a subsidiary branch of the Home Rule Confederation, which was established by John Ferguson in Glasgow, the Land League absorbed much of Irish nationalist activity in Greenock. Several local sections were established, and the John Dillon branch existed until 1900. Due to restrictions in the franchise, however, the voting power of the wider Greenock-Irish community was marginal before suffrage reform in 1868, and again in 1884–85.

Still, the Land League and Home Rule causes offered opportunities to prominent members of the Greenock-Irish enclave, who were eager to make their way in Scottish society, building bridges between the migrant community and indigenous population. Indeed, amongst the executives of the local Land League were members of the Irish skilled working and middle-classes such as John McGivern, a tailor, George Montague, a newsagent, Neil Haughey, a stationer, and Patrick and Samuel Fitzpatrick, both publicans. Moreover, Arthur Skivington, the branch president of the Greenock Home Rule Confederation, was a wine and spirit merchant, whilst the branch secretary, Hugh Cairns, was a provisions merchant. Such business interests often interfered with the nationalist cause. The majority of Greenock-Irish members of the Irish Land League (ILL) were publicans or spirit dealers. This led to a split within the ILL over voting intention for the Liberal party, who had close ties with the Temperance Association. The alcohol trade workers' opposition to the Liberal Local Option Bill in 1892 led the Greenock Spirit Trade Association, to which local Irish publicans belonged, to instruct its members to endorse the Unionist candidate, Thomas Sutherland. An Irish reader of the *Greenock Telegraph* countered this with an appeal not to sabotage the advancement of the Irish Home Rule cause:

Surely this will be a lesson to the men – the working men – who make up the Irish National League of Great Britain not to place in responsible positions the men whose interests are associated with the party opposed to Home Rule... the 'pot-house' proprietors.[62]

Nevertheless, the Irish nationalist movement in Greenock was firmly in the control of moderates with fairly respectable social positions and business interests in the town. Though they provided a respectable front for their communities, they were arguably driven by a desire for recognition and respect from the host population.

However, support for physical force Irish republicanism endured on the periphery of Scottish society, emerging from such class-tensions described above within the Greenock-Irish community, and with electoral politics writ large. Support of Irish nationalist activism offered salvation for émigrés of Erin adrift in an alien and tough waterfront environment. The rejuvenation of Irish republicanism in the decades after the collapse of the Fenian movement must be understood in the context of the cultural nationalist revival, which developed a more exclusive tone in the 1890s. Cultural nationalism was a traditionalist response to the political disparagement of the Parnell divorce ignominy, internal division in the parliamentary ranks and Liberal uncertainty over the delivery of Home Rule. Cultural nationalists sought either the restoration of Ireland's ancient Gaelic ways to inspire a revitalisation of 'native' values to build a sovereign nation distinct from the colonial relationship with Great Britain.

In Greenock, this cultural revival took the form of associational culture; organisations like the Ancient Order of Hibernians and Gaelic football clubs such as St Patrick's, Sarsfields, and Eire Og in Port Glasgow, fostered a sense of ethnic Irish identity in Greenock. Indeed, this new ethnic and cultural confidence led members of the republican Young Ireland Society to stand in defiant separation from electoral politics. In the process, they distanced themselves from the majority of the Greenock-Irish community. The pursuit of Gaelic ethnic virtues would ultimately be attained through political separatism. By rallying and maintaining support for anti-British sentiment and emotional Irish nationalism, Irish republicans appealed to simple expatriate feeling, evoking images and memories of 'home' through organisational meetings, and readily accessible writings and songs. In short, Irish republicanism in Greenock provided a portable identity – a way of 'being Irish' outside Ireland.

The Young Ireland Society in Greenock organised weekly lectures, usually followed by a debate and singing of national songs. Events were planned around the most important dates in the Fenian calendar – 4 March for the birthday of Robert Emmet, 17 March for St Patrick's Day and 23 November to commemorate the Manchester Martyrs of 1867. Of all the Young Ireland Societies in Scotland, only the Greenock branch survived into 1899, and provided a welcoming platform to veterans of the Fenian movement in Scotland. Still, with the death of the Irish Republican Brotherhood leader in Scotland, John Torley, the Fenian movement in the country approached terminal decline.

Yet cultural nationalist endeavors were kept alive with the Cumann nGaedheal, which set about promoting Gaelic nationalism amongst Irish migrants in the west of Scotland. A Port Glasgow branch was established in 1907, which incorporated Fenian veterans to its ranks and was largely composed of supporters of Sinn Féin principles. The same year, a Scottish Executive was appointed to coordinate Sinn Féin activities across Scotland through monthly conventions. Patrick McCauley of Port Glasgow was chosen secretary. Nonetheless, Sinn Féin organisations struggled to compete with parliamentary nationalism as a sense of optimism was becoming palpable amongst the Irish in Scotland over the Home Rule momentum. In the aftermath of the Easter Rising of 1916 however, with an attempt to impose conscription on Ireland for the war effort, Sinn Féin became a unifying force for otherwise disparate nationalist groups. Growing in numbers, and decidedly republican in character, Sinn Féin became the dominant Irish nationalist movement in Scotland. When it became increasingly apparent that there was a lack of political will behind various Home Rule proposals, physical force methods were increasingly utilised.

II

Having played a relatively minor participatory role in the Easter Rising, the Greenock-Irish revolutionary dissidents came to the fore in the Irish wars, drawing upon lengthy experience from the Fenian movement, of gun-running, refuge and deceptive activity. Coordinated by the local Sinn Féin organisation and the Scottish brigade of the Irish Republican Army, separatist republican forms of politics, hitherto overshadowed by Land League and Home Rule activities, were given new impetus beyond ethnic Gaelic patriotism. Moreover, Greenock became a strategic location to recruit volunteers, and subsequently hide individuals on the run or sprung from prison during the Irish War of Independence.

By 1919, there were roughly 75 branches of Sinn Féin in Scotland. The Sinn Féin Cumann in Greenock was named after Roger Casement, who was hanged for treason for his part in the Easter Rising, for which he had attempted to secure arms from Germany. With over a thousand members, it was one of the largest divisions in Britain, and matched only by Dundee. Much of its activity was channelled into gathering money for prisoners and their dependants, and organising meetings and lectures. The Greenock Cumann raised and sent over £1,000 to Dublin within a two-year period.

In the months after the Rising in 1916, members of the IRB and Irish Volunteers in Scotland (later the Scottish Brigade of the IRA) established a system of transportation between Ireland and Greenock of guns, ammunitions and explosives. Michael Collins, a leading figure in the post-rising revolution, entrusted Wexford merchant seaman Joseph Vize to oversee the Scottish Brigade, and to take control of the supply chains of arms and ammunition between Irish and Scottish ports. The smuggling of arms and ammunition to Ireland was co-ordinated by James Nolan. An IRB member and associate of Vize, Nolan infiltrated the Clyde Shipping Company to ensure the safe delivery of essential items:

> I was given a list of firms in England and Scotland who would be sending consignments [of arms, ammunition and potassium chlorate] to reputable merchants in Counties Waterford, Wexford, Kilkenny and Tipperary... Having access to the ships' manifests in my capacity as manifest clerk, I was aware before the ships' arrival in Waterford whether any such cargo or items were being carried.[63]

In an insight into the audacity of the operation, Nolan revealed that a network of seamen from across Britain with local knowledge of the major ports ensured the safe passage of supplies:

> Those who assisted me in this task of getting in stuff were six Irishmen, four Scotchmen, a Welshman and two Englishmen... to call to specified addresses in Liverpool, Glasgow, Plymouth, Southampton, London and Greenock for parcels...[64]

As well as utilising his maritime connections for supplying much-needed weapons, Vize sought to expand the Scottish Brigade of the IRA by recruitment through local Sinn Féin clubs. From Dublin, Michael Collins ensured that the IRA was properly trained and regimented by adopting a proper army command structure. By 1921, the Scottish Brigade consisted of five battalions, containing a total of 31 companies. The largest battalion, the 1st, was centred on Glasgow, with nine companies, including 150 British Army veterans. Other battalions were located in Lanarkshire, Edinburgh and Dundee. The 5th Battalion had constituent companies in Greenock, Port Glasgow, Paisley and Kilmarnock.

The 5th Battalion, Company B, was formed in 1919 under the command of Sean Wilson, and John Mannering and Tom Kershaw served as captains of the Company over different periods. The Company also contained two veterans of the Easter Rising, brothers Andrew and James Murphy, and some former members of the British Army. The majority of members were Scottish-born, and worked in Greenock as factory workers, dockers, barmen, and even schoolteachers. By 1921, B Company contained approximately 200 members.

The most significant operation carried out by B Company was an incursion on Fort Matilda naval base near Gourock in 1919, which was used as a training base for the 3rd Battalion of the British infantry regiment, the Royal Scots Fusiliers. In an audacious raid, B Company acquired up to 60 rifles from the base.

The strength of Sinn Féin in the west of Scotland caused considerable anxiety. Glasgow CID reported on a Sinn Féin meeting in Greenock, held in the League of the Cross Hall in Patrick Street, at which 37 clubs were represented. This letter states that there were 30,000 Sinn Féin volunteers in the west of Scotland, 20,000 revolvers, 2,000 rifles and plenty of ammunition:

> Delegates were instructed to inform their several battalions that an order might be received at any time to mobilise, and to be ready to act either in Ireland or in Scotland as might be required.[65]

Beyond the 'enrolled' members of Sinn Féin and the IRA, a wide range of activists and sympathisers provided the necessary facilities, resources and protection. B Company were given permission to train in secret in St Mary's Chapel Hall, as well as Duncan Street Hall, which was later to become St Patrick's Church. B Company also had its own chaplain and medical orderly. Family ties and ethnic networks between Ireland and Greenock also proved advantageous to provide 'cover' for IRA members who were under surveillance from Dublin Castle, including Maurice Collins, who was involved in the Easter Rising and became an IRA intelligence officer. Collins' main task was to intercept the mail of the 'Black and Tans' officers. After his home was continually raided, Collins received orders from Michael Collins to escape to Greenock. Maurice Collins left Dublin in December 1920 dressed as a priest, in clothes lent to him by his cousin, Father Maurice O'Shea. Upon arriving in Greenock, Collins was met by a Mr. McGivern,[66] who arranged for lodgings, and secured him a job as a manager of a pub in town. Collins held the job until July, and was popular with his employer:

> During the whole time I was with him he only knew me as Jack Kennedy and had no idea that I was 'on the run'. When the whole thing was over and the Treaty [the Peace Treaty of 1921] signed we corresponded and I gave him full particulars of my reason for taking up employment with him. He then invited my wife and myself for a holiday which we gladly accepted.[67]

After the Civil War, and the spectacle of Irishman killing Irishman, the activities of the republican movement went into decline. Though the Sinn Féin Cumann in Greenock continued, its membership subsided. Once the Irish Question was largely settled in the eyes of the Greenock-Irish, they increasingly participated in mainstream Scottish politics. With priorities closer to home such as social regeneration, working conditions and housing the immediate concerns, they largely began to turn to the Labour Party, who managed to harness the 'Catholic vote' to significant effect. However, while the majority of Irish Catholics in Greenock were not members of Sinn Féin or the IRA that does not mean that they were necessarily hostile to the aims of the republican movement. The Easter Rising and its aftermath, like the Great Famine, became embedded within the psyche of the Greenock-Irish enclave, whether Irish-born or not. It was a lasting reminder of their roots, and their 'curious middle place'[68] between a Scottish and Irish Catholic identity.[69]

Homecoming

Billy Kay

AT THE LAUNCH of the Scotland and the Easter Rising project in April 2015, a number of people commented that such a gathering for a potentially divisive subject like this could not have taken place until comparatively recently. True. And I would not have attended such an event until very recently. To be precise, my disaffection from what had once been a strong affinity with Scots Irish history and culture was finally broken after the Scottish Independence Referendum on 18 September 2014. One of the few positives I took from the grief of a No vote then was the fact that the majority in the Scots Irish heartlands of Glasgow, Lanarkshire and Dundee had voted Yes and in my eyes had at last realised that the natural home for an expression of their political and cultural traditions was in an independent Scotland. Seeing them come home at last, I could once again embrace the shared heritage that binds me as a Scot to Ireland – a tradition gently and beautifully expressed in a poem often attributed to Henry Joy McCracken, who along with Wolfe Tone was one of the leading figures of the radical United Irishmen movement of the 1790s. 'The Social Thistle and Shamrock' contains these lines:

> The Scotch and Irish friendly are,
> Their wishes are the same.
> The English nation envy us
> And over us would reign.
> Our historians and our poets
> they always did maintain
> that the origin of Scottishmen
> and Irish are the same...
> And to conclude and end my song
> may we live long to see
> the thistle and the shamrock
> entwine the olive tree.

To me, as a Scottish nationalist, identifying with 1916 and the successful independence struggle of a fellow Celtic nation was the most natural thing in the world. I was born in 1951 and growing up in Galston in Ayrshire a huge influence on me was the family of the burgh's provost for many years, John Murray. John had moral integrity and high principles, a devout Roman catholic who was elected again and again in a mainly protestant town. John was a self-educated socialist, a personification of the dignity of the working man of that era and a defender of his rights. He and his brother James were miners, and they were looked after by their sister Annie. So was I. As a greetin wean, I was handed over the hedge to Annie who gave me sweeties to pacify me. When I was home in Galston, I continued to visit until the last of them died in the late 1980s. The Murray living room was a shrine to catholic saints and Irish missionaries, and I was taken by Annie to Mass at St Sophia's. She had studied French at Glasgow University but had to give up her studies to help look after the family. She still though had a display case with a collection of blue cloth-covered Hachette classics from French literature, which I borrowed and read when I began studying the language. Thus wes a 13-year-auld boay in a cooncil hoose in Ayrshire learnit the steirin words o Racine an Molière, an some o their lines are still thrang in ma heid till this day!

The Murray family roots were in the West of Ireland, so I was also exposed to story and song from there, but they were Scots speaking Lowlanders like me and thirled to their Scottish as well as their Irish identity. Others have written extensively of sectarianism being 'Scotland's Shame', but the handful of families we knew who were sectarian were regarded by the respectable working class as low life scum. Significantly perhaps, one of those families had an Irish name so their roots were probably among the Orange communities in Ulster. For while the majority of the Irish who came to Scotland in the 19th century were Roman Catholic, and often Gaelic speakers from areas like Glencolumbkille, the Rosses and Gweedore in West Donegal, it is estimated that up to 25% of the migrants were Ulster Protestants, descended no doubt from those Lowlanders of the last major migration in the other direction in the 17th century.

With rare manifestations of sectarianism despised, and being raised in this mixed cultural environment, there was no barrier between me and people of Irish origin. On the contrary, their Irishness was attractive and as I got older and got involved in the folk revival of the 1970s, it was the exciting wave of exhilarating music played by Planxty and the Bothy Band which influenced young musicians reinventing our own vibrant musical traditions in bands like Ossian, Silly Wizard, the Tannahill Weavers, Battlefield Band and Jock Tamson's Bairns. As a student in Edinburgh I shared a flat with friends from the Creggan in Derry, and Banbridge in County Down, and started going to traditional music events in Buncrana and Gweedore. As a result of contacts made, I am proud to say that long before Celtic Connections was on the go, I organised one of the first Celtic Music events staged in Scotland, with Ar Log from Wales, Ossian from Scotland and *Ceoltoiri Altan* from Donegal.

What had attracted me first to Donegal was the wild fiddle music of the county, and I was intrigued to discover that several times every week there were privately run minibuses that picked up people all over Glasgow and dropped them off all over West Donegal. I took one of them and it was that bus's itinerary that later gave me the title of my first programme on this vibrant cultural connection, *From the Gorbals to Gweedore* – a title used for the very first programme in my oral history series from 1980, *Odyssey*, a television programme, a chapter in a book, and even a fine tune by the Highland musician and composer, Blair Douglas. In that first trip I stayed at an inn in Gweedore called Hiudi Beag's run by the kindly Gallagher family. It was a mecca for local musicians, among them the influential fiddler Francie Mooney, whose whole family turned out to play as *Ceoltoiri Altan*. The descendant of the family group *Ceoltoiri Altan* is of course the famous contemporary band *Altan*, which has the stirring fiddle and exquisite voice of Francie's daughter Mairéad Ní Mhaonaigh at its core.

One of the results of this influence was that airs and songs from Irish history became part of contemporary Scottish culture from the 'March of the King of Laois' to the 'Lamentation of Limerick', from 'Patrick McBride' to 'Down by the Glen Side'. Regarding the latter, one of the most stunning uses of music I have ever witnessed on television came in the Ken Loach series *Days of Hope*, set in Ireland in the years after the 1916 Rising. There, the great traditional singer Tríona Ní Dhomhnaill plays a young girl who defies the British soldiers billeted in her house and holds them spellbound as she proudly sings 'Glorio, Glorio, to the Bold Fenian Men':

> Some died by the glenside
> Some died 'mid the strangers,
> And wise man have said
> Their Cause was a failure;
> But they loved dear old Ireland
> And never feared danger,
> Glory O, glory O,
> To the Bold Fenian men!

You can see the clip of Tríona singing the song on YouTube, and even outwith the context of the back story of the drama it still has tremendous emotive resonance. Magnificent.

Another factor that bound all working class Scots together in the Central

Belt of Scotland was their adherence to the Labour Party. The Murrays and my own family were very much old Labour from the Home Rule tradition of Keir Hardie, who founded the Independent Labour Party in 1893, and RB Cunninghame Graham, who founded the Scottish Labour Party in 1888. John Murray was so much old Labour that he refused to take expenses when he went off on burgh business to Edinburgh. Even then back in the 1960s, he looked down upon the growth of career politicians in the party who regarded politics as a means of advancement for themselves rather than the people they served. What he would have made of the present hierarchy of the people's party would be unprintable. His attitude though was well expressed by an ex miner from Fife, Derrick McGuire, in my BBC Radio Scotland series on the history of Scottish Nationalism *The Cause*: 'Ye talk aboot folk birlin in their graves... Keir Hardie's should be fitted wi a rev-coonter!'

A brilliant writer with roots in the Scottish Irish experience, William McIlvanney also gets close to this dilemma in his novel *Strange Loyalties*: '"Scottishness may have been a life, but Britishness can be a career". You are not where you come from but where you can go'.

During the Referendum campaign I spoke at a number of gatherings around the country including a Labour for Independence event in Kirkcaldy, organised by Alan Grogan with an impressive array of speakers including Jeane Freeman and Tommy Sheppard. My contribution focused on the frustration so many people felt at the sight of Labour career politicians, many of whom came from this Irish-Scottish tradition, making sure that their wealth and privilege would be preserved with the continuation of the British State... and the Deil tak the hinmaist in society:

A few months ago the House of Lords had what they called a debate on Scottish independence. A clip from it was televised showing Baroness Liddell of Coatdyke obsequiously addressing 'the Noble Lord, Lord Lang' and agreeing with his Lordship that Scottish Independence would be the end of the world as they knew it... a world of elite privilege and power. Baroness Helen's contribution was followed by another extremely wealthy scion of the people's party, Lord Robertson, who suggested that giving political power to the Scottish people would unleash the forces of darkness. When I hear the increasingly hysterical ranting of Labour placemen, I recall the words of Oliver Brown writing in the *Scots Independent* on the effects of Winnie Ewing's breakthrough victory for the SNP in 1967: 'a shudder went through the Scottish members of Parliament frantically looking for a spine to run up'.

Thir anti Scottish interventions o major Labour figures gars me grue at the scunnersome decline in a pairty my Ayrshire an Fife mining grandfaithers luikit up til aw their days. So like many whose natural political home was the Labour Party, I feel not that I have left the party, but that the party has left me. Only with the radical shake-up of Scottish Independence can it return to its core ideals and again become a voice for the Scottish people, rather than the voice of a privileged, self-serving elite.

From Helen Liddell, John Reid and Jim Murphy in politics, to James MacMillan, Eddie McGuire and Andrew O'Hagan in the arts, there has been a significant strand in the elite of the Irish-Scottish community which has been patriotically pro-British and often virulently anti-Scottish independence. Given the popular Irish Republican culture many of them imbibed in West Central Scotland, to a Scottish nationalist and republican like me many of their pronouncements have been inexplicable, bordering on objectionable. And not to only me. Over the years I have given speeches at major conferences in Northern Ireland exploring Scottish/Irish links. At one, during a particularly politically sensitive time there and before a divided audience, the organiser said that I had got the balance about right according to the number of nodding and shaking heads he had observed! The last conference I spoke at was in April 2014 and the statement that got the noddin and shakin heids stunned into immobility was the irony of the fact that the descendants of these Irish republicans in Scotland, along with a small rump of what once had been a substantial loyalist tradition, now formed together one of the strongest unionist blocks in a Scottish political landscape that was shifting irrevocably toward Scottish Independence! With the dramatic expansion of SNP representation in recent years and the strength of the Yes vote in former Labour heartlands, I now realise that this huge Labour Unionist block vote has finally crumbled. It may well decline to the point that it represents a rump similar to the aforementioned loyalist vote.

For all of us who now passionately desire Scottish independence, again there are positive pointers from the Irish experience. In another interview I did for *The Cause*, the eminent historian of Scottish nationalism from Strathclyde University, Richard Finlay suggests that future historians looking back on this period may well regard devolution and the creation of the Scottish Parliament as the starting point for the independence that inevitably ensued. In the same way that people would date Irish Independence:

They would talk about either 1916 or 1922 because that starts the process. So in some sense I think we've already sort of passed the threshold of what to all intents and purposes, people in the future will look back and say, ye know, 1997 – that's when Scotland becomes independent.

For Scotland, as with Ireland, 'it's comin yet for aw that.'

Whatever the future does hold, for this commentator at least, recent developments mean that I can return to my enjoyment of Irish culture and appreciation of the immense Irish contribution to contemporary Scotland. It is as if you have found a way to balance pride in Ireland and belonging to Scotland. Welcome home. I will leave the last word to Father Canning and the story that ended the 1980 radio documentary *From the Gorbals to Gweedore* and the chapter of the same name in the book I edited, *Odyssey Voices from Scotland's Recent Past*:

> They first regard themselves as Scots, there's no doubt about it, after all it's a poor hen that despises her own nest, ye see. But by and large I'd say that they are proud of their ancestry, and some of them indeed are more Irish than the Irish are themselves. I can think of an old lady for example in the last parish I was in and she was furious when the parish priest had introduced a redecoration scheme and removed St Patrick's statue. She said afterwards that the parish had never had a day's luck from the day he was moved.

James Connolly's Stations

Phil Kelly and Aaron Kelly

For Sarah Kelly

ON 18 SEPTEMBER 2014 at a seminar organised by the Reform Group commemorating the centenary of the signing into law of the Home Rule Act, John Bruton, the former Fine Gael Taoiseach, told the Royal Irish Academy that Scotland's independence campaign and referendum offered Ireland the lessons of hindsight:

> The reality is that, in 1916, Home Rule was on the statute book and was not about to be reversed. If the 1916 leaders had had more patience, a lot of destruction could have been avoided, and I believe we would still have achieved the independence we enjoy today.[70]

Hindsight presumes an agreed version of this Irish past and the Scottish present. It makes both respectively homogeneous histories rather than heterogeneous and ongoing processes with multiple, conflictive forces, problems and possibilities. It is the self-styled liberal-reformist default position to deem all Irish Republicanism as a mythic, violent excess beyond the parameters of democratic and progressive reason and statehood. For example, Richard Kearney's revisionist equation of 'myth and terror' insists on 'mythological essence' as the DNA of Irish Republicanism imprinted upon all its strands, from Fenianism through the Rising, state Republicanism or nationalism in the South, to the Provisional IRA during the Troubles.[71] As David Lloyd has pointed out, this ahistorical and homogenising wisdom itself smacks of the mythological, in this case offering a foundational myth of the modern state's rational self-evidence:

> Social critics, historians or journalists, limited by rigid categories and ideological assumptions from grasping new forms of struggle and resistance, fall back on the ascription to those whose acts they do not understand of a consciousness outside the pale of modernity and civility. Those being the terms that legitimate the state, whoever opposes the state must be consigned to the pathology of pre-modern modes of thinking.[72]

The apparently objective 20/20 vision of Bruton's hindsight also seems to have encountered liberal mists in its 1914/2014 comparison as it journeyed across the Irish Sea. To Bruton, the current SNP dispensation in a devolved Scotland, on the verge of a democratically attained independence as and when it so votes, serves to chide revolutionaries with the peaceable promise of full democracy both then and now. Bruton's argument is underpinned by a faith in history as a benign, neutral continuum whose inexorable progress is stalled unnecessarily and futilely by dark violence:

> Scotland has had a home rule government, and a home rule parliament, and a majority in that parliament was later democratically won by a party that wanted complete independence. That could have happened in Ireland too – 90 years ago [...] All that has happened in Scotland without loss of life, without the bitterness of war. Ireland was given a similar opportunity 100 years ago this week, to move through Home Rule, towards ever-greater independence, gradually and peacefully, when Home Rule for Ireland became law on September 18, 1914. Ireland could have followed the same peaceful path towards independence that Scotland is now considering taking.

Notably, Bruton's history slips somewhat – 90 years, 100 years – very tellingly and strategically. For, in order that 1916 appears as intemperate destruction, this revisionist rationality must disavow the ways in which dominant histories are already and constitutively violent. It was of course by 1914 that imperialist war machines could add mass industrialised slaughter to the list of crimes by which elites rationalise their sovereignty over the name of progress. Turning the Absolute Spirit or *Geist* of Hegel on its head, Theodor Adorno once wrote of history's arc as 'the teleology of absolute suffering' rather than the inevitable revelation of positivity.[73] Bruton's faith in history as decreed and self-realising progress – in which the abstraction of history itself and elite emissaries like Bruton hand down to people what they should not expect too soon – forgets the vast forces of colonial and economic exploitation which made the world what it was one hundred years ago and what it is today. It also seeks to deny people the right to challenge those forces by rendering resistance as recalcitrance to the preclusive promise of reformism. It is never too early or too late to fight against imperialism and tyranny. It is never too early or too late for the *demos* to disrupt what elites define as democracy. If anything, the radical strands of 1916 coalesced with agitation such as that taking place on the Red Clydeside opposing conscription and urging workers to fight their true class enemies. The success of such an ethical project would have prevented the millions of deaths that ultimately prolonged empires proprietorially presided over by squabbling, inbred cousins.

Ignoring the esurient feuds of elites, the Bruton model assumes an *a priori* British parliamentary democracy facilitates an Irish one. Bruton's self-realising civics elides a number of key problems alive in Scotland and the world today as well as in the history of the Irish state and indeed in the history of his own political party. Bruton claimed:

> Given that this is a parliamentary democracy, one of the oldest surviving ones in Europe, one that did not descend into totalitarianism during the 20th century, it is important that we should celebrate parliamentary achievements. Remembering democratic, non-violent achievements should be part of the civic education of our nation.

This seemingly progressive pedagogy elides – as do the official versions of Irish history – the fact that Eoin O'Duffy and the leadership of Cumann na nGaedheal who founded Fine Gael were resoundingly fascist. In these terms, a figure like Michael Collins is today retained and commemorated as a symbol of a more measured and accommodating republicanism or nationalism echoing all the way through to the Peace Process in the North, at the same time that the Blueshirts are quarantined as a distinct, rogue organisation. O'Duffy lost his leadership role with Fine Gael because he was a moron and not because he was a fascist. Such reactionary conservatism – which now glosses itself as today's voice of reason – was not the monopoly of Fine Gael and includes its own false opposite, Fianna Fáil, with whom it more properly shares complicity in the ongoing inequity and injustice of the Irish state. In reclaiming the radical currents of 1916 from the myths of official history we should remember that in 1936, on the 20th anniversary of the Rising, communists and socialists, including James Connolly's son Roddy and the Scottish MP Willie Gallacher, were assaulted at the Easter parade, just as Connolly House in Dublin had been attacked repeatedly in March 1933. The main political parties and the Church offered illicit sanction to such action and explicit licence to groups such as the Saint Patrick's Anti-Communist League and the Irish Christian Front.

The political Fortinbras which usurped the radical potentials of 1916 resulted in a state in which 98% of the British imperial administration was left intact and in which moral blights like the Victorian workhouse persisted in Gaelicised and Catholicised forms well into the 1960s. The Irish state afforded prominence to figures such as Father Denis Fahey, a man so anti-Semitic that he suspected Hitler of being manipulated by hidden Zionist hands, or the 1916 veteran Patrick Belton, whose political career spanned both Fine Gael and Fianna Fáil, and who opposed O'Duffy's mission to send troops to support Franco in Spain solely on the basis that Irish fascists should take care of domestic business first. The revisionist amnesia which misremembers 1916 will never be able to acknowledge that the egalitarian and democratic energies embodied by people like James Connolly could have resisted such reactionary injustice and saved Ireland from itself had they been the basis of a new, post-colonial society rather than conservative, hierarchical nationalism. Instead, just as surely as all the differing constituencies of 1916 are lumped together into the one bitter violence, Bruton's highly typical revisionist history gathers all these state-sanctioned forces of intolerance, reaction and tyranny into a resolved narrative of civic development whose reasonable heroes have helped to move Ireland from irrational tumult. In so doing, the very event that might have brought full democracy to Ireland becomes the trauma from which a sham, delusional version of democracy must take therapeutic flight.

James Connolly suffered many indignities during his life. Having endured the squalor of working-class Edinburgh himself, he was also compassionately attuned to the sufferings of others, as so clearly demonstrated by his politics. Doubtlessly informed by his time in the British army too, his activism spanned Ireland and Scotland as well as the USA. As a migrant and socialist his politics are always more than narrow parochialism. His most famous work, *Labour in Irish History*, accounted not only for proletarian politics in Ireland but also for the plight of the working class in Britain and elsewhere, and ultimately demanded global revolution. In addition to the indignity of his execution – to which he responded with dignity in a manner that characterises his capacity to do more than just repeat the prevailing logic of the world back to itself – further indignity has been heaped upon his memory by its official state commemoration which affixes his name to a train station at the same time that it disconnects his politics. To such tokenism can be appended his translation into a nationalism that is really the codeword for nepotistic elites, and his dismissal as a man of violence by Bruton or revisionists and liberals. From the left, Connolly is sometimes branded naïve for throwing in his lot with Pearse. It is, however, evident that he saw 1916 as one part of a set of processes that would only become revolutionary when they became global uprisings and that he had a very sharp sense of the pitfalls of nationalism:

> After Ireland is free, says the patriot who won't touch Socialism, we will protect all classes, and if you won't pay your rent you will be evicted same as now. But the evicting party, under command of the sheriff, will wear green uniforms and the Harp without the Crown, and the warrant

turning you out on the roadside will be stamped with the arms of the Irish Republic.

Now, isn't that worth fighting for?

And when you cannot find employment, and, giving up the struggle of life in despair, enter the Poorhouse, the band of the nearest regiment of the Irish army will escort you to the Poorhouse door to the tune of St. Patrick's Day.

Oh, it will be nice to live in those days...[74]

As with those who fought against Franco's fascism in the Spanish Civil War in columns honouring and continuing James Connolly's politics rather than making superficial use of his name, Connolly's shining vision should not be allowed to be halted at the historical stations of nationalism and post-nationalist revisionism in which history has already reached its consensual terminus. Instead Connolly's commitments serve as lessons for today's world and for the land of his birth. Poverty and inequality do not disappear because elites fly new flags. The only problem with 1916 was not its timing but that its revolutionary constituents got eclipsed by its reactionary ones. Anyone truly committed to a Scotland based on equality, rather than a nation which spends a century pretending things are getting better and that independence means supplication before the power of global capital, needs to remember that it is not the national question which comes first and then other matters can take care of themselves. As Ireland has sadly proved, an independent Scotland must establish itself foundationally on the basis of that equality. Otherwise the state will naturalise hierarchy as the law, reframe inequality as rational worldviews, make disenfranchisement mean democracy, and understand the exclusion of millions of people as governing consensus. Post-1916 Ireland would do well to remember that what is called the War of Independence in many ways relied upon the emergence of the Irish Soviets from 1919 onwards where radicalised workers (not just the industrial working class but also unskilled workers, landless rural labourers, peasants, the dispossessed) revolutionised large parts of the country, north and south. They did so in abeyance of British imperialism, right-wing nationalism, and supposedly leftist figures like Constance Markiewicz who ordered the IRA to disrupt them. Most notably, the Limerick Soviet survived long enough to issue its own currency. The Cleeve's creamery dynasty was taken over by its workers under the slogan: 'We make butter not profit'. This was echoed in Bruree, De Valera's part of the world, by the mill workers who seized their factory under the banner: 'We make bread not profits'.

So when thinking of a better world, let us recall that we have already been told that humanity cannot live by profit alone. Comparably, Scotland should remember Connolly alongside the Red Clydeside, alongside John Maclean and those such as Seamus Reader or Margaret Skinnider who committed themselves to republican socialist struggles without borders. These voices would make Scottish democracy incommensurate with business opportunities for Donald Trump or placations with fellow members of NATO. With 1916 as their handbook, the grassroots members who have dragged the grammar of the SNP leadership to the left should consider how and why *The Sun* newspaper might still endorse the party and why the SNP looked to the Celtic Tiger for its economics, since so did George Osborne. The Celtic Tiger began with a repeal of the Wealth Tax in the Irish Republic that was itself nominally designed to redress a situation wherein 10% owned 40% of the nation's wealth. Lowering corporation tax is not an anti-austerity measure. If an independent Scotland constitutes itself on equality rather than lying to itself, then it must also confront the fact that the UK is constitutionally sectarian and if a monarchical Scotland retains the same head of state it will be constitutionally sectarian too at the highest level. Scottish sectarianism is not just the preserve of the bigots who rip down plaques to James Connolly's memory and try to disrupt marches in his name. The vile ridiculousness of such scum extends to accusing Connolly of sectarianism and their political illiteracy provides cover for any future Scotland based on protected intolerance and hierarchy.

The century since 1916 brutally demonstrates that if people wish to challenge domination and win freedom in order to attain real democratic sovereignty then they cannot do it from within the very system constructed to subjugate them. Ireland has painfully shown this, as have recent events in Greece where democratic citizenship has been remaindered by corporate balance sheets, so that the leadership of an apparently radical party does deals with 'financial realism' that even the IMF finds unwise. For the liberal gradualists like Bruton the world is already a democratic place but this reformism will only ever offer 'change' that was not worth waiting for. The self-appointed Isaac Newtons of liberalism's gravitational reason can wait for their fruit to confirm the existing laws of the world. But, as Che Guevara's *foco* model of revolutionary struggle insisted, 'the revolution is not an apple that falls when it is ripe. You have to make it fall'.[75] Connolly's actions in 1916 and those on the Clyde were similarly designed to spark revolutionary movement and to rupture the continuum of domination rather than awaiting the promise of reform. The only true democratic redress for mass social movements is as stark today as the choice faced by those who assembled in Dublin in the Easter of 1916.

Back in 1964 Margaret Skinnider considered the inequalities of Irish society by quoting the foundational words of the Republic back at the state which annexed its name in order to compare the remuneration of Teachtaí Dála with the neglect of pensioners:

> It will be interesting to note if salary increases envisaged for TDs will also operate from October 1st next. The Proclamation of 1916 declared 'its resolve to pursue the happiness and prosperity of the whole nation and all its parts, cherishing all the children of the nation equally.' Have the members of the Government forgotten this, and do they realise that but for many of these pensioners they would not be in the positions they now occupy?[76]

Why indeed should the people quivering in their beds at night be pensioners worrying about how to heat their flats or buy food? The poor and dispossessed of the world already know that all actions have consequences since they daily feel the full weight of the decisions of the powerful. It is time for the rich to acquire the knowledge that actions have consequences, so that it is they who are quaking in their homes. 1916 instructs that full democratic equality requires those who want and need it to fight on and to fight hard against the grinding, obdurate violence of the world. Unless those who hoard power in the name of being reasonable relent then this will always be a fight to the death, for one side or the other. How better it will be to live together as equals in a world where freedom is finally shared by everyone.

A Slant on Connolly and the Scotch Ideas

James Kelman

RADICAL HISTORY REMAINS marginalised within our culture. Discoveries we make come about through word of mouth and other flukes. 'What actually happened?' 'Where did we come from?' 'Who are we?' We root about and dig away on our own. What we find is that a great deal of material exists, and it is good material. But it is not in the public domain. We just do not know about it. Essential strands of our history are not generally accessed through popular media and ordinary educational resources. We contend with sectarianism, racism and assorted prejudice; historical misrepresentation, disinformation, falsification, and occasional outright lies, alongside everyday British state propaganda.

As a Protestant boy growing up in Glasgow the name of James Connolly meant little to me. Connolly was an Irish name anyway, or Catholic. But Catholics were Irish, if not by birth. I became aware he was an Irish leader who met an early death fighting for Ireland. Later again I discovered he was Scottish-born, that he lived as an adult in Scotland, had Scottish friends and comrades with whom he remained in contact throughout his lifetime.

I edited and introduced the autobiography of the Clydeside activist Hugh Savage.[77] In his formative years Hugh was a stalwart of the Communist Party of Great Britain (CPGB); one of a group of young people befriended by Harry McShane.[78] In the introduction I wanted to give a background to this and a physical presence to a few of the names to whom Hugh referred, from the 1880s through the 1914–18 war and the period following the formation of the CPGB. The name of James Connolly appeared to great effect. I came to realise he was of primary importance, and that his life is at the heart of the radical history of Britain and Ireland.

Here in Scotland his presence in radical history is not simply assured, it is seminal, by which I mean that when we focus on him we discover the lives of figures crucial to the period. In discovering the lives we gain insight into the people themselves, into their thought as well as action. But for Connolly's enduring friendship with John Carstairs Matheson our knowledge of Matheson's contribution would have been scant, and knowledge of its significance perhaps lost altogether. Yet during his lifetime he was considered amongst the foremost Marxian scholars in Britain and Ireland. He, William Nairn and Connolly, three of the outstanding Marxian theorists of the period, were active north of the border. This when among their friends and comrades were key figures Keir Hardie, RB Cunninghame Graham, John Murdoch, David Lowe, George S Yates, Donald Macrae, Bruce Glazier, Tom Johnston and John Wheatley; and a younger generation that included John Maclean, Helen Crawfurd, Guy Aldred, John S Clarke, Willie Paul, Neil Maclean and Arthur MacManus.

Without this focus on the individuals much would be lost not only in regard to their lives and times but the discourse itself, how the theoretical path was followed and in the process cleared a little more. The early period of Connolly's adulthood was crucial in this respect. The ideas he encountered were at the heart of the political discourse of the day, and some foundational within the home intellectual tradition. William Morris had visited from the 1880s; Aberdeen, Dundee, Edinburgh, Glasgow, giving talks and taking part in meetings; eventually he was led to conclude:

> here in Scotland... you working chaps apparently found each your own way to Socialism without even being in contact, as we in London were, with foreign revolutionary influences, as that you have all come the same road, so to speak, and that road has simply been the road of the reading and political experience common to the more thoughtful of the Scotch working class generally. Our comrade, the Rev. Dr. Glasse of Edinburgh, tells me practically the same thing.[79]

He speaks in general terms from his experience of Scottish activists. Dr Glasse shares the observation, and is not the source. The ideas raised were not peculiar to Scotland but something about how they were raised or in how they were formulated either was peculiar to Scotland, or leastways set it apart from England. Nowadays strands in thought are traced in the democratic movement and in political economy from Adam Smith to Karl Marx who 'learned much from the Scottish historical school'. They are traced also in the '[development of] classical sociology to a stage where it was becoming remarkably similar, at least in its broad outlines, to Marxist sociology.'[80] Men such as 'Smith, Adam Ferguson, William Robertson, and John Millar [were pioneering] a materialist conception of history, which fully appreciated that category of social phenomena known as "the unintended consequences of social action."'[81]

Another line of thought appears in the controversy aroused by the place of religion and religious belief in the life of James Connolly. It surfaces in the well-known letter he wrote to Matheson in 1908: 'tho I have usually posed as a Catholic I have not gone to my duty for 15 years and have not the slightest tincture of faith left...'[82] while on the other hand, in prison awaiting death at the hands of the British State, he asked for Father Aloysius, and was given absolution. The personal side of this may remain secured. His political and philosophical position provides the basis of this short essay: Connolly's 'oft-stated belief, that one could be a Marxist in politics and a Catholic in religion without any question of conflict'.[83] At the outset of his essay 'Labour, Nationality and Religion',[84] Connolly quotes the Right Reverend John England, Catholic Bishop of Charleston, USA in 1824:

> a General Council is infallible in doctrinal decisions... Yet we deny to Pope and council united any power to interfere with one title of our political rights, as firmly as we deny the power of interfering with one title of our spiritual rights to the President and the Congress. We will obey each in its proper place, we will resist any encroachment by one upon the right of the other.

Many of his Scottish comrades, whether Catholic or Protestant, would have agreed. If one was to replace 'Catholic' with 'Christian' then a few more might have agreed. Most were aware of the issue and for a majority there was no issue. This may have been influenced by their reading of Marx and Engels but it had little to do with the veracity of Marxism. There was the 'natural' world and there was the 'spiritual' world.

The relationship between political and spiritual rights are perennial in most cultures. In Scotland the relationship was pivotal and peaked in 1843 not with Chartist struggles but with the Disruption of the Church of Scotland when 474 ministers 'voluntarily gave up their homes and their livings rather than surrender the spiritual independence of their Church.'[85] They walked out after a ten-year dispute, resigning on what was seen as one basic issue, that they might 'hold fast the noble heritage of Christian truth and sacred principle...' It had become

> impossible not to recognise... the path of duty [and] that it has been given to the Free Church to gather into her communion so much of what constitutes the strength of Scotland – the intelligence, the faith, and energy of her people...[86]

The testimonies of clergymen directly involved were not published for 40 years or more, into the 1880s, and a new edition quickly appeared in 1893. This was a time of intense political activity within the left and various political formations were founded.[87] Yet some of the more heated discussion could have begun not from political immediacy but from 'older issues' now resurfaced, reinvigorating an older debate derived from 'biblical awareness, and the broader political arguments which claimed that freedom had been lost by departing from biblical and Christian principles.'[88]

In 1820, which was less than 25 years before the Disruption, the weaver Andrew Hardie was in a prison dungeon awaiting execution. He wrote in secret his account of the proceedings that culminated in what he described as 'The Glasgow Rising in 1820', and he managed to have his account smuggled out. When captured he had been asked why he 'was in arms' and he replied, 'to recover my rights... annual Parliaments, and election by Ballot. Government ought to grant whatever the majority of the nation requested.'[89]

When I first read Hardie's account, back in the 1970s, I wondered what he meant by 'recover my rights'? When have working-class people and the majority population ever enjoyed such rights? Was it to do with the Clan system or some ancient form of 'communism'? Hardie was a devout man and the answer has its basis there. I quote the following from Helen Macfarlane from Barrhead in Renfrewshire who was two years of age when Hardie was put to death by the British State:

> Upon the doctrine of man's divinity, rests the distinction between a person and a thing. It is the reason why the most heinous crime I can perpetrate is invading the personality of my brother man, using him up in any way from murder and slavery downwards. Red Republicanism, or democracy, is a protest against the using up of man by man. It is the endeavour to reduce the golden rule of Jesus to practice. Modern democracy is Christianity in a form adapted to the wants of the present age. It is Christianity divested of its mythological envelope. It is the idea appearing as pure thought, independent of history and tradition.[90]

Macfarlane was acquainted with Marx and Engels personally. Her translation of the Communist Manifesto was the first in English, published in 1850. Her expression of the above is said to have been 'unique' in Britain and Ireland at that time but this ignores or fails to grasp the significance of the Scottish contribution. She had little difficulty in resolving the supposed incompatibility of radical politics and Christianity, and she was not alone north of the border.

The influence of Hegel may be paramount in the above quotation but a line is traced also through the Scottish intellectual tradition. The contribution of George Buchanan (1506–1582) is a place to begin: 'Among Scotsmen... a cosmopolitan; among the Humanists, a modern who anticipated revolution.'[91] His most influential work of non-fiction argued in favour of limited regal powers and the people's right to dispose of a bad king. 'God is the Supreme

King whom kings must obey. If kings depart from God, authority departs from them.'[92] These arguments were used by the founder members of the American Constitution and remained first principles of the democratic movement.

Aspects of Buchanan's thought are integral within the radical tradition: skepticism, the recognition that people have rights; that a separation of powers may exist between the people and the king; that a separation does exist between on the one hand the people and the king, and on the other: God the Supreme. Buchanan tutored Michel de Montaigne[93] whose intellectual influence was felt throughout Europe, acknowledged by Rene Descartes, skeptic supreme. Skepticism is dangerous by virtue of what it is: a challenge to authority. It may be the authority of a king, of a government; the right of one person, or group of people, to dictate to another. The challenge might be to the authority of a system, the authority of the Law, or the authority of one Church as opposed to another.

Most of those who developed philosophies and belief-systems prior to Descartes found the place of God in them. They had to, and not as a duty. It was more basic than that. They had to find the place of God because He exists. God was already present. The idea that He may not have existed was inconceivable. Descartes went on to provide a proof of God's existence. But why should God have required a proof? How could the burden of proof be on God?

'Let us suppose for the sake of argument that God does not exist' may be judged anathema. A scientist or thinker who begins from such an assumption is the enemy of religious fundamentalism and most religious authorities. The failure to account for God's existence is tantamount to denial. The failure to assume His existence is a denial. Any thinker who begins by questioning God's existence is a charlatan, a non-believer, an infidel, an atheist. Such skepticism is not just unforgiveable but blasphemy. The history of religious persecution is full of examples but so too the history of ideas. Buchanan appeared in front of the Inquisition. Descartes thought it safer to leave France to avoid the fate suffered by Galileo.

That God's existence might be 'unnecessary' was inconceivable. The presence of God is everywhere and everything. Logicians, mathematicians and scientists who try to create 'perfect systems' are doomed to failure. Only God is perfect. Only God is complete. The people and the king are one thing, God Supreme is another.

Here in the 'natural world' tyrannies exist. The ruling class owns the State and are at liberty to do what they like. Unless stopped by the Law. But the Law is their own invention; amended and devised by the ruling class for their own protection. Look to the natural world for answers but be warned on the dangers. No system can 'explain everything'. God alone is the explanation.

'Incompleteness' and 'imperfection' are characteristics of humankind. We are all less than perfect, we are all sinners. The affairs of people and kings belong to 'this world'; the affairs of God are beyond reach.

Any product of human thought must contain 'a space'. Any human receptacle, such as a brain or a mind, will contain 'space for the space'. For Christians and others who hold religious beliefs this 'space' is of God, and 'the space for the space' is also of God.

But problems continue to arise: How do we know things we have never experienced? If we are obliged to stay within the 'natural world' how do we account for 'non-natural matters'? Things exist in the 'inner world' that have no existence in the 'natural world'. Never mind 'the true nature of God', what about the true nature of 'mathematical truths'? Economic systems and political truths may be tested and verified in the world we confront on a daily basis, the world where we meet the neighbours and sign on as unemployed but how do we verify 'inner truths'? Where do we test them? Can we test a spiritual truth in the natural world? How do we recognise 'truth'? Is truth beyond our grasp? What about 'beauty' and 'goodness'? Can they exist in the 'real world'? Perhaps not. This would explain the existence of hypocrisy, greed, the abuse of power. It would explain also why certain horrors appear necessary. Rich people remain rich through the suffering of others. The suffering is necessary. People retreat from the 'outer world' into their own 'inner world' that they might endure the suffering of other people, stoically.

Political principles clash with spiritual tenets; spiritual principles with political tenets. Liberty, democracy, universal suffrage are fundamental ideas but where did they 'belong', the 'outer world' or the 'inner world'; the natural world or the spiritual world? How about religious and intellectual liberties such as freedom of speech, freedom of thought and freedom of expression. Should they exist in 'real life'? Are they to be treated as 'spiritual' or 'material'?

Newtonian mechanics exercised a tremendous influence in Scotland as elsewhere in Europe. People wished to bring the rigor of this into their formulations of the 'inner' as well as 'outer' worlds; perhaps 'natural laws' might govern areas other than the purely 'physical': what about the inner workings of men and women?

The concern becomes not the spiritual world, nor the necessity of God's existence, but that there is more to life than the 'natural world' and what we learn and experience from within it. Certain 'inner truths' appear to hold true when applied to the 'outer' world; 'inner truths' are discovered, or perhaps revealed, by our application of bodily-things in the material world. Science helps us discover 'deeper' truths, 'inner truths'.

Individuals intuit illogicalities within belief-systems and perhaps amend them, or search for deeper consistencies. Logical distinctions come to provide a sort of theoretical basis for new sects to arise within particular religions, for new ideologies to split from orthodoxy, for the development of science.

Are we stuck with 'separate worlds' demanding separate sets of tools and methodology. Or are these worlds compatible?

Another difficulty is 'precedence'. Politics and religion go hand in hand for some, but others say 'hand in glove' is more fitting: humanity the hand and God the glove. The 'spiritual' world is 'of God' and thus greater than the 'natural' world, the world of human beings. For others the 'spiritual world' is the hand and the 'material' the glove. People can believe whatever they want to believe, but keep it under lock and key. Your 'inner' world is your business. Spiritual beliefs are all well and good but cannot be allowed to interfere with the world of human affairs: to that extent the 'spiritual' is redundant or irrelevant, and can even be consigned to oblivion.

In Scotland the skepticism of David Hume provided a major challenge. The difficulty for those who wished to confront this was the power of his work. It took another of similar stature: Thomas Reid.[94] His answer to skepticism provided a move forwards: 'Nothing is more conducive to the spread of a movement than the discussions arising out of the efforts of a capable opponent to refute its principles.'[95] And the legacy of this intellectual war is present in 'ethics, aesthetics and the philosophy of mind... [found] in contemporary theories of perception, free will, philosophy of religion, and widely in epistemology.'[96]

Issues around the compatibility of 'separate worlds', whether or not the 'material' world may be 'embraced' or 'transcended' by the 'spiritual', connect to ideas on 'perfection', 'completeness', 'translation' and 'interpretation', and through this we gain insight into the work of Kurt Gödel whose:

> Incompleteness Theorems [are] among the most significant achievements in logic since, perhaps, those of Aristotle touch[ing] every field of mathematical logic... Gödel formulated and defended mathematical Platonism, involving the view that mathematics is a descriptive science, and that the concept of mathematical truth is objective.[97]

If people are one thing and God another, how can we ever know Him? Perhaps never. Our own 'imperfection' remains. We are never 'complete'. We will come to know what we need to know. God has His own way of doing it. Perhaps he gives us knowledge by some other method.

Gödel was often in the company of Albert Einstein who said of James Clerk Maxwell, a central figure in the Scottish intellectual tradition:

Since Maxwell's time, physical reality has been thought of as represented by continuous fields, and not capable of any mechanical interpretation. This change in the conception of reality is the most profound and the most fruitful that physics has experienced since the time of Newton.[98]

Logical headaches are central to the history of ideas. One of the foremost Presbyterian theologians of the 19th century was Dr Thomas Chalmers who in his early days preached at the Tron Church in Glasgow. He antagonised the political as well as religious establishment by speaking in defence of the radicals from the pulpit. The family of Andrew Hardie were members of the congregation. Andrew attended not only the Kirk sermons but the additional lectures Chalmers gave on astronomy. He was also a mathematician and in 1804 had applied:

> for the chair of natural philosophy at St Andrews, and again in 1805 for the same chair in Edinburgh University. An objection [was] made to his candidature for the latter chair, 'that the vigorous prosecution of mathematical or natural science was incompatible with clerical duties.'[99]

He came to Glasgow in 1812 and created an immediate impression by:

> reorganising the parochial system so as to provide a machinery by which the destitute and outcast might be visited and reclaimed, and the young instructed in the lessons and duties of religion.'

This was a time when many scientists and intellectuals were having to reconcile Christian accounts of creation with findings in the field, as for example in geology.[100]

But perhaps the two can be reconciled. We discover knowledge of God by observing the world about us but also by searching inside ourselves. In both instances this knowledge is revealed to us by God Himself. The 'outer' and 'inner' worlds are compatible. They have to be. Our knowledge is of God and belongs to us through Him. Whether by revelation or by our knowledge of the 'natural' world is beside the point, it is only through God that we come to know of it.

The operations of 'Natural theology' and 'revealed truth' were essential areas for Thomas Chalmers and one volume of his very many written works is entitled *Discourses on the Christian Revelation, viewed in connexion with Modern Astronomy*.[101] In 1827 he left Glasgow, having accepted the Chair of Divinity at Edinburgh University. By 1843 controversies surrounding man-made tampering with 'spiritual' matters reached a peak. Chalmers had become the leading figure of the Disruption. Following the walkout he found his position within Edinburgh University untenable and resigned. Only one year later, by this time into his 60s, Chalmers:

> set on foot a scheme for reclaiming the inhabitants of the West Port district in Edinburgh, a locality notorious alike for physical squalor and moral degradation. A staff of visitors was organised for the purpose of visiting the different families in this quarter; a school was opened in the close which had earned an unenvied fame as the scene of Burke and Hare's murders; and lastly, an old tannery loft was opened for worship on Sundays, Dr. Chalmers himself conducting the services.[102]

It is difficult to exaggerate either his prominence or the regard in which he was held during his lifetime. When James and Lillie Connolly married they came to live at 22 West Port and there is no question that his name and reputation would have survived. Just along the road from where he lived the Reverend Glasse preached at Old Greyfriars Parish Kirk, the friend Morris referred to earlier.

With Eleanor Marx, Edward Aveling and others, following their split from Social Democratic Federation [SDF], Morris had founded the Socialist League, '[advocating] the principles of Revolutionary International Socialism'[103] and was home to a variety of christian socialists, anti-parliamentarian socialists, Marxists and anarchists; diverse 'impossibilists' but very few 'reformists'. Dr Glasse organised talks and meetings and featured speakers included 'Andreas Scheu, Leo Melliet, Lawrence Gronlund... Prince Kropotkin, Stepniak, Henry George, and Edward Carpenter...'. Connolly and his brother John attended these talks and meetings and were acquainted with the Rev Glasse, well versed in the so-called 'clash' between Christianity and socialism.

In the earlier quotation Morris recognised that there might have been more to the Scottish comrades than an inspired reading of Marx, that 'the road of the reading and political experience common to the more thoughtful of the Scotch working class generally' might have had something to with it. This is not to say that they were unfamiliar with the work of Marx, but that there might have been a solid base from which to begin. Elsewhere Morris refers to a famous meeting at Glasgow's Albion Halls when he was heckled by Willie Nairn,[104] a stonebreaker from Brechin long settled in Glasgow. Nairn was a founder member of the Scottish branch of the SDF and was giving 'lectures based on Volume One of Marx's *Capital*' in the early 1880s, almost 30 years prior to John Maclean:[105]

[When] Morris rose to leave the meeting, [he] asked the question, 'Does Comrade Morris accept Marx's theory of value?' Morris replied emphatically, 'I do not know what Marx's theory of value is, and I'm damned if I want to know. It is enough political economy for me to know that the idle class is rich because they rob the poor.'

Morris' position held true for many radicals. For others it was not enough. The poor had been robbed by the rich for centuries, their own families among them: Connolly, Nairn, Keir Hardie, Wheatley, Bruce Glasier and other activists had grown up in desperate hardship. Something more than the most basic knowledge of the fact was required.

Connolly's position was shared by very many of his Scottish comrades of the period, perhaps more associated with members of the Independent Labour Party (ILP). Connolly knew David Lowe and Keir Hardie from his early days in Dundee and perhaps was present when 'Keir Hardie gave the opening lecture' for the first meeting of the Labour Church in Scotland.[106] He knew also another leader of the ILP: John Wheatley, who founded the Catholic Socialist Society and held meetings and discussions at his home in the east end of Glasgow. Connolly was one of the many visitors. Here he met the younger squad, MacManus, Bell, Paul. So too was Jim Larkin a visitor to Wheatley's home and he forces his way into this essay, doing his damndest for the last word, from a speech he made in 1913 in which he declared, in characteristic low-key fashion: 'the man that tells you it is impossible to be a Socialist and a Catholic is a liar.'[107]

This was not enough for Connolly, as with others of his generation in Scotland, there were ways into these ideas that seemed to demand exploration and the attempt to work things out for yourself. It was not enough just to 'know'. When we focus on the life and times of James Connolly here in Scotland we find a general intellectual integrity among his friends and comrades and, during their early years especially, a duty to the article of faith, whether the faith was religious or not. Most of them were punished by the State, some severely, enduring periods of imprisonment, suffering physical torture through force-feeding and excessive force, and some died young. Those who seek to raise doubts in regard to his integrity will have to live with the fact that Connolly was a good man and he was an honest man and, like countless others, was murdered by due process of the British State acting in a manner typical of any other tyranny.

Short Skirts, Strong Boots and a Revolver: Scotland and the Women of 1916

Kirsty Lusk

If you want to walk round Ireland, or any other country, dress suitably in short skirts and strong boots, leave your jewels and gold wands in the bank and buy a revolver. Don't trust to your 'feminine charm' and your capacity for getting on the soft side of men, but take up your responsibilities and be prepared to go your own way depending for safety on your own courage, your own truth and your own common sense.[108]

IN 1915, MILITANT feminism and militant nationalism were both on the increase, but there remained a division between them. Countess Constance Markievicz, a suffragette, a socialist and a nationalist, was a strong critic of the subordinate role of the women's organisation, Cumann na mBan, to the male Irish Volunteers. In her speech to the Irish Women's Franchise League in October 1915, she complained, 'Today the women attached to the national movements are there chiefly to collect funds for the men to spend'[109], and stated that only in the suffragettes and Labour women was the spirit of ancient Ireland still in existence. 'Ancient Ireland,' she argued, 'bred warrior women and women who played a heroic part in those days. Today, we are in danger of being civilised by men out of existence.'[110]

If we switch 'existence' with 'the national narrative' then there was a strong prophetic element to Markievicz's words. The Easter Rising of 1916 has a powerful and ever changing legacy, one in which a masculine nationalist narrative bound with ideas of blood sacrifice has taken precedence over the twin concerns of labour and women's rights. In *The Proclamation of the Irish Republic*, nationalism, labour rights and gender equality were bound together in an appeal to the people of Ireland regardless of their creed. However, efforts to consolidate the different intents behind the Rising into one coherent narrative have led to the suppression of alternative narratives, including those of feminism and socialism, both through literature such as that of WB Yeats or Sean O'Casey, but also through political manoeuvring. In addition, the personal accounts of the female participants of 1916 are less well known and there are many that have gone unnoticed or remained unshared until recently. In the last few years, public and academic attention has returned to overlooked aspects of the major events in Irish history, particularly to lesser explored elements of the Easter Rising, such as the role of women, in preparation for, as participants in, and in the aftermath of 1916. It is through publications by authors such as Margaret Ward, Sinead McCoole, Liz Gillis and Ruth Taillon that the extensive participation of women in Irish politics during the revolutionary period is becoming known and understood, and that these women are beginning to be returned to the narrative which they had been 'civilised' out of.

It is estimated that more than 100 women took part directly in the Easter Rising.[111] Amongst these women was a 23 year old Coatbridge-born schoolteacher named Margaret Skinnider who fought as a dispatch rider and sniper, attached to the Irish Citizen Army, and who went on to write a personal account of her experiences of Easter week, entitled *Doing My Bit for Ireland* (1917). A militant suffragette known to the police, Skinnider became involved with the Irish Volunteers in Glasgow before joining the Anne Devlin branch of Cumann na mBan when it was set up in Glasgow in mid-1915. Through her childhood experiences of inequality while visiting Ireland on holiday with her family, Skinnider had developed a strong conviction of the necessity of Irish independence, which she combined with her belief in the necessity of gender equality and improved labour rights. With the advent of the First World War, it became apparent that action would be taken and the Anne Devlin branch of Cumann na mBan, Skinnider with them, were involved in raids at shipyards and mining facilities in the West of Scotland with the Irish Republican Brotherhood for arms, explosives and ammunition. It was not long before Countess Markievicz, to whom these supplies were being sent, heard of Skinnider's work with Cumann na mBan and invited Margaret to visit her in Dublin at Christmas in 1915. Skinnider travelled at night by ferry over the Irish sea, with bomb detonators hidden inside her hat, arriving safely despite her understandable fear of accidentally setting them off. Unsurprisingly, Skinnider highly respected Countess Markievicz, who proved something of an inspiration and she described her as 'the most patriotic and revolutionary woman in Ireland'.[112]

While in Dublin, Skinnider continued to help with preparations for the Rising, her work including drawing up plans of the Beggar's Bush barracks, putting her skills in mathematics to excellent use in assisting Countess Markievicz. She also passed herself off as a boy to the Dublin Fianna in case the disguise might be necessary in the future. Skinnider had joined a rifle club in Glasgow, one of many set up, ironically, to train women in case they were required to defend Britain, and she proved herself a better shot than any of the boys when taken to a local shooting gallery. It was also during this visit that she was first introduced to Thomas McDonagh, who gifted her the revolver she would go on to use during the Rising. At the start of 1916, Skinnider returned to Glasgow to continue her teaching career and to await news of the planned Rising.

Skinnider arrived in Dublin on Holy Thursday and joined the Irish Citizen Army at the recommendation of Countess Markievicz, who was an officer in the organisation. During Easter week, she was a member of the St. Stephen's Green contingent under Markievicz and Commandant Michael Mallin. Skinnider worked as a dispatch rider at great personal risk and was mentioned three times for bravery in dispatches to the General Post Office. By the Wednesday of Easter week, when there were fewer dispatches to be taken, she changed into her uniform at the request of Markievicz, and took a spot in the rafters of the Royal College of Surgeons to fight as a sniper against the British soldiers placed at the Shelbourne Hotel. 'More than once I saw the man I aimed at fall',[113] she recounts.

On Wednesday evening, Margaret Skinnider was part of a contingent sent out to set fire to a house so as to restrict the British retreat. When Councillor William Partridge broke the lock on the door, his rifle discharged and the flash drew the attention of the British forces. Margaret Skinnider was shot three times, receiving severe wounds to her spine and upper right arm, causing nerve damage which would trouble her for the rest of her life. She remained in the Royal College of Surgeons until the surrender order was given, at serious danger from pneumonia as well as her wounds. Skinnider survived her wounds and remained in St. Vincent's Hospital until she was fully recovered. Despite being questioned by the police, Skinnider was not arrested and succeeded in getting a special permit to return to Glasgow, thanks in part to her 'loyal Scotch accent'[114].

The most famous of the female participants from Scotland, Skinnider was by no means the only one, yet the influence of Scottish women on the Rising – and the impact of the Rising on Scottish women – is almost entirely unexplored. There are few surviving records of the Anne Devlin branch of Cumann na mBan prior to and during 1916. Skinnider travelled over to Dublin smuggling arms with a Miss O'Neill and she references Lizzie Morrin, a dressmaker who made clothing with hidden pockets for unobtrusive smuggling of ammunition. The lack of records is compounded by some personal resistance to acknowledging connections with Scotland by those who were involved in the Rising.

Nora Connolly O'Brien (1893–1981) was born in Edinburgh, Scotland, the second daughter of James Connolly and Lillie Connolly. In her early years, the family moved frequently for Connolly's work and O'Brien spent time in

America, Dublin and Belfast, as well as Scotland, during her youth. Later an activist, a member of the Irish senate (nominated by the Taoiseach Eamon de Valera) and a writer, O'Brien authored a number of books relating to Irish independence, including two particularly focused on her father and his ideals, entitled *Portrait of a Rebel Father* (1935) and *James Connolly Wrote For Today – Socialism* (1978). Apparently, at the age of eight, Nora 'saw her father speak in Glasgow and, from then on, was a devotee of his socialist politics'[115]. Like Skinnider, O'Brien assisted in the preparations for the Rising and the pair went on to become firm friends. She also worked closely with her father and Countess Markievicz. O'Brien not only helped with bringing in 900 rifles at Howth, sitting atop the rifles in taxis to hide them while moving them through the city, but she also smuggled Liam Mellows (who was to be deported) back to Ireland from Leeds by dressing him as a cleric, and informed her father of the orders from Eoin MacNeill against mobilisation of the Irish Volunteers. It was O'Brien who snuck James Connolly's last statement out of Dublin Castle, despite being searched, and she would go on to write her account of the events of Easter Week, *The Unbroken Tradition* (1918), while staying in New York with Margaret Skinnider. Like Skinnider, it was her connections with Scotland that allowed O'Brien to leave Ireland. When travelling to America, she gave her name as Margaret Connolly and provided Skinnider's Glasgow address instead of her own, subverting expectations by playing on the same stereotype of Scottish loyalty. O'Brien remained reluctant to discuss her Scottish roots in any detail for most of her life, contrary to her sister Ina Connolly Heron who provided a statement to the Bureau of Military History Archives that detailed their father's past and his political involvement in Scotland.

In writing of Scotland and the Easter Rising however, it is important to go beyond the active participants in the struggle and to acknowledge the more subtle, perhaps unintentional, influences. The suffrage movement was one that reached across borders, as was the labour movement. In hospital, Margaret Skinnider spoke to her fellow patients and nurses about the work of the Scottish suffragettes. According to Skinnider:

We had very few Irish revolutionists in Scotch prisons. Two hundred of them were brought, during August, to Barlinnie Prison but they were allowed to stay only a short time. Far too much sympathy was expressed for them by the Irish in Glasgow and by Scotch suffragettes, who made a point of going to visit them and taking them comforts.[116]

There were other Scottish suffragettes who had a lasting influence however.

Head of the Women's Liberation Front, Ishbel Hamilton-Gordon, Marchioness of Aberdeen and Temair (1857–1939) was instrumental in providing first aid training to women in Dublin. Her husband, John Campbell Hamilton-Gordon, was the first Marquess of Aberdeen and Temair, and Lord Lieutenant of Ireland in 1886 and from 1905–15, and Lady Aberdeen courted controversy by opening the lessons to anyone who wished to be taught, not just those loyal to the British Empire, and thus provided valuable training to members of Cumann na mBan. Lillie Connolly appealed to Lady Aberdeen in 1913 when her husband, James Connolly, was on hunger strike in prison, having been arrested for his part in the Dublin Lockout. Lady Aberdeen demanded his release and it was discovered that her husband, the Lord Lieutenant had already given the order for him to be freed from prison.[117]

Margaret Ward is entirely correct when she states:

> We need to read about the concerns of the suffrage movement; we need to know what women in the labour movement were saying and doing; and women whose political sympathies were with the unionist cause also need to have their voice recovered for this generation.[118]

Unless these alternative voices are brought back into the narrative of the Easter Rising then there are glaring gaps in our understanding of the legacy of 1916 and the confluence of events and motivations that brought about the Rising. Scottish-born women such as Margaret Skinnider and Nora Connolly O'Brien who wrote personal accounts of 1916 are thus incredibly important figures in reconfiguring that narrative.

The events of Easter week had a lasting legacy for women's rights as well as Irish Independence. Margaret Skinnider, recalling an argument with Michael Mallin during Easter week, wrote:

> My answer to that argument was that we had the same right to risk our lives as the men; that in the constitution of the Irish Republic, women were on an equality with men. For the first time in history, indeed, a constitution had been written that incorporated equal suffrage.[119]

In this respect, the Proclamation of the Irish Republic was a revolutionary document, a positive step forward for gender equality (despite all the signatories being male). The ideal was more challenging to put into practice however. Kathleen Clarke recounts that:

> [when the Proclamation] was signed that night, it represented the views

of all except one, who thought equal opportunities should not be given to women. Except to say that Tom [Clarke] was not that one, my lips are sealed.[120]

During Easter Week, women were turned away from a number of garrisons throughout the city by leaders including Eamon de Valera and many of them attached themselves to the Irish Citizen Army in the General Post Office instead of the Irish Volunteers as the ICA were more accepting of women in their ranks. This tension between the Proclamation and political practice may to some extent explain the reluctance to approach the reality of women's participation in 1916, highlighting an element of hypocrisy. When Margaret Skinnider applied for her military pension in 1925, she was told it only applied to 'soldiers as generally understood in the masculine sense'[121]. Skinnider would not receive her pension until 1938. Gender equality remained an ideal rather than a reality and still does to this day. In that respect, the Proclamation is not just a document of important historical value but also a reminder of what is still to be achieved.

With the Celtic Revival, the Dublin Lockout and Easter week as well as the suffrage movement, women in Ireland were more politically engaged than ever before. The events of the Easter Rising reached beyond militaristic endeavour. They also triggered revolutionary change in constitutional politics. In 1918, Countess Markievicz, as a member of Sinn Féin, was elected to the British House of Commons as the first female Member of Parliament. Markievicz did not take her seat. She was still in jail, and in any case Sinn Féin refused to take their seats, instead establishing the Dáil Éireann. In 1921, Markievicz would go on to become the first Irish female cabinet member as Minister for Labour.

In a speech at the Scottish Parliament on 14 March 2015, to the Scottish Women's Convention, Scottish First Minister Nicola Sturgeon stated that:

Scotland has always turned out women with big political ideas and I have been fortunate in that a number of strong women blazed a trail before me in Scottish politics.[122]

The source of that legacy stretches beyond Scottish politics. Sturgeon noted the impressive female representation in the Scottish Parliament:

Standing in this chamber each week for FMQs, before a female Presiding Officer to debate with two other female leaders it could be easy to forget how much more work we still have to do.[123]

We owe the continued and expanding involvement of women in politics to those who have provided the inspiration for young women and there is no doubt that the Scottish independence movement, like the Irish independence movement, has encouraged political engagement amongst women, particularly young women. Countess Markievicz was the first female MP, Nicola Sturgeon is the first female Scottish First Minister and both have encouraged young women to engage not just in politics but every aspect of civic life. 'Many still perceive politics as an unfriendly place for a woman to be. That must change,'[124] Sturgeon insisted. Markievicz took the first step on a long journey towards achieving gender equality in political representation and Nicola Sturgeon has taken another, insisting on a gender balance in her cabinet. There is an echo of Markievicz's appeal to the young women of Ireland in Sturgeon's appeal to the young women of Scotland:

> When I became First Minister four months ago, I said in this chamber that I hoped that my election would send a strong, positive message to all girls and young women in Scotland – if you are good enough and if you work hard enough, nothing should hold you back, the sky is the limit. No glass ceiling should ever stop you from achieving your dreams.[125]

Coatbridge-born Margaret Skinnider was 23 years old when she was shot three times in the spine and upper right arm while fighting for Irish independence as a member of the Republican forces during Easter week. At the same age, all I had to do was walk five minutes to my nearest polling station and put a cross in the correct box to signal my wish for Scottish independence. Both endeavours failed to gain independence. It would take years of struggle before Irish Independence was finally – if not fully – achieved, and Scottish independence is still a hope for the future for many. What is clear though is that while equal suffrage is a reality, true equality for women is still something to achieve and real independence for the nation needs to entail gender equality. By bringing female voices back into the narrative of the Easter Rising perhaps it will be possible to take a step towards reconciliation and a fuller understanding of the importance of its legacy for Scotland today.

Irish Kin under Scottish Skin

Kevin McKenna

SOMEWHERE OUT THERE, perhaps, is a geopolitical relationship counsellor who might help people who encounter conflict in their emotions about the lands from which they were sprung. I fancy that most of her customers would be people like me who, for most of their adult lives, have struggled to measure their loyalty to the land of their birth and to the land where their ancestors were born.

As a fourth generation Irishman (I think that means that my great grandparents were born in Ireland) I have tried to convince myself that my relationship with Ireland has never been strong. Ireland has been the mother who gave me up for adoption and I have been the reluctant son, torn between love and resentment. Such is the contradictory love-hate relationship my generation of Scots-Irish has with the old country. On special occasions we reconnect and, drink having been taken, I am comfortable in my Irishness and I become that object of derision on either side of the water, the Plastic Paddy. These occasions have receded as I've got older though, and today I would insist that I have never felt more comfortable in my Scottish skin.

Yet there have been regrettable occasions when I have taken my Irishness out of the closet and for a night out. At these times, again when drink has been taken, I have sought to add a degree of the theatrical to my existence by putting on what I fancy is a very entertaining Irish accent, rarely taking account of the feelings of any Irish people in the company and forgetting how cringeworthy is an Englishman trying out a cod Scottish accent. To be sure.

On these occasions I am fond of exaggerating my Irishness, usually to wind up my Presbyterian Scottish friends or to impress women from an Irish background like mine. My favourite and most regrettable way of doing this was to exaggerate the Irishness of my name, which is plain old Kevin Joseph McKenna. Sometimes though, I'll allow a cheeky wee Patrick to creep in there too, this being my Confirmation name. Kevin Joseph Patrick McKenna. It's more Irish than Kathleen O'Hanlon's shawl. But it's not as Irish as Kevin Joseph Patrick ALOYSIUS McKenna. Admittedly, the added nomenclature is in direct proportion to the amount of Bacardis I've shifted and at this point my companions are waiting for me to break into the Riverdance.

Some other offences must be taken into account such as laughing at Ian

Paisley's description of the south as a 'Priest-ridden banana republic'... in the good Doctor's Ulster roar, or ridiculing Saint Bono when he turned up at a Glasgow concert venue and began clicking his fingers. 'Every time I click my fingers another child dies of starvation,' said Bono. 'Well stop clicking your fuckin' fingers then,' came a Glaswegian voice from the audience.

Permit me, if you will, to reach for a football analogy (favoured by all those lacking in imagination) to define the pattern of my patriotic relationships. If Scotland were ever to reach another major finals series in my lifetime then, of course, she would be my first preference. Very quickly though, Scotland would be knocked out and then my support would transfer to Ireland. In a match between Scotland and Ireland there is no conflict at all and I will support the country of my birth.

In my teens it was fashionable to display love and affection towards Ireland and it was considered a duty almost to study the origins, conduct and aftermath of Irish history from the republican perspective. Thus, at university, my friends and I joined the Troops Out movement and mixed with bar-room intellectuals who talked endlessly about the Easter Rising, not in the context of Ireland's relationship with Britain but from the perspective of Marxism and the continuing struggle of workers everywhere.

These good but very zealous people took rather a dim view of us in our Celtic scarves who insisted on buying Guinness all night long and were word perfect in the 'Broad Black Brimmer', a song that was pressed into service halfway through the fourth pint. That or 'Sean South of Garryowen'.

We, in turn, disdained their lofty idealism and were suspicious of their pernicious anti-clericalism. These reedy-voiced, combat-jacketed atheists didn't give a flying fuck about Catholic Ireland and the restoration of the 32 counties, they simply viewed it as a laboratory in which to experiment with their formulas for an international workers' revolution. This was our first emotional and spiritual conflict over Ireland, but there was another one unravelling in my own home, one that I suspect was being played out in the bedrooms and living rooms of many Irish Catholic households across the West of Scotland.

In the early 1980s universities and colleges throughout west central Scotland encountered a significant influx of undergraduates from working class, Irish-Catholic households. These were third and fourth generation Irish who had lately begun to grow uncomfortable and not a little resentful of the social and cultural contracts their parents had struck with civic Scotland.

We grew up in households where gentle Irish rebel songs of the 'Johnson's Motor Car' oeuvre were occasionally belted out and where my father's rendition of 'Danny Boy' signaled that the party was over. But in my early school years 'the Troubles' came (it was always whispered) and so all those songs which were considered to possess even the merest hint of rebellion or of armed struggle were jettisoned in a mass act of self-censorship and were rarely heard of again. My parents, you see, along with many others, were fearful of causing offence in a country where they still considered themselves to be immigrants confessing a faith that was still to be feared and to be treated very carefully. At a time when the BBC and the British press were reporting Ulster in a grotesquely one-sided way it was best to stick with 'Danny Boy' and 'Molly Malone'.

But the multitudes of their sons and daughters who, in the early '80s, were the first fruits of their grandparents' self-sacrifice and discipline, seemed to possess more strident, even belligerent, feelings about Ireland, the Potato Famine, 1916 and the civil rights issues of the Catholics in Ulster. It is impossible to discuss matters pertaining to the Irish diaspora in Scotland without talking about Celtic Football Club. It is simply impossible to overstate the importance of Celtic to the Irish Catholic community in Scotland. The Glasgow University Celtic Supporters Club, founded in 1970, was in 1981 the single biggest club affiliated to the Students Representative Council.

On Holy Days of Obligation four masses were filled to their capacity and then, in October 1981 there was the Hunger Strikers incident. This was when a motion to support Bobby Sands and his fellow hunger strikers in the H-Block at Long Kesh prison was debated at the Glasgow University Union. The motion was carried in front of a tumultuous crowd and the decision made headline news across the UK and beyond. It wasn't difficult to detect a sense of disbelief in the reporting of the event and in its analysis. 'What just happened?' How did one of Britain's oldest and most revered educational establishments fall into the hands of this republican rabble?

Many of the students who thronged the debating hall that day went on to reach the top branches of the UK and Scotland's legislative and judicial executive. Others began to storm the citadels of those professions which their parents and grandparents had struggled to break down owing to their faith and heritage – newspapers, the law and the financial services. Yet while making their way in Scotland, for the most part they left their passion and fervour for the Byzantine politics of Ulster in that debating hall. From time to time it received an outing at Celtic Park, especially in those games against Rangers. Even as Scotland was changing and becoming more self-confident so, I believe, were the Irish Catholics. We had made our point and fulfilled our grandparents' dreams, when they disembarked from the boats that carried them away from famine, of making a better life for their descendants.

Some memories from that time though, still make me squirm. My brother had chosen to study quietly at an engineering college where he became firm friends with Craig, a lovely Protestant lad from Ulster whose parents were keen for him to study in Scotland to get away from the trouble in his own country. Thereafter, I can barely recount this tale without wincing. It's a car crash from here on in.

Our Gerard had invited Craig to stay for the weekend and my parents were delighted because it meant that their efforts to guide us away from sectarianism and division seemed to have borne some fruit. Craig had been given my bedroom for the weekend as I was in Aberdeen for a Celtic match. But no one had told me about this arrangement, otherwise I would have removed the giant poster of Bobby Sands which hung over my bed, fighting with Che Guevara for dominance of the wall space.

My brother was just bewildered but my dad was ashamed and furious. And so when I walked in the door, euphoric at a rare Celtic victory at Pittodrie he said, 'You are a bloody fool, what the hell do you know about Bobby Sands? How dare you embarrass our family like this?'

'I'm the one who ought to be ashamed,' I replied, 'at how much my family has forgotten where it came from.' And then he hit me... the only time he ever did so.

Perhaps though, my comfort in my Scottish skin and the way in which I have allowed my Irish heritage to fade gently away comes simply from complacency and indolence of the 'I'm alright, Jack...' strain. Not long ago I was challenged eloquently by the Scottish academic, Joe Bradley who took me to task when I told him I now felt more Scottish than Irish. 'I was born here, educated here and work here. I can count on one hand the number of times I've been back to Ireland,' I said. 'My parents and grandparents were born in Scotland.'

'So when did 1,000 years of Irish blood become Scottish in less than 100?' asked Joe.

Last year I was compelled once more to address the conflict between birth and heritage; my Scottishness and my Irishness. I accepted an invitation to speak at an event in Letterkenny organised by the Donegal Diaspora Committee which explored the impact of immigration from Ireland to the rest of the world. The title of my talk was 'A reluctant Irishman in Scotland' and while preparing it I was forced to confront my complacency and denial.

I live in a Scotland which still remains uncomfortable with its citizens who are of Irish descent. The ridiculously drawn out process by which Glasgow is reluctantly and slowly agreeing to have a memorial to the Irish Famine has become embarrassing. The Great Famine, more than any other event, shaped Glasgow's destiny. In not having a Famine memorial Glasgow stands alone among those cities where there is a significant Irish immigrant population. Likewise St Patrick's Day Parades and other public displays of Irishness outside of football matches are rarer here than in other cities with comparable histories of Irish immigration. And 2016 looks like being the first real opportunity to mark the Easter Rising, led by James Connolly, a Scot of Irish heritage.

The reasons this remains the case are similar to the reasons Neil Lennon, the former manager and captain of Celtic FC was physically assaulted more than a dozen times during his 11-year career in Glasgow… and the victim of an attempted murder bid. Yet it is over-simplistic to blame old-style anti-Catholic bigotry for this.

Lennon's career at Celtic occurred at a moment in history in Scotland which has seen the main Christian churches decline in influence and an erosion in the traditions and hegemony of the Church of Scotland. A well-known Glasgow lawyer and Rangers supporter Douglas Kilpatrick is uncomfortable with the easy assumptions about the opprobrium that surrounded the Celtic manager. 'To some in my tradition, Lennon represents the sum of all fears, and religious prejudice on its own does not explain all of this,' Kilpatrick once told me. 'The influence and sense of entitlement which has sustained many working-class and middle-class Protestants has declined in the last decade or so. Some Scots just can't cope with this all at once and their response is suitably atavistic. But it will pass. There is too much healthy respect and goodwill between the majority on either side for it not to.'

Those from an Irish Catholic background are looking in the wrong direction if they still feel that classic, Orange anti-popery is to blame for any of the belligerence that remains in Scotland towards their faith. Instead they should look to Holyrood and to civic Scotland where Catholicism and indeed any other expression of mainstream Christianity is becoming annually less tolerable as the 21st century progresses. The debate over gay marriage and faith schools and the fate of two experienced Catholic midwives who refused to participate in abortions has revealed an aggressive strain running through all of our main political parties which holds that all vestiges of Christianity must be wiped from the face of civic Scotland. And it would be even better if they could criminalise some aspects of traditional Catholic and Christian teaching in the process.

Following a century of progress, success and advancement Irish Catholicism may be facing a challenge greater than anything posed by traditional and influential Protestantism. Ironically, it is to evangelical Protestantism that the Catholic Irish must now look to make common cause against a greater threat. Remembrance of the Easter Rising in Scotland may offer an opportunity to re-examine religious identities and to interrogate secularism as well as sectarianism.

'Pure James Connolly': From Cowgate to Clydeside[126]

Willy Maley

ON 11 OCTOBER 2010, *The Scotsman* newspaper ran an item entitled 'Scot in line for top Irish title'. The Scot was Edinburgh-born James Connolly, the title that of Ireland's greatest historical figure. Connolly came fourth of the five shortlisted candidates, but he beat Bono. The winner was not a Scotsman with an Irish name but an Irishman with a Scottish name, John Hume. And not just a Scottish name but also a great-grandfather, Willie Hume, from the Lowlands of Scotland, who emigrated to Donegal during the reign of Victoria.[127]

In recent years, Irish and Scottish critics have argued for Connolly's Scottishness, an aspect of his identity often airbrushed out of historical accounts. Successive British and Irish commentators of varying political persuasions have their own reasons for sidelining Scotland in official versions of 'Anglo-Irish' history. Unionists adhere to a British identity, where Scottishness can be an unnecessary complication, while for nationalists the perception persists that the Ulster-Scots connection provided – and still provides – a backdoor to Britishness. Yet according to Murray Pittock:

> By most measures of nationality, James Connolly was a Scot: described as 'Scotto-Hibernian' even in Dublin (where he came from Edinburgh at the age of 28), he spoke with a Scots accent and named his daughter, born in 1907, 'Fiona' after William Sharp's alter ego.[128]

As Owen Dudley Edwards observed in a pioneering essay:

> The first thing to remember about James Connolly and Irish tradition is that he was born outside it. He was Edinburgh born, his parents were Monaghan emigrants to Edinburgh.[129]

Edwards argues – as does James Kelman elsewhere in this collection – that Connolly's socialism was made in Scotland:

Looking up from the squalid and almost lightless depths of the Cowgate, the young Connolly could learn Marxism simply by seeing the stately folk walking far above him on the fashionable George IV Bridge which swept above the slums below. He could see he was a proletarian long before he could hear he was Irish.[130]

Edwards makes fun of the Irish tendency to render invisible Connolly's Scottish origins:

In Irish tradition, Connolly was born at the age of 28 in Dublin in 1896, in the manner of Mr. Furriskey in *At Swim-Two-Birds*, when he was not born in Clones at the age of 0 in 1870. But in fact, he was of course born at the age of 0 in Edinburgh in 1868, and therefore his view of Irish tradition was never wholly Irish.[131]

Edwards insists that Connolly's 'immediate heirs' are to be found 'not among the Irish republicans but with such figures as John Maclean of Scotland'.[132] Connolly wasn't just born in Edinburgh – the youngest of three sons. He lived in Scotland till he was 28. Connolly supported Hibernian Football Club, founded in 1875 by Canon Edward Hannan, an Irish priest based in Edinburgh's Cowgate, known as 'Little Ireland'. Connolly didn't just support Hibs; he carried the players' kits and did other odd jobs at the ground. He left school at ten and worked in a printer's, a bakery and a tiling factory. He also worked at the Edinburgh *Evening News*. Connolly's formative political influences and socialist principles were formed in Scotland.

Which is not to say that the Scottish claim to Connolly is uncontested. Those whose families left Ireland in the wake of Famine feel part of a great diaspora, and thus entitled to self-describe as Irish. Many Irish and Scottish socialists had cross-cultural connections and cross-water connections. They included Willie Gallacher (1881–1965), born in the Irish ghetto of Sneddon, Paisley in 1881, who played a key role in founding the Communist Party of Great Britain in 1920–21; and Ulster Scots Socialists like William Walker (1871–1918), the Belfast Protestant who challenged Connolly, and David 'Davy' Robb Campbell (1874/5–1934), the Belfast Protestant who supported Connolly. John Wheatley (1869–1930) is another key crossover figure. Born in Bonmahon, Co. Waterford, in 1869, his family moved to Bargeddie, near Glasgow, in 1876. Wheatley became a leading Scottish socialist, joining the Independent Labour Party in 1906, and founding the Catholic Socialist Society in the same year. The Dublin Lock Out of 1913 and the Glasgow Rent Strike of 1915 showed solidarity across the water.[133] Speaking in March

1918, Cathal O'Shannon claimed that:

> Glasgow and Dublin are the two cities in these countries that lead the van in the militant army of Labour, and from them, if from nowhere else, we may expect a bold lead.[134]

One of the most radical Scottish socialists of the time was John Maclean (1879–1923). According to James Hunter:

> Both Connolly and Maclean – the two most outstanding Marxist revolutionaries so far produced in these islands – were born to Gaelic-speaking parents. And they devoted no small part of their considerable abilities to reconcile socialism with the nationalisms of their respective countries.[135]

The phrase 'respective countries' ignores the fact both were born in Scotland and took an interest in the politics of Ireland and Scotland. In the summer of 1907, during the strike by dockers and carters, Maclean spent a few days in Belfast with Jim Larkin. Maclean reflected on the risks of sectarianism:

> The strikers and thousands of workers knew that they must cease quarrelling about Catholicism and Protestantism, because thus they would be playing the game of the capitalists. I believe religious riots are a thing of the past, consequent upon the eyes of the people having been opened to the scurrility of the party press and to the treachery of the party politicians, both Nationalists and Unionists alike.[136]

Belfast-born Ulster Scot William Walker reminded Connolly in their exchange in Scottish socialist magazine *Forward* in 1911 that Scottish Presbyterianism and Protestantism more broadly had played a progressive part in modern Irish history, including labour history. According to James D Young: 'The role of *Forward* in providing Maclean, Connolly and Larkin with space to expound their views testified to the developing links between the left of the Scottish and Irish workers' movements'.[137] Walker stood unsuccessfully as Labour candidate for Leith in the general election of January 1910, so he had Scottish connections in the neighbourhood from which Connolly sprang. In fact, Connolly and Walker had both stood for office in Scotland, Connolly unsuccessfully contesting elections to Edinburgh Council in 1894 and 1895.

Irish-Scottish connections in their modern form date from the Ulster Plantation presided over by King James VI and I in 1609, an event that transformed their relations to the benefit of England and the emerging British state. Connolly expressed his view on Ulster and the Scots in an essay written for *Forward* on 12 July 1913. He sympathised with the presbyterian planters as victims of English colonial manipulation in a passage that anticipates the views of Alasdair Gray in his pamphlet on Scottish independence, to the effect that the Ulster plantation was designed to divide and rule the Irish and Scottish. According to Gray:

> A large body of English settlers might have held Ulster down, but very few English wanted to settle in a hostile and much poorer land [...] Jamie did what could only be done by a Scottish king ruling Ireland with an English army: he colonised Ulster.[138]

As Jonathan Githens-Mazer puts it:

> Sectarianism blinded Catholic and Protestant to common exploitation by English elites who introduced or settled outsiders in Ulster to exploit them for personal gain.[139]

Connolly maintained that:

> while the Plantation succeeded from the point of view of the Government in placing in the heart of Ulster a body of people who, whatever their disaffection to that Government, were still bound by fears of their own safety to defend it against the natives, it did not bring either civil or religious liberty to the Presbyterian planters.

And went on to conclude that:

> the only hope lies in the latter combining with the former in overthrowing their common spoilers, and consenting to live in amity together in the common ownership of their common country [...] I have always held, despite the fanatics on both sides, that the movements of Ireland for freedom could not and cannot be divorced from the world-wide upward movements of the world's democracy. The Irish question is a part of the social question, the desire of the Irish people to control their own destinies is a part of the desire of the workers to forge political weapons for their own enfranchisement as a class. The Orange fanatic and the Capitalist-minded Home Ruler are alike in denying this truth; ere long, both of them will be but memories, while the army of those who believe in that truth

will be marching and battling on its conquering way.[140]

In 1914, as the prospect of partition loomed, Connolly attacked those who:

agree in front of the enemy and in face of the world to sacrifice to the bigoted enemy the unity of the nation and along with it the lives, liberties and hopes of that portion of the nation which in the midst of the most hostile surroundings have fought to keep the faith in things national and progressive [...] the betrayal of the national democracy of industrial Ulster would mean a carnival of reaction both North and South, would set back the wheels of progress, would destroy the oncoming unity of the Irish Labour movement and paralyse all advanced movements whilst it endured.[141]

Connolly had spoken in Glasgow on 15 October 1910, so he was certainly attuned to events there. James D Young confirms Maclean's views on Connolly's awareness of Scottish developments in the run-up to Easter 1916:

Connolly was aware of what was happening on Red Clydeside. In the 20 November, 1915 issue of the *Workers' Republic*, he attacked the suppression of 'Free Speech in Scotland' [...] At much the same time, he published an article entitled 'Glasgow Gaels Will Fight' in which he reported on a meeting in the Sinn Féin Hall, London Street, Glasgow... In an article on 'Scots Labour Men and Lloyd George', Connolly published a report in the *Workers' Republic* saying that the majority of Clydeside workers at the famous meeting in Glasgow were anti-war.[142]

Connolly's intimate knowledge of the Scottish scene was mirrored by the growing activism of other Irish-Scots increasingly exercised by events across the water.

In the aftershock of Easter 1916, and after a spell in prison, Maclean moved closer to Connolly's views. According to Gavin Foster, when Maclean visited Dublin for the first time in July 1919, 'he was exposed to the large British military build-up in Ireland and was forced to confront several of his ideological blind spots on the "Irish Question"'.[143] As James D Young remarks:

From 1 May, 1919, Maclean was committed to the Irish cause as a part of a worldwide anti-imperialist struggle. When he, John Wheatley, and Countess Markievicz spoke at the Glasgow May Day in the presence of

100,000 workers, Irish tricolours were openly carried among the crowd and the Soldiers' Song was sung along with the Red Flag.[144]

In 1920, Maclean wrote one of the most forceful pamphlets on the Irish situation from a Scottish perspective. *The Irish Tragedy: Scotland's Disgrace* (1920) had a postscript that stated:

> Since writing this pamphlet the *Glasgow Herald* in a leader on Tuesday, June 8, 1920, entitled 'The Army in Ireland', gloats over the fact that Scots regiments are pouring into Ireland and others are held in readiness. It seems the Scots are being used to crush the Irish. Let Labour effectively reply.[145]

In his General Election Address of 1922, standing in the Gorbals, Maclean declared:

> I was arrested and taken to Edinburgh Castle as a prisoner of war, was bailed out, and was sentenced to penal servitude for three years at Edinburgh High Court on 12 April 1916. When Jim Connolly saw how things were going in Edinburgh he resolved on the Easter Rebellion in Dublin, the beginning of Ireland's new fight for freedom, a fight that can only end in an Irish workers' republic based on communism.[146]

According to David Lloyd, one of a number of critics to revisit Connolly's work in recent years:

> There is no doubt that the concept of 'Celtic communism' lends itself potentially to an idealizing nationalism that seeks to trace in the past the contours of a benevolent and undegraded national spirit. But Connolly's deployment of the concept in *Labour and Irish History*, *The Reconquest of Ireland* and elsewhere, though a consistent element of his socialist project, is if anything precisely opposed to such idealizing.[147]

Several Scottish writers have certainly drawn inspiration from Connolly as an activist rather than an idealist. According to Chris Harvie, Hugh MacDiarmid 'had several streams running through him, one of them Ireland and the Easter Rising of 1916, where poets had apparently changed a nation'. Harvie points out that 'to younger Scottish socialists like MacDiarmid, politicised by the war and the industrial struggles of the Red Clyde, Connolly became a hero.'[148]

The Scottish reclamation of Connolly can be seen in Irvine Welsh's novel

Bedroom Secrets of the Master Chefs (2006), an extract from which appears in this collection. In that same novel, one of Welsh's characters reflects:

> As a young man back in the sixties, I became interested in politics. Particularly the national question. I wondered how it was that most of Ireland was free, while Scotland was still in servitude under the English Crown. I looked around at the New Town, its streets named after English royalty due to that toady Scott, while a great, Edinburgh native son and socialist leader like James Connolly merited little more than a plaque on a wall under a shadowy bridge.[149]

The following year, in the short story collection *If You Liked School, You'll Love Work* (2007), Welsh has another character say of a particularly stirring speech that it was 'Pure James Connolly'.[150]

James Kelman is another Scottish writer who has acknowledged Connolly as a relatively unsung Scottish socialist, and has pointed to the lost legacy of the left nationalism of the early 20th-century, a nationalism that was thoroughly internationalist in outlook:

> Now it's just assumed that if you are not parliamentarian, then you have no politics, and that's a really extraordinary reaction to what started happening about a hundred years ago when the debate was much more sophisticated politically, and there was such a great divergence amongst socialists. It was probably valid to have a belief in self-determination, to have a position like James Connolly or John MacLean.[151]

In this regard, Kelman has spoken of the way in which the Irish question has dropped out of sight in Scottish political culture:

> Part of the extraordinary thing is the marginalisation of Irish politics in relation to Scottish radical history. I would say that you cannot get an understanding of radical politics, probably throughout the UK, but certainly in Scotland, without understanding the significance of Irish politics as well. Take James Connolly for example. About 20 years ago [in 1989] when a young refugee Ahmad Shaikh, a boy of 21, was murdered in a racist attack and a protest march was organised, police said it couldn't take place. The reason why was because one of the groups marching in solidarity was the EIS, the teachers' union. It was the local branch, which carried on their banners a portrait of James Connolly, the Irish Republican martyr who was murdered by the British government in

1916. The extraordinary thing about all of this was that James Connolly was actually an Edinburgh man, he's Scottish. He didn't go to Ireland until his early 20s. His father was Irish, but he was born less than a mile from where we were about to march. You know there are a lot of ironies; a lot of Scottish-Irish people, because of the indoctrination and propaganda, don't even know that James Connolly was Scottish. I'm talking about guys who are maybe 75 years of age who are Scottish Catholics. They're not necessarily Republican because the whole thing's a kind of mish-mash. But when I speak to them about James Connolly they will know that type of background – and until that kind of background is known by everyone, there will never be a real understanding of radical politics in this country. These areas are still marginalised or suppressed.[152]

Another aspect of Connolly's life often overlooked – in addition to his Scottish birth and upbringing – is his time in the British Army, which he joined under-age in 1882, and from which he deserted in 1889, subsequently joining the Scottish Socialist Federation in 1890.[153] Many Irish and Irish-Scottish men and women passed through the ranks of the British Army. Thomas Maley, father of the Celtic manager Willie, was a sergeant in the Royal North British Fusiliers. Willie Maley himself was born in the barracks at Newry in 1868, the same year that James Connolly was born in Cowgate. But Connolly's own military connections have a particularly bitter twist to them, as Easter 1916 had another poignant Scottish dimension. Connolly's eldest brother, John, had joined the British army ahead of James, in 1877, aged 15, possibly serving in India. While James deserted to become a socialist and die fighting for Ireland, John stayed on. When James was speaking in Dundee in 1913, he didn't appreciate John turning up to hear him in the uniform of Edinburgh City Artillery. Shortly after James's execution in Dublin, John died in Glasgow, and, 'as an honourable discharged veteran corporal' was buried in Edinburgh with full military honours.[154] The two brothers who served in the British Army met very different ends on either side of the Irish Sea, but their fates testify to the ways in which Irish-Scottish relations are shaped by empire, war, migration and plantation.

'Mad, Motiveless and Meaningless'?
The Dundee Irish and the Easter Rising

Richard B McCready

THE IRISH IN Dundee are often forgotten about when considering the history of the Irish in Scotland and the wider Irish diaspora. Dundee had among the largest population of Irish-born residents anywhere in Scotland, indeed in Britain. The Irish in Dundee played a key role in the politics of Dundee and paid close attention to events in Ireland. In terms of the Easter Rising one of its leaders, James Connolly, lived in Dundee in the late 1880s.

This chapter will examine the initial reactions of the Dundee Irish to the Easter Rising, it will also examine the events which took place in the period after the Rising in the run up to the establishment of the Irish Free State.

Dundee in the first half of the 19th century was a rapidly expanding town. Dundee recorded remarkable rises in its population between the decennial censuses. For example between 1821 and 1831 the population rose by 48% and between 1831 and 1841 it rose by a further 38%. Amongst these statistics there were a very high proportion of Irish-born people in Dundee. In 1841 9% of the population of Dundee had been born in Ireland. In 1851 this proportion had risen to 19%, meaning that in 1851 roughly one in five of the population of Dundee had been born in Ireland. These remarkable figures make Dundee one of the most Irish cities in Britain.

As the Easter Rising leader James Connolly commented during his stay in Dundee in 1888:

> You could hear at once... the brogue of every county in Ireland for there is not a county in the Emerald Isle but what sent its representatives here. I should think Dundee has, in proportion a stronger Irish population than any other town in Great Britain.[155]

The Irish made up an extremely important part of Dundee's population, and the Irish community was larger than these figures suggest as a result of the children of Irish immigrants considering themselves to be Irish. In Scotland as a whole the Irish formed a proportionately significant element in the population. The Irish in Scotland, though numerically a smaller number, made up a larger section of the community than the Irish in England. Within that community there were places, like Dundee, where the Irish were far more concentrated.[156]

Even numerically Dundee was in the top five towns with an Irish-born population in 1851 and still held on to this position in 1871.[157]

This Irish community in Dundee remained strong into the 20th century. The Irish played a very significant role in Dundee politics, for example in the 1908 By-election when Winston Churchill attended Irish nationalist meetings and stated that his victory was a 'Victory for Ireland!'[158]

The Easter Rising in 1916 was one of the pivotal events in modern Irish history. Its effects and the events which followed it had a profound effect not just on Ireland but also on the rest of the United Kingdom. The Rising and subsequent events had a lasting impact on the Irish diaspora, not least in Dundee.

The *Dundee Advertiser* for the Tuesday of Easter week 1916 reported that 'Sinn Féin volunteers' had had their 'Easter manoeuvres' cancelled and that Sir Roger Casement had been captured in the attempt to land German weapons. The same edition also carried the first reports of 'disturbances' in Dublin. The *Advertiser* was convinced that the Rising had only taken place with the assistance of Germany, though it was pleased to point out that 'happily... the great majority of Irishmen are animated by... loyal feelings... and are whole-heartedly hostile to Germany.'[159] A correspondent to the *Advertiser*, 'Erina', presumably a member of the Dundee Irish community stated that if Ireland ever hoped to be free then:

> there is no tyrant [the Irish] should resist, like the German, who tramples on their religion, derides their cross of hope and will treat them as he treated Catholic Belgium if he is allowed to land on the Isle of Saints.[160]

The *Dundee Advertiser* believed that the Rising brought shame on Ireland – the *Advertiser* was pleased to say that the Rising was 'happily' unsuccessful.[161]

It was not just British Unionist opinion which riled against the rebellion. The Rising shocked the leader of the Irish Nationalist Party, John Redmond, who told the House of Commons of his 'horror' and 'detestation' of the Rising.[162] The vast majority of Irish opinion shared Redmond's viewpoint in the immediate aftermath at least. The Birmingham Irish deplored and 'emphatically condemn[ed] the rebellion'; the Tyneside Irish felt the same. The New Zealand Hibernians abhorred the rebellion; the Queensland Irishmen deplored the Rising pointing out that Irish soldiers in the present war, by their valour and devotion have demonstrated their loyalty to the Empire. The New

York United Irish League strongly condemned the 'conspiracy' which had been organised by men 'who never had, and never will have Ireland's welfare at heart.'[163]

The attitude of the Dundee Irish followed that of the Irish elsewhere. On Easter Sunday Father Michael Fahy, a curate at St Patrick's Church in Dundee, had given a lecture entitled 'Ireland of the future under Home Rule.'[164] The Easter Rising came as a shock to the Irish community in Dundee. The *Dundee Advertiser* said that Dundee Irishmen were indignant at the actions of the Sinn Féiners.[165] One 'prominent member of the United Irish League' in Dundee said that the Sinn Féin movement contained:

almost every crank, sorehead, and disappointed official in Ireland, who were 'agin' everything and everybody who was opposed to them, and as such they were as much a menace and an annoyance to Ireland as they were to the Empire.[166]

The Dundee branches of the United Irish league, Irish National Foresters and the Ancient Order of Hibernians met jointly in Dundee on 1 May 1916. It is significant to note that this meeting took place before the executions of the leaders of the Rising began. Nevertheless the representatives of the Dundee nationalists passed the following resolution:

That we deeply deplore the recent occurrences in Ireland, and condemn in the strongest manner possible the actions of the parties responsible. The revolt in Dublin to our mind, is not only an act of treachery to the Empire, but also to Ireland, which after a long struggle is now on the threshold of a new era. We earnestly trust that the Sinn Féiners, and those associated with them in their mad, motiveless, and meaningless work may soon be compelled to give way, and before long law and order will again reign in Ireland's capital.[167]

FL Crilly, TP O'Connor and John Redmond thanked the Dundee Irish for passing this motion.[168] The *Dundee Advertiser* claimed that there were no Sinn Féin supporters in Dundee. To the *Advertiser* the rebellion was about egotism, its translation of Sinn Féin as 'ourselves' demonstrated the selfishness of the movement, according to the *Advertiser* it was a movement which 'cuts off the nose to spite the face.'[169] The magazine *Punch* carried a cartoon which portrayed Sinn Féin as a serpent.[170]

One of the leaders of the Easter Rising, James Connolly, was relatively well known in Dundee. He had lived in the town in 1888, as we have seen. Connolly was said to have relatives resident in Dundee and had visited often to speak on Labour issues. Those who knew him in Dundee were said to be surprised that he had become involved in the Rising.[171]

The Dundee Irish had called for law and order to be restored in Dublin – the British authorities interpreted this by executing the leaders. The *Dundee Advertiser* was a supporter of this policy. According to the *Advertiser* 'mercy' towards the rebels would be a sign of 'intolerable weakness.'[172] Just under two months later the *Advertiser* commenting on the sentence passed on Sir Roger Casement said that 'it is unhappily true in the history of Ireland that the executed rebel lives on as an influence and the pardoned rebel passes into insignificance.'[173] Indeed it has been stated that 'the deaths of the rebels... sealed the 1916 rising in the image of sacrificial martyrdom.'[174] The executions are often said to have had a profound effect on public opinion in Ireland. Leon Ó Broin has stated:

> By the end of 1916 the Sinn Féin leaders from being fools and mischief-makers, almost universally condemned, had been converted by the operations of martial law into martyrs for Ireland. Before the executions, TP O'Connor said, 99% of Ireland was Redmondite since then 99% had turned to Sinn Féin.[175]

Many of those who were involved in Irish politics felt that it was the execution of the leaders that changed public opinion; this was the view of many moderate nationalists such as Stephen Gwynn, the erstwhile Redmondite MP.[176]

The change of attitude can be seen in the Dundee Irish as early as June 1916. Sinn Féin prisoners were held in Perth prison and the UIL made efforts to ease the lot of the captives. The *Dundee Catholic Herald* carried details of how to visit the prisoners.[177]

In the period after the Rising support for an Irish Republic amongst the organised Dundee Irish was muted, by 1922 support for Sinn Féin would make a substantial contribution to the defeat of the senior Member of Parliament for Dundee, Winston Churchill.

Major events such as the death of the Lord Mayor of Cork, Terence MacSwinney, on hunger strike in 1920 had a profound effect on the views of the Irish in Dundee. Thousands of the Dundee Irish turned out on a weekday to process through the city to a Requiem Mass at St Joseph's Church.[178]

The Sinn Féin supporting Archbishop of Melbourne Daniel Mannix visited Dundee in 1921. Mannix spoke to a large meeting of the Dundee

Irish and told his fellow countrymen to support Sinn Féin and Labour. His visit is often credited with turning the Dundee Irish against their MP Winston Churchill and Churchill subsequently lost the 1922 election in Dundee. In this period the IRA was also active in Dundee and three people were arrested for gunrunning in Dundee.

There can be little doubt that the Easter Rising was unpopular when it took place both in Ireland and amongst the Dundee Irish. Over time attitudes towards the Rising changed and had a remarkable effect on the subsequent history of Ireland and the Irish in Britain. In this respect the Dundee Irish mirrored what happened in Ireland where the Rising was unpopular at first and then over time people's attitudes towards it changed.

MacLean in the Museum: James Connolly and 'Àrd-Mhusaeum na h-Èireann'

Niall O'Gallagher

A POET WRITING in Gaelic one hundred years since the proclamation of *Poblacht na hÉireann* in 1916 has to come to terms with Sorley MacLean (Somhairle MacGill-Eain, 1911–1996). Born on the island of Raasay, off Skye, MacLean is widely considered the greatest Scottish Gaelic poet of the 20th century and among the greatest of all Gaelic poets. A committed republican and socialist – though his attitude to Marxism appears to have changed over the course of his lifetime – MacLean's support for independence for both Scotland and Ireland is addressed across his poetry. Part of that poetry's novelty when it first appeared in the 1930s and '40s lay in its attempt to integrate Gaelic and Scottish history into the story of the international workers' struggle. A central figure in that attempt was fellow Scottish socialist, James Connolly.

An Irish revolutionary from an Edinburgh slum, Connolly was an important figure throughout MacLean's career. The poet's fullest tribute to the leader of the 1916 Rising had to wait until the 1970s, the decade in which MacLean's earlier work was republished with facing English translations, the decade in which Scottish nationalism became a serious political force and in which bloodshed in Ireland reached levels not seen for decades. 'Àrd-Mhusaeum na h-Èireann' ('The National Museum of Ireland') describes the poet's encounter with the bloodstained shirt worn by Connolly at his execution, treated by this avowedly atheistic poet as a religious relic:

'Àrd-Mhusaeum na h-Èireann' (1970)

Anns na làithean dona seo
is seann leòn Uladh 'na ghaoid
lionnrachaidh 'n cridhe na h-Eòrpa
agus an cridhe gach Gàidheil
dhan aithne gur h-e th' ann an Gàidheal,
cha d' rinn mise ach gum facas
ann an Àrd-Mhusaeum na h-Èireann

spot mheirgeach ruadh na fala
's i caran salach air an lèinidh
a bha aon uair air a' churaidh
as docha leamsa dhiubh uile
a sheas ri peilear no ri bèigneid
no ri tancan no ri eachraidh
no ri spreaghadh nam bom èitigh:
an lèine bh' air Ó Conghaile
ann an Àrd-Phost-Oifis Èirinn
's e 'g ullachadh na h-ìobairt
a chuir suas e fhèin air sèithear
as naoimhe na 'n Lia Fàil
th' air Cnoc na Teamhrach an Èirinn.

Tha an curaidh mòr fhathast
'na shuidhe air an t-sèithear,
a' cur a' chatha sa Phost-Oifis
's a' glanadh shràidean an Dùn Èideann.

The poem, which could be arranged in quatrains reminiscent of classical Gaelic poetry, is instead presented in a long verse-paragraph, followed by a final closing quatrain, almost like a museum exhibit with its accompanying caption or explanatory note. MacLean's diction is strikingly Biblical here. Words like 'gaoid' (XXI) and 'ìobairt' (XVI) recall the book of Leviticus when the God of the Old Testament instructs Moses on the prohibition on the unclean entering sacred places, and the sacrifices necessary for the atonement of sins. Connolly's shirt becomes the 'còta anairt naomha' of Leviticus, his chair the 'caithir-thròcair' on which God himself will appear, the Museum an 'ionad naomh' which only the pure may enter. The Province of Ulster, however, is the 'stain... in the heart' that should prevent the poet from approaching the sacred place. That prohibition applies in particular 'to every Gael, who knows he is a Gael'. MacLean's definition is at once inclusive, Connolly himself being the child of Irish immigrants, born in the Scottish capital far from the Gaelic language's traditional heartlands, and compulsory – those who don't accept MacLean's deification of Connolly are dismissed for false consciousness. Repetition in the long verse-paragraph gives it an almost liturgical quality, as does the obsessive, but not quite regular monorhyme on 'é'. Liturgy, like other kinds of religious ritual, aspires to a significance outside of time. This is made explicit in the final 'captioning' quatrain, where Connolly, having lost his name and become simply 'the great hero' is seen at once sitting in the executioner's chair, fighting in Dublin's General Post Office and sweeping streets in Edinburgh. Connolly's life is collapsed into one moment, just as the years between 1916 and the time of the poet's own 'witness' ('cha d' rinn mise ach gum facas') are elided such that both sets of events occur simultaneously. MacLean's poem was prompted by a visit to Ireland in 1970. 'Àrd-Mhusaeum na h-Èireann' is explicitly concerned as much with the 'evil days' in which it was written as with those of James Connolly.

MacLean's technique, using religious rhetoric for his atheistic political purposes, had been long established in his poetry by the time he wrote 'Àrd-Mhusaeum na h-Èireann'. While he is now best known, particular outside the Gaelic world, for another later poem, 'Hallaig', MacLean's reputation still largely rests upon a sequence of love lyrics written in the 1930s and '40s, and never published in full during the poet's lifetime. The 18th poem in MacLean's *Dàin do Eimhir* bears the title 'Prayer' and presents James Connolly as a secular saint:

from 'Ùrnaigh' (Dàin XVIII, 1939?)

An iarr mi mo chridhe bhith glainte
bho anfhannachd mo ghaoil ghlain ghil,
an iarr mi spiorad 's e air fhaileadh
eadhon gum faighear anns a' bhoile mi
cho treun ri Dimitrov no ri O Conghaile?

MacLean's panoply is expanded in his long poem on the Highland Clearances, 'An Cuilithionn', in the couplet 'Toussaint, Marx, More, Lenin, / Liebknecht, Connollaigh, MacGill-Eain' ('An Cuilithionn' (1939), VII: 100-101), where the last name given is the Gaelic form of MacLean's own surname, referring here to the Scottish socialist John Maclean (1879–1923). In the *Dàin do Eimhir* the claims of love and politics compete. The speaker is torn between taking up arms for the Spanish Republican cause or staying at home with his beloved, of whom he would therefore be unworthy. The language of purity is here too as the speaker asks his heart to be 'cleaned' of his love's weakness, but this is set in a paradoxical tension by the repetition of the word 'glan' in the following line's reference to his 'pure, fair love', rehearsing a cliché from the Gaelic song tradition. MacLean's 'anns a' bhoile' seems to echo the 'passionate intensity' of Yeats' poem of 1919, 'The Second Coming', though the poet's verdict recalls Yeats on Connolly and his fellows in 'Easter, 1916', which asks whether 'excess of love / Bewildered them till they died'.

MacLean's speaker departs from Yeats in asking to be purified of love so that he will be able to take part in revolutionary struggle. By the time of 'Àrd-Mhusaeum na h-Èireann', that process seems to have been completed, with politics, even war, winning out over the 'excess of love' for which he chided himself in his earlier poetry.

A more disillusioned poem, named for Connolly, remained in manuscript during MacLean's lifetime:

'Seumus Ó Conghaile'

Aig bànadh an là ghil am bhliadhna nan Sia-Deug
tràighte, faoin-lag, cràdhte, fo chreuchdaibh,
ceangailte gu dlùth ri cathair nam pian dhut-
seadh, tilgeil t' anam an làthair Mhic Dhè uat,

nan abradh neach riut madainn an là ud
gum biodh daoine an-dràsta air feadh do thìre
bhiodh bochd is nochd; gun an dùil ri aon rud
ach an-shògh is call, is iad beò an dèirce.

MacLean is now best known to English readers through Seamus Heaney, who translated 'Hallaig'. In a lecture at the Edinburgh Festival given six years after Sorley MacLean's death, Heaney praises the poem, attributing to its author a resignation about the future of the culture he had come to represent:

'Hallaig' is at once historical and hallucinatory, a poem in which the deserted homesteads of a little settlement on the Island of Raasay are repopulated by a vision of 'a fair field full of folk'. It arises out of MacLean's sense of belonging to a culture that is doomed but that he will never deny.[179]

Seamus Heaney's MacLean is a very different poet to the one we encounter in 'Àrd-Mhusaeum na h-Èireann'. Readers may well be unsettled by MacLean's poetic response to the 'evil days' of Ulster in 1970, with its talk of ritual sacrifice and its deification of Connolly the martyr of 1916. Heaney's 'Hallaig' is a much safer poem, his MacLean the last representative of a culture now neatly consigned to history. While MacLean deified James Connolly, he himself has been merely canonised. Heaney's hagiography is convenient for all those who believe that the Gaelic language, and its literature, belongs in a museum. A century since the events Sorley MacLean helped to mythologise, his poetry continues to resist.

'Scotland is my home, but Ireland my country': The Border Crossing Women of 1916

Alison O'Malley-Younger

ON MONDAY 24 APRIL 1916 Padraig Pearse stood on the steps of the General Post Office in Dublin and proclaimed an Irish Republic, declaring 'the right of the people of Ireland to the ownership of Ireland and to the unfettered control of Irish destinies, to be sovereign and indefeasible'. In the six days that followed, battle raged between the British Army and the combined forces of several distinct groups, among them the Irish Volunteers, the Irish Citizen Army and Cumann na mBan. After much carnage, this culminated in the surrender of the rebel forces to the Indian-born veteran of colonial conflicts in Egypt, Burma, and the Boer War, Brigadier-General WHM Lowe, on Saturday 29 April. According to Sean O'Casey, 'this display was a sign to the governing classes to at least consider the dumb wish of an aspiring people'. Instead, it was 'followed by fire and bloodshed.'[180]

It is widely acknowledged that Pearse not only prophesied this 'fire and bloodshed', but lauded it as a 'cleansing and sanctifying thing' which would free the nation from 'slavery', and restore what he saw as its 'lost manhood'.[181] However, while Pearse's messianic rhetoric appears to mark the Easter Rising as a solely male affair, an expanding body of scholarship has shown that women, across a variety of classes and ranks, were key participants in the events of 1916 through their contribution to cultural and political organisations including the Gaelic League, Sinn Féin, the Irish Citizen Army, *Inghinidhe na hÉirean* (Daughters of Erin), and Cumann na mBan (Council of Women).[182]

The founding document of the Irish Volunteers, agreed at a meeting in Dublin on 25 November 1913, emphasised the need for manly resistance while acknowledging that 'there will also be work for women to do'.[183] This women's work was seen as subordinate to the military and strategic efforts of the men. As Margaret Ward has argued:

> The history of Cumann na mBan is, above all, an account of the tensions generated by this subordination and of the repeated attempts by some women to establish a degree of autonomy for themselves.[184]

In what follows I hope to foreground the ways in which two of these women, Margaret Skinnider and Constance Markievicz, neither of them born in Ireland, gained a degree of autonomy in the hyper-masculine world of revolution, due to a cross-water Celtic connection which traversed borders, boundaries and barriers of class, clothing, gender, religion and nationality. Indeed, during a time in which, as Ward observes, 'there [was] too much testosterone fuelling the national struggle',[185] Markievicz and Skinnider stood alongside numerous others as activists as opposed to auxiliaries, 'asserting their claim to be part of the shaping of the nation' which they, like many others, hoped would unite the forces of republicanism and socialism under the auspices of national self-determination.[186]

Constance Markievicz was an unlikely rebel. Born in London on 4 February 1868 and raised in the picturesque and privileged surrounding of Lissadell House in Sligo, Constance Georgina Gore-Booth, according to Anne Marrecco, was 'a being born to be happy in the surroundings which her destiny had allotted to her', a society beauty, and 'a child by right of the Ascendancy'.[187] Yeats celebrated her in the poem 'In Memory of Eva Gore-Booth and Con Markievicz', published in 1933, as one of two beautiful sisters 'in silk kimonos' enjoying a hazy summer evening in the manse of Lissadell. An artisan who travelled and studied in both Paris and London, she married a Polish nobleman, Count Casimir Markievicz, and in time gave birth to a daughter Maeve. And yet, as Marreco points out:

> She is chiefly remembered because when a handful of desperate men in 1916 changed the political face of Ireland forever, she was in the thick of the fray.[188]

Such a comment recalls Sean O'Faolin's suggestion that Markievicz:

> came within reach of the antennae of men acting deliberately where she acted by instinct, men searching consciously and deliberately for their own type where she searched with blind feelers.[189]

Notably, as in many descriptions, Markievicz is diminished as a passive gadfly on the backsides of desperate male heroes, or discounted as an over-theatrical, shrill-voiced idealist, incapable of fully comprehending the business of men into which she has stumbled. As Louise Ryan points out, the fact that she was a leader of men is conveniently overlooked, the fate of many female figures engaged in conflict.[190] Equally the Countess' courage in battle, skill at arms, leadership and inspirational qualities are ignored in order to concentrate on her physicality, in particular her clothes, depicted as a risible and flamboyant copy of a male uniform. If we take this image of mock-machismo at face value, as Diana Norman argues, 'Countess Markievicz is disappearing like the Cheshire Cat in *Alice* and what remains is not a grin, but a swagger'.[191] Elsewhere, equally distorted and ignored, the figure of Margaret Skinnider is consigned to the myth of Markievicz, as a lovelorn and lonely fan-girl, defined by her devotion to the 'Rebel Countess'. For example, in his review of Skinnider's memoir, *Doing My Bit For Ireland* (1917), Joshua Wanhope sarcastically observes:

> The countess according to Miss Skinnider seems to have been a veritable superwoman. She was a dead shot, and Miss Skinnider relates no less than five killings – not woundings – to her account. Whenever her finger pressed the deadly trigger a Britisher was sure to bite the dust.[192]

Perhaps, as Lisa Weihman has suggested there is an element of 'romantic adoration', idealisation, and, perhaps homoeroticism in Skinnider's often rhapsodic accounts of Markievicz, but this should not detract from either of their actions in relation to 'nationalism, socialism and feminism'.[193] As Sikata Banerjee observes:

> The Countess's and Margaret Skinnider's political activism clearly disrupted the scenario that envisioned 'male' soldiers protecting Mother Ireland as outlined by both Pearse and the Irish Volunteers.[194]

Who was Margaret Skinnider? Born in Coatbridge near Glasgow in 1892, the child of Irish immigrants, she was a Scottish schoolteacher, suffragist and nationalist who became one of about 3,000 Volunteers present in Glasgow in 1914. A commanding officer of the Glasgow-based Ann Devlin branch of Cumann na mBan, she was one of only two women (and 28 men) who regularly carried weapons and intelligence from Glasgow to Dublin in the run-up to the Rising. Her account of the Easter Rising, published in New York in 1917 as *Doing My Bit For Ireland* (a title picked by the publisher that Skinnider never liked) may be romantic, but it is also revealing and with all its highly personal and polemical aspects it remains an important contemporary historical document.

Skinnider details her military training and her gradually escalating involvement with armed struggle in Ireland:

> In Glasgow I belonged to the Irish Volunteers and to the Cumman-na-

mBan, an organisation of Irish girls and women. I had learned to shoot in one of the rifle practice clubs which the British organised so that women could help in the defence of the Empire. These clubs had sprung up like mushrooms and died as quickly, but I kept on till I was a good marksman. I believed the opportunity would soon come to defend my own country.[195]

By her 'own country', Skinnider meant Ireland. As she put it, 'Scotland is my home, but Ireland my country'.[196]

Skinnider was invited to Dublin at the end of 1915 to meet Markievicz. As Skinnider recalled, the Countess:

had heard of my work in the Cumman na mBan and wanted to talk with me. She knew where all the men and women who loved Ireland were working, and sooner or later met them all, in spite of the fact that she was of Planter stock and by birth of the English nobility in Ireland.[197]

Skinnider crossed the Irish Sea with detonators in her hat, and the wires wrapped under her coat. She slept on the detonators and was later told the pressure could have set them off.[198] She scouted out a barracks for bombing, and her map of the target was passed on to James Connolly, whom she then got to meet. Some sense of the Irish history that was part of Skinnider's home life in Scotland can be gauged from one exchange after her return from this trip:

When I told my mother on my return of the plans for Easter, she shook her head. 'There never was an Irish rising that someone didn't betray it,' she said. 'It was so in '67, and before that in 1798.'[199]

Pondering her Irish inheritance, Skinnider then made a highly revealing observation:

Fortunately, Glasgow is two fifths Irish. Indeed, there are as many Irish there as in Dublin itself, and the spirit among the younger generation is perhaps more intense because we are a little to one side and thus afraid of becoming outsiders.[200]

That younger generation were making hard decisions on the hoof, and in the context of a bloody imperialist war that was laying waste to the youth of Europe:

In February, when conscription came to Scotland, there was nothing for members of the Irish Volunteers in Glasgow to do but to disappear. I knew one lad of 17 whose parents, though Irish, wanted him to volunteer in the service of the empire. He refused, telling them his life belonged to Ireland. He went over to fight at the time of the rising, and served a year in prison afterward.[201]

Skinnider, like Constance Markievicz, cross-dressed for convenience, passing as one of the Glasgow Na Fianna Éireann, in a green Fiann shirt and saffron kilt in lieu of knickerbockers, as she relates with pride:

When I told Madam I could pass as a boy, even if it came to wrestling or whistling, she tried me out by putting me into a boy's suit, a Fianna uniform. She placed me under the care of one of her boys to whom she explained I was a girl, but that, since it might be necessary some day to disguise me as a boy, she wanted to find whether I could escape detection. I was supposed to be one of the Glasgow Fianna.[202]

It is fitting that Skinnider dressed thus, given that the Glasgow branch of Na Fianna Éireann was one of the most militant and active contributors to Republican activism in the run-up to the Rising. According to Skinnider, after a try-out of her outfit, 'The boys took me for one of themselves'. She could drill, signal and gun-run as well as any boy too. Yet she would dress in female garb when necessary, aware that a woman was less likely to be strip-searched by British soldiers than a male. This was particularly effective when she was gunrunning and undertaking dispatch work when she could fade in and out of male ranks undetected. As her memoir recounts, this was a source of great pride to her.

Skinnider was one of a number of women who consciously or unknowingly responded to Markievicz's call, issued in the November 1909 edition of *Bean na h Éireann* in which she exhorted women to:

Arm yourselves with weapons to fight your nation's cause. Arm your souls with noble and free ideas. Arm your minds with the histories and memories of your country and her martyrs, her language, and a knowledge of her arts, and her industries. And if in your day the call should come for your body to arm, do not shirk that either.[203]

Margaret Skinnider did not shirk from arming her body. With other members of Cumann na mBan, she carried ammunition and arms, and helped to make cartridges for combatants. She acted as a dispatch carrier and sniper. She was shot, and wounded while scanning the area around St Stephen's Green on the

Wednesday of Easter Week. Like Markievicz, Skinnider subsequently became heavily involved in Irish party politics. They were comrades-in-arms who stood for the causes of Suffragism, Feminism and Nationalism in the face of colonial and class oppression in what Yeats describes as the 'casual comedy' that birthed the 'terrible beauty' of modern Ireland.

As well as fighting alongside Skinnider and Connolly, Constance Markiewicz was no stranger to Scotland or to Scottish influence in Ireland. In December 1908 Yeats agreed to have Constance's husband Casimir Markievicz's work staged at the Abbey, where Constance played her part:

> In *The Dilettante*, a society farce set in a shooting lodge in Scotland, she played Lady Althea Dering, who professes her love to Archibald Longhurst, a man who is not her husband.[204]

According to Lauren Arrington:

> If *The Dilettante* is in any way an allusion to real life, it is in its reflection of Constance's commitment to female friendships, a conviction that she enacted outside the theater in her campaign for suffrage and in her growing connections with the nationalist movement.[205]

Fifteen years later Markievicz was not just treading the boards in a play set across the water, but was there speaking to various groups 'in an attempt to unite Communists and Irish Republicans in Scotland'.[206] On this stage she was equally passionate:

> In Glasgow at the end of January 1923, she spoke to the communist Irish Republican Organisation in Scotland and declared that 'she was a Communist but their first duty was to clear the British out of Ireland, then they could have any form of Republic they liked,' echoing James Connolly's stance in the months prior to the Easter Rising. On the whole, Markievicz was unrestrained in her support for Bolshevism during her Scottish tour.[207]

As the centenary of the Rising approaches, in the midst of the commemorative ebb and flow, it is worth recollecting the words of Markievicz, spoken in June 1921 on the rights of Ireland, and 'crushing, cruel and grinding' capitalism:

> While Ireland is not free I remain a rebel, unconverted and incontrovertible. There is no word strong enough for it. I am pledged as a rebel because I

am pledged to the one thing – a free and independent Republic... I know what I mean – a state run by the Irish people for the people. That means a Government that looks after the rights of people before the rights of property... My idea is the Workers' Republic for which Connolly died.[208]

For Connolly, the pressing problems of social injustices, and the subjugation of the disadvantaged outweighed any narrow-gauge notion of nation. For Markievicz also, self-determination was a driver for political change that would lead to recognition of the rights of the Irish people. This she felt would occur as a natural consequence of being freed from British rule. As the case of Skinnider makes clear, these aspirations were not confined to the people of Ireland, but part of what Willy Maley and Niall O'Gallagher call 'a cross-water dialogue'.[209] In the current political climate, such a dialogue, focusing on the rights of people before the rights of property is just as valid and necessary today as it was in 1916. Indeed, as Maley and O'Gallagher conclude, this 'Celtic connection is essential for a proper understanding of our recent past, and an informed debate about the future'.[210]

To Rise for a Life Worth Having

Alan Riach

> *Scots steel tempered wi' Irish fire*
> *Is the weapon that I desire.*

THUS HUGH MACDIARMID, in 1932. Metaphoric or literal, this affirmation of complementarities makes explicit a relation comprehensively reappraised and reinvigorated by MacDiarmid and other writers, artists and composers from 1916 to 2016, in ways still vital with inventive possibilities.

In the closing lines of 'On a Raised Beach' (from *Stony Limits*, 1934), MacDiarmid wrote this:

> It is not more difficult in death than here
> – Though slow as the stones the powers develop
> To rise from the grave – to get a life worth having;
> And in death – unlike life – we lose nothing that is truly ours.

In other words, the struggle continues as perennially in humanity as the stony beaches move across geological time, and acknowledging mortality, we still try to achieve an independent, self-determined 'life worth having' in defiance of all those forces trying to compel us to believe it could never be done. 'To rise from the grave – to get a life worth having' may be the imperative that gives preference to the connotations of a 'rising' (as opposed to a 'rebellion') that applies in Scotland, or anywhere, as much as in Ireland.

MacDiarmid was keenly aware of the imperative, moved by it, committed to its enactment. He was in British army barracks in Sheffield, England, between 24 and 29 April 1916, and was to serve in the Royal Army Medical Corps, in Salonika and France, contracting cerebral malaria, returning to Scotland in the wake of the Great War and the Russian Revolution as well as the Easter Rising. In the 1970s, he said of the Easter Rising, 'If it had been possible at all I would have deserted at that time from the British army and joined the Irish.' He noted that he had at one time been gun-running for the Irish, and recollected:

The picture of Casement hanged, and Connolly taken out on a stretcher and executed, are two of the great rallying points of my spirit in its eternal and immeasurable hatred of everything English.

After the overthrow of the Tsarist dynasty in Russia in 1917, MacDiarmid was planning a study of 'The Soviet State' and already beginning to imagine an independent Scottish intervention in imperialism. The twin ideals of Celtic republicanism and international socialism were realities for him, in the aftermath of what was one of the bloodiest decades in modern history.[211]

In the 1920s, his efforts for Scotland were political as much as literary, and came directly out of the cradle of ideas and ferment of actions generated by James Connolly in Ireland and John Maclean in Scotland, and before Maclean in Glasgow, John Murdoch (1818–1903), land reformer, in the Highlands of Scotland, active in the 1870s and 1880s. MacDiarmid acknowledges him in *The Company I've Kept* (1966): 'the crofters' leader – Maclean's agrarian counterpart.' In 1925 Murdoch's manuscript autobiography was deposited in Glasgow's Mitchell Library. More work is still to be done.

For MacDiarmid, and contemporary and later Scots poets, engaged in both politics and literature, Yeats was inspirational, not only as poet but also as statesman, committed to the full complexity of literary understanding and social engagement with the realities of anti-imperial modernity. His example was taken both by MacDiarmid and then by Sorley MacLean (especially in his poem, 'At Yeats' Grave'). MacDiarmid and Yeats have been studied closely through contrasts and comparisons.[212] Still, there remains much to take forward. The imperatives of Yeats and MacDiarmid cannot be relegated to history. The poet Aonghas MacNeacail (b.1942), in his poem, 'not history but memory' in *A Proper Schooling* (1997), emphasises this point: 'when i was young / it wasn't history but memory'. A monoglot Gael on the Isle of Skye till the age of five, his education was equally monoglot in English, although most of his teachers were also Gaelic speakers. The damage had been done long before. The 1872 Education (Scotland) Act, which introduced compulsory education, did not even acknowledge the existence of Gaelic. MacNeacail observed in 2015:

> the language once spoken by Scottish royalty is now on the margins, but it continues to attract a creative energy that produced, in Sorley MacLean, one of the major poets in any language, as happily acknowledged by Seamus Heaney, among others, and is still delivering poets, novelists, playwrights and songwriters the equal of any working in other languages. That the state of the language, and attitudes to it, prompt strong political reactions should hardly surprise anyone with any knowledge of our experience.

So the Gaelic component in the declaration of self-determination enacted by the Easter Rising is a key element whose value remains essential in 21st century Scotland, in defiance, generally, of the social, educational, institutional and political establishment. This is the long-term cultural legacy of MacDiarmid's opposition to what he called 'the English ethos': not to be dismissed as mere xenophobic, reactionary racism, but rather a detailed, nuanced, sensitised journey of understanding those components of human identity that distinguished Scotland, and connected the Scots and Irish peoples in a cultural history that had been neglected or deliberately suppressed by the British Empire. The writers and artists since MacDiarmid confirmed multifaceted Celtic identities which, despite 19th-century pro-Gaelic men of letters like JS Blackie or Robert Buchanan, up until 1916 had been neglected or considered solely the provenance of Gael or Irish Celt. The example of Ireland, even with its liabilities of violence, remained a key cultural co-ordinate point. This was keenly felt by another native Gaelic-speaker, Iain Crichton Smith (1928–98), writing in 'For Poets Writing in English Over in Ireland', from his collection *The Exiles* (1984):

> Do the stones, the sea, seem different in Irish?
> Do we walk in language, in a garment pure
> as water? Or as earth just as impure?
>
> The grave of Yeats in Sligo, Innisfree
> island seen shivering on an April day.
> The nuns who cycle down an Easter road.

The choice of the words 'April' and 'Easter' is not accidental. In this poem, Crichton Smith recognises an affinity of identity in the languages, ambiguously pulling in different directions, Irish Gaelic, Scots Gaelic, English, but gestures towards the distinction from English-language English writers: 'When did Bleaney / dance to the bones?' Philip Larkin's glum character in his poem 'Mr Bleaney' is profoundly foreign to the Celtic legacy noted here, but, Crichton Smith implies, the pathos of the human story is ours as much as his, his as much as ours: 'I must go home. / To English? Gaelic? O beautiful Maud Gonne, / the belling hounds spoke in what language to you?' Yeats is addressed: 'creator of yourself' and: 'Another world is echoing with its own / music that's distant from the world of Larkin.' We are 'poised between two languages' – not only Gaelic and English, but youth and age, authority and vulnerability, the violence of immediate action and the commitment and patience that cultural meanings and forms of art require.

This should alert us to a much more complex and comprehensive world of relations, influences and interconnections, in all the arts in Scotland and Ireland from 1916 to 2016. The Rising in Ireland lit a fuse for the Scottish Renaissance, as MacDiarmid named it in 1922, using Patrick Geddes' term 'Renascence' from the 1890s, and thus intrinsically connecting to the political, literary and artistic Bengal Renaissance, resisting British rule in India in the 19th and early 20th centuries, which culminated in the work of Rabindranath Tagore (1861–1941), whom Yeats championed, and Indian independence in 1947. In each case, political and artistic work was interconnected and aligned with modernity and radical forms of modernism in the arts. The French philosopher Denis Saurat recognised this in his appraisal of 'La Renaissance Ecossais' in 1924. Yet these were also affirmations of ancient ideas of 'renaissance' meaning simply rebirth, decided acts of cultural rejuvenation, a healthy appetite for regeneration, in opposition to reactionary ideals of imperial authority and the foreclosures of conservatism.

Revolutionary modernism for Scotland, as for Ireland, entailed a revitalisation of rural and non-urban forms of language, social order and communal affiliation. Or as MacDiarmid put it in *In Memoriam James Joyce* (1955): 'All dreams of "imperialism" must be exorcised, / Including linguistic imperialism, which sums up all the rest.' Regenerating older traditions in the modern world was revolutionary in Scotland because it opposed the deadening hand of imperial hierarchy and the pretentiousness of cultural 'sophistication'. It returned the artistic elites to contact with the potential of people, generally, as surely and closely as JM Synge heard, internalised, and wrote in the idioms of rural Irish speech through his residences in Wicklow and the Aran islands, or as Jack Yeats saw, sketched and painted the people of Sligo and the west. Their art is no more naive than MacDiarmid's or MacLean's, and as advanced as that of Brecht or Munch.

In his book *Modern Scottish Painting* (1943), JD Fergusson says that the point about the modern movement in painting of around 1903–13, and especially the work of the cubists Picasso and Braque, was to acknowledge:

the resemblances the average person finds in modern painting to ancient painting, I mean Stone Age and that sort of ancientness... When things are brought down or come down to fundamentals they do resemble each other in spite of many thousands or perhaps hundreds of thousands of years of time.

Modern painting, or modernism in all the arts was:

an attempt to get back to fundamentals, and it succeeded... So there's nothing *out of order* about really modern painting resembling really ancient painting, which was in its time of course really modern...[213]

The significance of this for us is that the artistic and political revolutions enacted in modernism in Ireland in the work of Synge, Joyce, Yeats, Sean O'Casey, Flann O'Brien and others, and in Scotland in the work of MacDiarmid, Lewis Grassic Gibbon, Neil Gunn, Nan Shepherd, Catherine Carswell, Willa and Edwin Muir and others, are, along with the political ideals of egalitarianism, self-determination and opposition to imperialism, all related in their attempts to get back to 'the fundamentals'. So Fergusson, like Picasso, is only as 'advanced' as the work in the caves at Lascaux.

In 1926, on the 10th anniversary of the Easter Rising, the National Theatre, the Abbey Theatre in Dublin, staged O'Casey's *The Plough and the Stars*, presenting the events of 1916 from the perspectives of women and the working class, and asked, has anything changed? And answered, not much. Protests were intense. Among the audience were people who had fought or lost loved ones not only in the rising but in the civil war that followed. They wanted something that would tell them it had been worthwhile, and O'Casey was not giving them a celebration. The play honours the dead and gives respect to Ireland by tearing apart myths of purity and exceptionalism. The audience was outraged. Yeats responded by elaborating the idea that national identity might be characterised in two ways. One is by national vanity (nothing could be better than us), the other is by national pride (in which we can take all the criticism that comes). Yeats advocated a state where pride is a fragile, vulnerable thing, and the anxieties that go with vanity are superseded by that sensitive confidence of maturity. Confidence is not arrogance. In other words, you neither cringe ('we're just not good enough'), nor do you vaunt your ego ('we're incomparable, always right') – rather, you think about it, seriously. Maybe the lesson is that the best nation state would be one in which people were at ease with their own plurality, and open to revision. This was made possible, perhaps, in the late 19th century, when readership, audience, public sensibility, began to fragment and diversify. The work of Robert Louis Stevenson addresses local and international readers, children, travellers, colonials, imperialists, tribes of many kinds, just as printed work is becoming more widely available and commercialised interests are exploiting new readerships eagerly. The Celtic Revival contemporary with Stevenson is not really opposed to the rise of modernism: it runs into it, as Declan Kiberd reminds us in *Ulysses and Us: The Art of Everyday Life in Joyce's Masterpiece* (2009). And it resumes with new vigour after the Second World War: bloody revolutionary modernism led to political disasters but the arts show other ways.

Such elective affinities between Ireland and Scotland might be demonstrated in the connections of specific works by a range of writers, artists and composers, in their engagement with Celtic myths. For Scotland, the long legacy of the Rising is an acknowledgement of the shared history of Celtic identities, from the old gods, through Cuchulain and the warrior cycle, to Ossian and tales of the Fianna. The legacy calls for heroism but pomp calls for satire and subversion. In 'The Statues' (1938), Yeats asks: 'When Pearse summoned Cuchulain to his side, / What stalked through the Post Office?' He calls upon 'We Irish', born of 'an ancient sect' but 'thrown upon' a 'filthy modern tide' to climb 'to our proper dark' that the beauty of 'a plummet-measured face', a (perhaps terrible) beauty arising from the depths of history, may be seen in full understanding. The mysteries or ambiguities in these lines are multiple but there is surely commitment to both heroic aspiration and genuine humility. If there is nobility here, it is vulnerable. Samuel Beckett also invokes Cuchulain in *Murphy* (1957): the hero is now embodied in a statue in the Post Office, and the icon of self-sacrifice is the focus for the novel's suicidal Neary, in a scene of radically iconoclastic comedy, or, simply, hideous farce.

Old stories tell of Cuchulain learning the arts of war from Skathach, at Dunskaith, just off the Isle of Skye. This generates a different, fiercely feminist reading of not his but *her* story, centred in Scotland, in Janet Paisley's novel *Warrior Daughter* (2009). The novel is written self-consciously post-Easter 1916, validating feminist priorities.

From pre-Christian oral traditions, to the plantation of Ulster, to Irish immigration into early 20th century Scotland, the national identities are reciprocal, never wholly cut-off and defined. Thus the Scots language of Burns is shared and branches out among a whole school of Ulster poets. Joyce, preferring Finn and the outlaws (last minstrels, outsiders) rather than warrior-heroes, prefigures MacDiarmid's preference for the 'Hjok-Finnie body'.[214] And Ossian the bard is most curious not only from Macpherson but in the visual arts, from the astonishing drawings and sketches of Alexander Runciman (1736–83) to the montage photographs of Calum Colvin, especially his *Blind Ossian* (2001). Celtic gods and warriors inhabit the symbolist, figurative art of John Duncan (1866–1945), with *The Fomors* and *The Riders of the Sidhe*, while JD Fergusson's magnificent *Danu, Mother of the Gods* uses the symbolism of the Celtic Revival to address a later, distinctly 20th century world, and in his drawings in embellishment for MacDiarmid's *In Memoriam James Joyce* (1955), Fergusson brings art, literature and music together in the Celtic Ogham script, just as the poem sings praises of all forms of human creativity throughout time and across the world, from the

Ancient Edda to Tarzan of the Apes. The recuperation of the Celtic myths in modernist work was, and is, triggered by the conjunction of abstraction and reality signalled across a century by Easter 1916.

As for connections in specific instances, think of these. In the visual arts in Scotland, the proto-impressionist Gaelic-speaking William McTaggart (1835–1910), in the 1890s, painted a series of major canvases on two major themes – the coming of Columba to Scotland from Ireland, and the leaving of Scotland by emigrants. One theme portends regeneration, in spiritual, social, political reality, most evident in the only great work of art ever to rise from what we might call a school of art: Iona's *Book of Kells*. The other depicts immediate and recent catastrophe, and portends the politics of resistance the 20th century would bring, and this points forward to, for example, the outdoor sculptures of Will Maclean, commemorating the Clearances in Lewis and the western isles. In music, the ancient 'Deirdre's Farewell', sung as she prepares to leave Scotland to return to Ireland, might contrast with 'Fingal's Cave' by Mendelssohn (1809–47), celebrating his exhilarating arrival in a Scotland made new by international Romanticism. But then come forward to modernist composer Erik Chisholm (1904–65), and his 'Ossian' Symphony No. 2 (1939; recording 2007) (CDLX 7196), where the Celtic stories evoke opposing forces gathering in the rise of Fascism in that decade; or his 'Ossianic Lay' from 'Preludes from the True Edge of the Great World' (1943, recording 2004) (DRD0223); or the dense and complex masterpiece, 'Night Song of the Bards: Six Nocturnes for Piano' (1944–51; recording 1998) (OCD639). These are Scottish classical music examples drawing on the shared Celtic myths with immense conviction and intensity, and infused with modern, contemporary political purpose.[215]

One further example. 'The Birlinn of Clanranald' was composed by Alasdair Mac Mhaighstir Alasdair in the aftermath of the Jacobite rising of 1745 and the massacre at Culloden in 1746, and its author was an officer in the Jacobite army. It has been translated a number of times, most significantly after 1916 by Hugh MacDiarmid, with help from Sorley MacLean, in 1935. Why is this significant? The poem reflects upon social and human disaster in ways that go further than literalism. It presents a clan and a crew of men working in extreme co-ordination, disciplined and intuitive, but they and their vessel are subjected to a storm of unprecedented violence, a natural imposition that calls up unpredicted inimical forces. The courage and skills of the crew and the strength of the ship carry them through, but at a cost, and without any sense of inevitability. The safe harbour they come to is Carrickfergus, in Ireland, and the connection their voyage makes, between the Celtic west of Scotland and the Irish coast, is, also, a signal of an ancient kinship, across differences, of the Celtic peoples and the human needs of all people, opposed to inimical forces in nature and anti-human forces in the political world.

Looking back on Easter 1916 after 100 years, the rallying point of regeneration doesn't confirm militarism or violence. Inimical forces are always ready to break into the worlds we might make for ourselves, family, friends, companions. Human greed and vanity will always seek to restructure the world and our best responses to it. But in poems and music, paintings and sculptures, the structures of ships, the design of our parliaments and dwelling-places, art of all kinds, how our states are run, there are ways to oppose and resist both natural and unnatural impositions.

Easter 1916 recollected may be a reminder of failure, violence, bloodshed, vicious state reprisal, and how public sympathies change, but in a broader context, and in more intimate ways, it may also be an enactment of virtues: different co-ordinate points, strengths, suppleness and subtlety, loyalty, determination, hope: a play, a drama, a weathering of storm, coming to rest in the prospect of a future, in Scotland as in Ireland, most apt for 2016.

'Let the People Sing': Rebel Songs, the Rising, and Remembrance

Kevin Rooney

'Your deeds they would shame all the devils in hell.
Ireland, Iraq, Afghanistan. No bloodstained poppy on our hoops'

THE SLOGAN ON a huge banner unfurled at Celtic Park at a match against Aberdeen on 6 November 2010 was part of a protest against the club's decision to mark Remembrance Day with players sporting poppies against their green and white jerseys and fans asked to stand for a minute's silence. Like me, Celtic supporters involved in this protest identified with the traditions of anti-imperialism and Irish republicanism. One of our heroes is James Connolly, the socialist republican who led the 1916 Easter Rising against British rule in Ireland and the slaughter of World War One. The first line of the slogan on the banner was taken from a well-known ballad entitled 'James Connolly', made famous by the Wolfe Tones on their 1972 album, *Let the People Sing*. Connolly himself knew the power of songs and slogans. In 1903 he wrote 'A Rebel Song', the opening verse of which runs:

> Come workers sing a rebel song, a song of love and hate
> Of love unto the lowly
> And of hatred to the great.
> The great who trod our fathers down,
> Who steal our children's bread,
> Whose hands of greed are stretched to rob
> The living and the dead.[216]

Over 100 years later these words still resonate with Celtic supporters who revere Connolly and his politics. In a tolerant society people should freely express their culture and identity and celebrate political figures they admire. Introducing *Songs of Freedom*, Connolly stated that:

> no revolutionary movement is complete without its poetical expression. If such a movement has caught hold of the imagination of the masses they

will seek a vent in song for the aspirations, the fears and the hopes, the loves and the hatreds engendered by the struggle. Until the movement is marked by the joyous, defiant, singing of revolutionary songs, it lacks one of the most distinctive marks of a popular revolutionary movement, it is the dogma of a few, and not the faith of the multitude.[217]

Yet reaction to the poppy protest was fierce. John Reid, the then Chairman of Celtic FC and former Labour Home Secretary advocated banning the protesters from Celtic Park for life. A legitimate peaceful protest against the glorification of war was denounced, with one MP calling on the club to 'lance the boil' of rebellious fans and police pledging to track down the culprits. The vilification of the protestors was shocking in its own right. But an aspect of the demonisation of the fans that went largely unremarked was the blatant hypocrisy. As a Labour Party member Reid would have attended events and marches where comrades paid tribute to Connolly as a trade union activist who argued for the need to unite catholic and protestant workers in the fight against British rule in Ireland.

I have spent the last four years campaigning against and conducting research on an illiberal piece of legislation introduced by the Scottish government to outlaw 'offensive' communications at football games. The Offensive Behaviour at Football and Threatening Communications (Scotland) Act 2012 has outlawed slogans like that on the offending banner on Remembrance Day, pro-republican or loyalist football chants, and a whole host of traditional Irish rebel songs celebrating figures like Connolly. Singing rebel songs, now deemed by the authorities to be offensive and sectarian, can lead to arrest and prison sentences of up to five years for fans. The OBA claims to protect free speech and freedom of expression. It spells out 'for the avoidance of doubt' how preachers, comedians, artist and atheists are free to criticise religion. Yet such exemptions make the legislation even more elitist, draconian and contemptuous of working-class people. It is okay for middle-class types to say certain things at a performance at the Edinburgh Fringe but woe betide people at a football game saying such things! In this respect it is contemptuous of people who attend what is still a largely working class sport. The disdain shown for ordinary people is compounded by the dishonesty built into the law, which lies in its equation of people who sing political songs celebrating the struggle for Irish independence with hatred of others' religion. Celtic fans singing about Connolly or the Easter Rising are wrongly judged to be voicing hatred of Protestants.

The politics of remembrance has always been political, as the story of the founding of the modern Irish state and the partition of Ireland makes clear.

Remembrance Day, and remembrance of World War One more generally, was a card to play in defence of the new political arrangement, and a commemoration to be viewed with suspicion by those for whom 1916 was more about the GPO than the Somme. As Clair Wills puts it in her study of Easter 1916 and its aftermath:

> On Remembrance Day 1922 James Craig, Prime Minister of the newly formed Northern Irish state, asserted that 'those who passed away have left behind a great message to all of them to stand firm, and to give away none of Ulster's soil.' This loyalist message was relayed at Remembrance services throughout the North as 11 November was remoulded as 12 July, echoing the cry of 'No surrender'. Five years later the Cumann na Gaedheal government had to deal with a petition to turn Merrion Square – directly outside the Houses of the Oireachtas, or Parliament – into a Great War memorial park. There was immediate concern that Remembrance Day parades, passing directly under the windows of the Dáil, would prove a focus for anti-government agitation [...] By 1926 the idea of noble sacrifice at the GPO was firmly established as a foundation stone of the new Irish polity.[218]

The fear of the Dublin government was that the focus would be on the Great War as founding moment rather than the Easter Rising. Craig, the son of 'a whiskey distilling millionaire of Scottish origin', made explicit the link between Remembrance, Union and Empire.[219] Remembrance is not a neutral act.

The 100th anniversary of the Easter Rising is an opportunity for an intellectually honest debate about Connolly's legacy. We can bring history alive by discussing how Connolly's principles and values might relate to issues like free speech and civil liberties in Scotland today. Celtic FC is a Scottish football club whose origins can be traced to post-Famine Ireland, founded in 1888 by an immigrant Irish priest, Brother Walfrid, to raise money to feed the often-destitute Irish of Glasgow's East End. This history explains the historic attachment of many Celtic fans to leaders like James Connolly who fought against the British regime that inflicted such suffering on their ancestors. The radical and republican section of the Celtic support looks up to Connolly not for sectarian reasons but its polar opposite – a sense of universalism and solidarity with other oppressed peoples. Yet it is this history that has proved so problematic for politicians in recent years. Celtic and Rangers have gone out of their way to cleanse their club of any links to Irish politics and implemented a bewildering list of rules, restrictions and bans of any displays of support for political groups or historical figures in Ireland. The laws banning 'offensive' communications were merely the logical endpoint of years of policing the behaviour of those Celtic fans expressing an affinity with Irish republicanism of which the Easter Rising is a key element.

Academics will say 'context is everything'. Revising, debating and reinterpreting the history of the Easter Rising in new books and conferences is a world away from defending political chants on the terraces. They are right of course. Interrogating and debating Connolly's legacy is important and stems from a desire to better understand the past and its lessons for the future. But it sits uncomfortably with me that those best placed to understand the anti-imperialist tradition associated with a section of the Celtic support do not do more to challenge the criminalising of working class people who shout the 'wrong' slogan at a football match. I have sung 'The Boys of the Old Brigade' at football matches for decades. I see it as a tribute to the Easter Rising and my hero James Connolly. The only way I could get away with it in public now might be to give a rendition in a lecture theatre.

Scottish academics may want to interpret famous battles against England like Culloden and Bannockburn in various ways or differ in their analyses of the influence of William Wallace. Nobody is suggesting that references to these events and celebrations of Wallace in song by supporters of Scotland's national football team should be discouraged. Scotland fans singing 'Flower of Scotland' is acceptable. Remembering the wars of Irish liberation is banned on the terraces. Celebrating world wars and the British soldiers that died in them is officially sanctioned. These breath-taking double standards may have been lost on many commentators but not on some Celtic fans. The Green Brigade, a spirited and rebellious group of Celtic fans showed their eye for hypocrisy when they attended the match against AC Milan on 26 November 2013 and unfurled a banner showing images of William Wallace and Bobby Sands. The banner read:

> The terrorist or the dreamer
> The savage or the brave
> Depends whose vote
> You're trying to catch
> Or whose face you're trying to save.

For me Celtic stands for hope, aspiration and self-respect for oppressed working-class Catholics in both Scotland and the north of Ireland who in many other ways were the underdogs. While there are those in authority in Scottish football today who would prefer to forget this it remains the case that for many support for Celtic was synonymous with support for a United Ireland and those fighting for it. That's why supporters of Celtic and Rangers sang songs and chanted slogans about the conflict in Ireland rather than the skills of respective players. Ironically, one of the Wolfe Tones' most famous songs beyond their ballad of James Connolly is 'Let the People Sing', a song dear to the heart of Celtic fans, all the more so since the introduction of the OBA. It is belted out with a lot more gusto these days. A further irony is that this anthem appears on the 1983 Wolfe Tones' album, *A Sense of Freedom*, alongside 'Flower of Scotland'. Irish republicans identify with the struggle for Scottish independence. Why are they not free to sing about the struggle for Irish independence? Connolly belongs to Scotland and to Ireland. To Catholics and Protestants alike. He belongs to socialists, trade unionists, republicans and internationalists and no one deserves a prison sentence in modern Scotland for the crime of singing about his struggle.

We have a peace process in Ireland today and many young Celtic fans from Scotland are now third or fourth generation Irish with little or no interest in Irish politics or the history of their club's past political associations. There is what my dad would call the 'daft wee boy' element of fans shouting IRA slogans primarily to antagonise rival fans or the Glasgow police. And there is a small if dwindling section of fans like me who take our history seriously, who still see Connolly as our hero and still link our support for Celtic with our political outlook. It is such supporters that have been censored and criminalised by the new anti-free speech laws in Scotland. The irony at the heart of the new law against offensive communications at football is that there are fewer 'offensive communications' than at any other time in Celtic's history. In other words the media, police, football authorities and politicians decided to turn their fire on displays of support for Irish freedom or loyalism and sectarianism in Scottish football at the very moment in history when these were disappearing.

Those preparing to celebrate the centenary of the Easter Rising should seize on this occasion to show a new tolerance. James Connolly could, if we allowed him, be a unifying figure in present-day Scotland. He could bring together a section of Scottish people who have been marginalised by an illiberal law with the people who run Scotland and who themselves seek independence for their own country. That many Celtic fans singing 'rebel songs' also support Scottish independence is further reason for a change of heart. What a noble gesture it would be to mark the centenary of the Easter Rising by scrapping the OBA.

Taking a stand again imperialist wars and their commemoration is not always popular, or even legal, but it remains necessary. Connolly fought for freedom, and used songs of freedom as part of that struggle. He called for an end to partition, poverty and social inequality. The causes that Connolly fought and died for are still worth fighting for, as is a genuine internationalism even if a sober analysis would tell us these are still a long way off right now. One battle that could be won before the end of 2016 on the centenary of the Easter Rising and Connolly's death is the abolition of the OBA. One slogan we should rally round is 'Let The People Sing'.

Before the Rising:
Home Rule and the Celtic Revival

Michael Shaw

'THEY HAVE SEVERED the union of the flowers', noted *The Scotsman* in 1889.[220] Charles Stewart Parnell, the leading parliamentary advocate of Irish Home Rule, arrived in Edinburgh in July of that year to controversially receive the Freedom of the City, a document that was presented in a silver casket with thistles and shamrocks included in the ornamentation. Having been vindicated during the Parnell Commission, which disproved allegations that he had been involved in the murder of two Irish Secretaries, Parnell and Irish nationalism experienced a spurt of enthusiasm. When he visited Edinburgh, a crowd of 30,000 people greeted him, stretching from Lothian Road to Calton Hill.[221] The Liberal workingmen of Edinburgh stated that 'the mass of the people of Scotland were with the people of Ireland in their struggle'.[222] Contentiously, the Corporation of Edinburgh decided to prioritise Scottish-Irish connections in the casket design by omitting the rose, which represented England, and, together, the United Kingdom. Unionists were concerned: the relationships between the three kingdoms were shifting.

Many aspects of Scottish and Irish cultural and political life increasingly interacted towards the turn of the century. This mainly occurred because similar battles were being fought in both nations. The land wars, home rule campaigns and Celtic Revivals prompted many involved in these efforts to realise that their ends could be more effectively met through co-operation. Consequently, Scotland and Ireland often worked together to defy assimilation and express their desire for change within Britain. What I plan to briefly demonstrate here is that Scottish connections to the Easter Rising were not without precedent: they were part of a growing pattern of developments.

The latter half of the 19th century was a strange period in the history of Scotland's union with England: although Britain was triumphantly marching towards its imperial zenith, discontent was also stirring. Ireland's discontents have been well documented but Scotland's have received little attention. For too long, 19th-century Scotland has been understood as an unequivocally unionist domain, but, although there were no attempts to repeal the Acts of Union, there were nevertheless anxieties over Scotland's position within what was felt to be an increasingly assimilated British state. In 1851, a National Association for the Vindication of Scottish Rights was established to question the structure of the British political system, which often relegated the importance of Scotland and Scottish affairs, in the eyes of many. These concerns were enhanced by the pressures facing the crofters in Scotland (with limited access to secure, affordable land) and, consequently, criticisms of the union were amplified: Professor John Stuart Blackie, a scholar of Greek and Celtic Studies, was a vocal critic of land policy in Britain and an advocate of cultural and political recalibration in the British Isles, supporting the reestablishment of the Scottish Parliament. The land issue was also significant for encouraging many in Scotland to look to Ireland: the Highland Land League, modelled on the Irish Land League,[223] became an effective (if short-lived) political vehicle. The four MPs that the Crofters' Party returned (along with a further ally) in the 1885 General Election were instrumental in securing the Crofters Holdings (Scotland) Act, 1886.

But Scotland wasn't just looking to Ireland; Ireland's presence in Scotland had increased. The political interaction between the two countries was certainly encouraged by the large number of Irish emigrants who moved to Scottish cities like Glasgow in the 19th century. This shift created the conditions for fertile international connections (as well as long-lasting tensions). One of the most significant products of Scotland's shifting demography was the formation of numerous Irish Home Rule Associations throughout the country. The Glasgow Home Rule Association, which John Ferguson (an Irish immigrant) became president of at its inauguration in 1871, was one of the largest and most successful. These associations outside Ireland were helpful to the Irish nationalists who knew that they would need to gain support in seats across the UK to achieve a Home Rule majority in Westminster. Although they focussed on Irish Home Rule and land issues, 'the audience included "Irish and Scotch"' in Glasgow and it wasn't long before they started speaking to the developing interest in Scottish Home Rule – the Irish recognised that they could garner more support for their campaign if it brought benefits to Scotland too.[224] Between 1883 and 1890, the number of Home Rule branches in Scotland increased from 52 to 630.[225]

Although attempts were made to appease Scotland's growing dissatisfaction with the state of the Union (such as reinstating the Scottish Office in 1885, with a Secretary for Scotland), for many it was not sufficient. In 1886, the Scottish Home Rule Association was founded, advocating the return of the Scottish Parliament. It is often forgotten how significant this movement was – Westminster leaders started to campaign on a platform of 'home rule all round' and there were several debates about Scottish Home

Rule in Westminster from the 1880s onwards. Scottish Home Rule motions started to be carried in the House of Commons from the 1890s, leading to two bills which were carried by significant majorities on first readings in the House of Commons (in 1908 and 1911) and one that passed its second reading (1913). The issue was often closely related to the Irish Home Rule debate but, as Reginald Coupland argues, if the Scottish Home Rule movement was simply a parrot cry in response to Irish developments it would not have developed so far or remained on the agenda for so long.[226] Indeed, other political institutions responded to the appetite for a Scottish Parliament. The Scottish Labour Party, founded in 1888 by Keir Hardie and Robert Bontine Cunninghame Graham, made Scottish Home Rule a very firm part of its platform. One of the party's notable members was James Connolly – he wasn't simply born in Scotland, he was evidently concerned with Scottish political affairs too.

While Scotland was looking to Ireland for inspiration, Irish nationalists were also modelling their developments on Scotland. James Hunter argues that many of the Irish developments began in Scotland, noting that 'the link between [Gaelic revivalism and nationalism] is evident in Scotland much earlier than in Ireland', citing the Gaelic Society of Inverness (1871) – which was not simply cultural but vindicated 'the rights and character of the Gaelic people'.[227] Hunter also notes that Douglas Hyde was influenced by the Gaelic Revival in Scotland which was, he said, 'much healthier and more vigorous' than in Ireland.[228] With both nations drawing from and increasingly encountering each other politically, calls for a Gaelic Confederation surfaced and,[229] although this proposal did not advocate repealing the Acts of Union, it did imply radically reshaped unions that gave political autonomy and an international political voice to Scotland and Ireland. For many, the old incorporating, Anglo-centric unions needed to be challenged and a Celtic counter-hegemony was the way to do it.

It is unsurprising that these political filiations bred cultural connections too. Like their political distinctions, there were cultural differences between Scotland and Ireland but both nations were keen to resist cultural assimilation and a co-operative effort was palpably evident. The Pan-Celtic movement – embodied by the Pan-Celtic Congress – brought them together but often there were specific Scottish-Irish ties. For instance, several figures associated with the Easter Rising and Irish nationalism contributed to Scottish periodicals and pamphlets. Patrick Pearse, for instance, became an early contributor to Stuart Erskine/Ruaraidh Erskine of Mar's *Guth na Bliadhna* (*The Voice of the Years*) in 1905. The periodical was devoted to promoting Gaelic Revivalism, and Pearse's essay on '"Education" in the West of Ireland' – an attempt to raise Scottish awareness about the problem of anglicisation in Irish education – complemented this theme well.[230]

Patrick Geddes, the renowned sociologist and town planner, was also keen to highlight Scottish-Irish connections. He was one of the central figures of the Scottish Celtic Revival and his publishing company was responsible for producing *The Evergreen*, a Scottish and Celtic Revival equivalent to the decadent magazines of the so-called 'yellow nineties' that characterised the late Victorian era. Although this magazine promoted a distinctive 'Scots Renascence', Douglas Hyde (the Irish language scholar and first President of Ireland) contributed to two editions of the magazine and work by Katharine Tynan and Standish O'Grady also featured; Hyde would also contribute writings to *The Celtic Review*, another Edinburgh periodical that ran between 1904 and 1916. A further Celtic Revival success of Geddes' was his design for a mural series in the common room of the Ramsay Garden University Halls in Edinburgh (executed by the Scottish Symbolist painter John Duncan). This was a great period for Celtic mural painting in Edinburgh: Phoebe Anna Traquair – an Irish muralist closely connected to the Scottish Celtic Revival – was another figure who created many stunning murals, such as those for the Apostolic Church on East London Street. Geddes and Duncan's mural scheme chronicled several notable figures associated with Scotland, from the birth of the nation to the Victorian period. Geddes was particularly keen to emphasise the shared mythic roots of Scotland and Ireland: the Celtic warriors Fionn mac Cumhaill and Cuchullin form the beginning of this cycle. Another Scottish-Irish figure Geddes was keen to heighten awareness of was St Columba – not only did he include Columba in his pageants of history but his company published Victor Branford's *St Columba* in 1912. The centenary of Columba's death in 1897 certainly awakened interest in the Scottish-Irish connections that he and Iona embodied.

Columba was also an important figure in the writings of 'Fiona Macleod', a pseudonym of the writer William Sharp. Sharp, born in Paisley and educated in Glasgow, imagined this female personae living in the Hebrides writing mystical Celtic Twilight works, which proved to be hugely popular. Although many of the 'Fiona' works portray the Celts as a passing, mystical race, others have a tone of resistance to them and these aspects no doubt attracted the attention of WB Yeats who wanted Fiona to contribute works to his Irish theatrical revival;[231] *The House of Usna* is one of the products of Yeats' encouragement. Several in Ireland did not find Sharp suitably nationalist or Celtic enough though; it was necessary to assert some distance between Sharp and Ireland's movement, reflecting one of the main features of the Scottish-Irish relationship in this period,[232] contested cooperation.

Outside the Celtic Revival, cultural sympathy with Ireland was developing too. Arthur Conan Doyle, a Scot of Irish descent and twice a candidate for the Liberal Unionists in Scotland, made a striking conversion to the cause of Irish Home Rule in 1911, influenced by his friend Roger Casement, on whose behalf he petitioned the British Prime Minister in 1916. Robert Louis Stevenson, who was deeply concerned with reunifying and reclaiming Scotland, was also a supporter of Irish Home Rule, although he turned away from the cause when the violence of the movement became apparent to him. The title of his essay 'Confessions of a Unionist' is deeply revealing – Stevenson's eventual unionism was one of real discontent.

Clearly, it is wrong to see the Scottish-Irish connection in the period before 1916 as strongly unified in its resolves; due to their different circumstances and objectives, there were limits to the collaboration between Scotland and Ireland. Nevertheless, ties between the two nations certainly developed in this period and it is important to see the Scottish involvement in the Easter Rising within the context of these reawakening connections. Geddes repeatedly stressed that 'it is not for London to educate Iona; it is for Iona to educate London'.[233] For both nations, reidentifying with each other (in this case, via Iona) could be a key way of loosening their ties to Britain and asserting their identities.

'Hibernian's most famous supporter'

Irvine Welsh

THE BOY WAS going to a party in the Canongate and he asked her to come along. She agreed; she didn't want to go home […]

As they walked in the cold night he talked effusively, seeming fascinated by her green mane, and told her that this part of town used to be known as Little Ireland. He explained that the Irish immigrants settled here, and it was in these streets that Burke and Hare murdered the poor and destitute in order to provide bodies for the medical school. She looked up at his face; there was a hard set to it but his eyes were sensitive, even womanly. He pointed over to St Mary's Church, and told her that many years before Celtic in Glasgow, the Edinburgh Irishmen had formed the Hibernian Football Club in these very halls. He grew animated when he pointed up the street, and told her that Hibernian's most famous supporter, James Connolly, was born up that road and had went on to lead the Easter Risings in Dublin, which culminated in Ireland's freedom from British imperialism.

It seemed important to him that she knew that Connolly was a socialist, not an Irish nationalist. – In this city we know nothing about our real identity, he said passionately, – it's all imposed on us.

Irvine Welsh, *Bedroom Secrets of the Master Chefs* (2006), p. 3, published by Jonathan Cape. Reproduced by permission of The Random House Group Ltd.

Scotland 2015 and Ireland 1916

An Afterword by Owen Dudley Edwards

I

The Bigger Picture

Catspaw. Though why catspaw? I mean, what have cats got to do with it?'
'The expression derives from the old story of the cat, the monkey and
the chestnuts, sir. It appears –'
'Skip it, Jeeves. This is no time for chewing the fat about the animal
kingdom. And if it's the story about where the monkey puts the nuts,
I know it and it's very vulgar...

PG Wodehouse, Joy in the Morning (1947)

THE GREAT WAR of 1914–18 brought about the 1916 Easter Week Rising in Ireland. Their interdependence is eloquently expressed in *The Road to Sarajevo* (1968), the classic history of the advent of the assassination of the Archduke Franz Ferdinand written by Tito's biographer and guerrilla comrade, Vladimir Dedijer, the last three words of whose book are 'Connolly and Pearse'. The war was integral to the Rising in its origin and course, but it also shaped its reality. It was a UK disaster, and a German triumph, bringing Germany its greatest propaganda victory. Or so it was at the end of 1916. Having harvested so fine a crop, the Germans squandered it from the beginning of 1917. Had they kept their heads it might have enabled them to win the war. Instead they caused it to become a world war, which they lost.

We say 'the UK' and we must continue saying it as far as 1916 is concerned. There is an unspoken historiographical conspiracy between British unionism and Irish chauvinism, agreeing that Ireland was never really conquered by England and never could be. This releases the British unionist from the admission of a failure which might not have been inevitable, and the Irish chauvinist from suspicion that separation from Britain was not necessarily a 700-year-long demand of the Irish populace. The truth was that in 1916 Ireland was a clear if controversial part of the United Kingdom and that terms such as 'the British army' are misleading and unhistorical. In strict constitutional accuracy 'Britain' was merely a geographical expression (as

Metternich had remarked of Italy a century earlier). The United Kingdom of Great Britain had ceased to exist on 1 January 1801, when the United Kingdom of Great Britain and Ireland came into legal existence. The army was Irish no less than British. Its most famous general in the century preceding 1916 – Wellington – was Irish, its leading military textbook writer – Wolseley – had been its commanding general within living memory and was Irish, its leading generals in the Boer War of 1898–1902 were Roberts (not born in Ireland but loving to be called Irish) and Kitchener (born in Ireland and hating to be called Irish), and its two most visible generals at this point of the war – John French and Henry Wilson – were Irish. The Irish gave their lives and limbs in more or less the same sacrificial numbers as did the English, Welsh and Scots. The Easter Week Rising pitted Irishman against Irishman, and four of its seven Proclamation signatories reflected British origins – Tom Clarke from infancy in the Isle of Wight, James Connolly from birth in Edinburgh, Patrick Pearse's English father, Thomas MacDonagh's English mother. The mix even infects historians. My English Protestant grandfather (Walter Dudley Edwards) was a socialist and pacifist who opposed the 1914–18 war, my Irish Catholic grandfather (James Florence O'Sullivan or Sullivan) served for the UK in the war with Irish nationalist pride.

Paul Fussell's *The Great War and Modern Memory* (1975) is one of the great books of historical and literary criticism. It argued that the conflict of 1914–18 overshadowed the English-speaking popular vision of UK war experience when looking back throughout most of the ensuing century. It suggested that World War II in retrospect had its memories often conditioned by World War I. Notably it felt that Joseph Heller's novel *Catch-22* (1961) really partakes of World War I attitudes although set in World War II, above all in the intrigues of its self-advancing protagonists. Fussell (possibly himself a victim of the mislabelling of 'UK' as 'Britain') made little use of Ireland (although granting star treatment to the Irish poet-scholar Robert Graves), but we can help ourselves to his conclusions with little difficulty. In particular, *Catch-22* has a haunting relevance to Ireland. In that novel we encounter US General PP Peckem obsessed with the hope of supplanting US General Dreedle. In 1916 certain officials in the UK armed forces wanted an Irish insurrection, which they intended should be easily but overwhelmingly defeated. The relevant officials in the German armed forces also wanted an Irish insurrection, which they intended should be easily but overwhelmingly defeated. It remains moot as to whether certain leaders of the Irish insurrection in their turn wanted it to lose, charismatically but clearly. Their nominal object was the separation of all the Irish counties from the UK rather than permit a devolution scheme which allowed six counties to opt out: catch-32, in fact. As for the 20th century, 1916 overshadowed all Ireland for its duration whether in the Ulster Protestant cult of the horrific slaughter of the Somme or the Irish nationalist sense of the Easter Rising as the defining moment of Irish identity.

If the image of a country in the eyes of its neighbours be reckoned on the prominence of its human products in public life, and Ireland's highest achievers were military, Scotland's were Prime Ministerial. In the 20 years before the Great War it had supplied three premiers – Rosebery, Balfour and Campbell-Bannerman – and the present incumbent, Asquith, was MP for East Fife. Paradoxically, UK public opinion in 1916, especially when managed by cartoonists or comedians, seems usually to have seen the Scots as soldiers, the Irish as politicians. In fact the Irish could claim to have modernised and democratised the House of Commons under O'Connell in 1829-41 and Parnell in 1880–90, but the Irish nationalist bases of both leaders' movements discouraged valorising Westminster the nominal heart of the Empire, despite Irish and Scots having given much to and frequently profited more from Empire itself. In the Great War Scottish regiments were still venerated cannon-fodder, but Kitchener as War Minister indulged his personal prejudices with criminal folly to favour pointedly the recruits from Ulster Unionist pre-war rebels while the many Irish Catholic volunteers were devoured but disdained. The makers and shapers of public perception in UK journalism and literature since 1890 sometimes seemed to irritated Englishmen to consist entirely of Scots and Irish, though generally resident in London. Scotland in 1916 had no creative giants of the stature of Shaw, Yeats or the largely unknown Joyce, but (like Wales) continued vital in the diffusion of reading and learning through such cheap editions as Nelson's Classics driven by the firm's employee John Buchan, now the UK's master-propagandist in administration and creativity from his latest war thriller *Greenmantle* to his apparently endless volumes of *Nelson's History of the* War (whose leading rivals were the successive instalments of the Irish-descended Scotsman Sir Arthur Conan Doyle's *The British Campaigns in France and Flanders*). But the stage Scots and stage Irish continued to gibber from the music halls and the supposedly humorous *Punch* with what were usually the same jokes seasoned by a century. Public opinion had never been more basic to a war effort, and for all of the UK's incessant war propaganda campaigns, there was ominous journalistic opposition to it on the Red Clydeside as well as on the green Liffey.

But the prime target of German propaganda was the USA, whose involvement in support of the Central Powers was evidently an impossibility, but whose restraint from military support of the Triple Entente was vital. Up to the Easter Rising the UK was clearly winning the propaganda war, less because of actual coups so much as natural features such as common language, accessibility of UK press, assimilation of British Americans, prominence of pro-Ally public figures from Theodore Roosevelt to Henry James – as well as apparent German war crimes such as the German submarine U-20 torpedoing of the RMS *Lusitania* killing 1,198 passengers and crew on 7 May 1915. The *Lusitania* was in fact justifiably sunk according to the laws of war since it carried contraband munitions but that remained hidden for 20 years, the bill of lading being carefully concealed by President Woodrow Wilson. As it was, sympathisers (or at least empathisers) with Germany, notably in the German-American Midwest, argued that the Allies' naval blockade was cumulatively as deleterious to humanity as the submarine toll on ship passengers, but the submarines gave the press their needed headlines. (We may notice, in passing, that the County Cork jury – since Ireland was the land closest to the sinking – gave the inquest verdict on the victims of the *Lusitania*, charging murder against the Kaiser. If the UK was not unanimous on such issues up to that point, it was pretty close to unanimity.) The crimes of German soldiers, particularly in Belgium, were wildly exaggerated by Allied propaganda, but there was enough ugly reality to them to disgust neutral observers more especially as the victims were suffering in a country whose neutrality Germany had violated.

It was therefore a good propaganda coup when Sir Roger Casement the unquestionably heroic evangelist against exceptionally brutal slavery in the Belgian Congo appeared in wartime Germany seeking aid for an Irish nationalist insurrection. The epiphany was welcome but to prolong its effect more was required. Essentially the rape of Belgium eventuated in innocent victims. To be most satisfactorily offset, innocent victims of UK rape were needed. German scholarly achievement in English and Irish history and antiquities would have placed relevant precursors at German warlords' disposal – the Spaniards had attempted a major invasion in support of Irish allies in 1600, the French in 1796 and 1798. These attempts had failed, and while one of the major causes of war was Germany's challenge to UK mastery of the seas, any attempt comparable to the French 15,000 soldiers in 1796 (which storms at sea prevented from landing) must run the UK naval gauntlet: the Battle of Jutland starting at the end of May 1916 would show how dim such German dreams would prove. Where Germany was winning naval supremacy was not on the sea but under it, and some troops could be landed in Ireland. Obviously they would not win. But Casement's like-minded Irish friends might be led to believe they would, all the more when one them arrived in Germany – Joseph Plunkett, one of the future signatories of the Easter Rising Proclamation – happily imagining himself to be re-enacting Wolfe Tone's recruitment of French Revolutionary allies in 1796. And the Germans had only to look at their own Belgian record in reality and in Allied propaganda to gain hope that the UK would fall into a similar trap: brutal repression in meeting the immediate challenge of local pro-German rebellions in Ireland. Casement might not prove a very effective recruit, but he would make a magnificent martyr. We may not know how far the Germans actually ensured that British naval intelligence would be fully conversant with Casement's odyssey from Ireland to pro-German Irish in America, thence to honoured reception and parade in Germany, and all the way back to Ireland.

The Germans took care to have him openly seek to recruit Irish prisoners of war from the German concentration camps. They also took care that several of these prisoners who refused to accept release under his sponsorship requiring enlistment in German armed services, would be sent back to the UK in nice time to give evidence in Casement's trial. When Casement was tried in London two months after the Easter Rising the danger for Germany existed that the UK authorities would lapse into compassion or even wisdom, perhaps even respond to public pressure for a reprieve for the famous humanitarian. An outcry such as that at the German execution of the humane and innocent Edith Cavell in October 1915 might offset such compassion. Nine months is a long time in war, so between Casement's trial and execution another innocent victim of German ruthlessness was produced, Captain Charles Fryatt, who had fought off submarines trying to attack his ship, was captured by clever stratagem some time later, and held until 27 July 1916 when he was tried and sentenced to death (confirmed by the Kaiser) and executed with predictable UK outcry. Casement was already sentenced to be hanged on 3 August 1916 and Fryatt's death sealed his fate. Meanwhile the expected doomed Easter Rising had indeed been put down with heavy slaughter in Dublin and subsequent executions from 3 to 12 May 1916 of its Proclamation's seven signatories as well as of several minor figures such as Patrick Pearse's brother Willy, and the boys' author Michael O'Hanrahan, whose relative innocence was obvious to Dublin if not to London. If the responsible UK official, General Sir John Maxwell, had been in German pay, he could not have done better from Germany's point of view. The resultant American indignation ran far beyond the confines of Irish-America. The public meetings in the USA featured such prominent speakers as Bainbridge Colby who would ultimately be President Wilson's last Secretary of State. In particular, the Democratic Party, traditional political home of most American Irish, demanded a passionate support of continued American neutrality and from the floor hijacked its platform to demand an anti-war campaign when renominating Wilson in Convention in St Louis in June 1916. The UK's arrogance in mail censorship and blacklists of US business firms garnished the dish. Ireland must have been the high point in German propaganda success. Meanwhile on 4 May 1916, the morrow of the executions of Patrick Pearse, Thomas MacDonagh and Thomas J Clarke (the latter a US citizen naturalised in 1905), the Germans issued what was known as the *Sussex* pledge (following the torpedoing of the *Sussex* on 24 March 1916 with 50 lives lost), whereby no passenger ships were to be sunk, merchant ships to be sunk only if carrying weapons, and lives of all passengers and crew protected.

If the Germans had left matters there, and held true to the *Sussex* pledge, they would probably have won the war, since the USA would have had no basis for ending its neutrality, the UK was on the verge of bankruptcy and Russia was near revolution. Wilson chafed under such restrictions on his conduct in a war whose outcome he yearned to determine whether in American peace or war, but Congress would require real grievances to vote for war should he deliver it a War Message. The long-suffering German ambassador to the USA, Graf Johann-Heinrich von Bernstorff, remarked in his post-war memoirs that if Germany had chosen the best policy she would have maintained absolute observance of American neutrality throughout the war. The second best policy would have been to go absolutely for victory sweeping legalities of neutrality out of the way with utterly unrestricted submarine warfare. What Germany actually did, he reflected, was absolute folly, that of pursuing both policies. In January 1917 Hindenburg and Ludendorff took control of German policy and announced unrestricted submarine warfare. The USA went to war against the Central Powers in April, though as an Associate Power to the Triple Entente, not as an Ally (as it would ultimately show in unilaterally accepting German offers of armistice in November 1918).

II

The Disuniting Kingdom

...the Tory Rebellion was not merely a brutal attack upon an enfeebled opponent – that is to say, political; it was not merely the impassioned defence of impossible privileges – that is to say, economic; it was also, and more profoundly, the unconscious rejection of an established security. For nearly a century men had discovered in the cautious phrase, in the respectable gesture, in the considered display of reasonable emotions, a haven against those irrational storms which threatened to sweep through them. And gradually the haven lost its charms; worse still, it lost its peace. Its waters, no longer unruffled by the wind, ceased to reflect, with complacent ease, the settled skies, the untangled stars of accepted

*behaviour and sensible conviction; and men, with a defiance they could
not hope to understand, began to put forth upon little excursions into
the vast, the dark, the driven seas beyond. When Mr Bonar Law incited
the Army to mutiny, his boat was already out; when Sir Edward Carson
played upon the fury of Orange Ulster, he had left the haven, too; and so
with Mr FE Smith, and Lord Halsbury, and Lord Hugh Cecil, and the rest.*

*Would they manage to keep afloat, by baling out with some little
political bucket? Would they sink? Would they put back? These questions
were never settled; for, alas, the waters in which they found themselves
were soon to be adventured upon by the whole western world, to be widely
strewn with the wreckage of Liberal faiths, and to encompass us all today.*

George Dangerfield, *The Strange Death of Liberal England* (1935)

The Strange Death of Liberal England is 80 years of age, yet its prose still
enchants, still risks beguiling its readers into perhaps undue acceptance of
its fascinating thesis that the Great War saved the United Kingdom from
revolution, menaced as its stability was by the rebellions of the Tories, the
women, and the workers. Books must reach their end – in all senses – and
naturally the end of that one was the outbreak of war. But history is never
as final as its books. Granted, the suffragettes, led by Emmeline Pankhurst
and her daughter Christabel, became passionate supporters of the war effort,
which her other daughter Sylvia, allied with the embattled workers, opposed.
But in Britain and Ireland countless workers volunteered for war service,
many to keep their families alive especially when they had lost their jobs to
employer vengeance for labour militancy. It is the Tory rebellion which proved
the strongest survival. They had been ready to commit treason in opposing the
legal implementation of Irish Home Rule passed by the Commons, delayed
for the two years permitted to opposition in the Lords, and ratified by George
V, but as they and their Protestant Ulster working-class followers enlisted for
legal war service, they remained ready for any eventuality which would enable
them to undo the Home Rule settlement. As the Curragh Mutiny had shown,
they had Irish allies amongst army command, Catholic as well as Protestant.
The Liberals retained power from the 1910 elections only by the support of
their Irish nationalist allies led by John Redmond, but when the Tories forced
coalition on Asquith on 17–27 May 1915 they drove from office former
defector from their ranks Winston Churchill and the victim of their press
witch-hunts the allegedly pro-German Lord Chancellor Haldane, probably
the most brilliant Scot in political life. Haldane had in fact modernised the
army when Secretary for War, to the good fortune of the UK forces when war

came. The Tories provided as the leading English Law Officers Sir Edward Carson (Attorney General) and FE Smith (Solicitor General) who before the war had mobilised Orange Ulster to oppose the law. Bitter Irish memories of prominent nationalist MPs of the early 1850s who sacrificed their election promises at the chance of office ensured that Redmond could not accept a government post until implementation of Home Rule (suspended for the duration of the war). It was a psychological wound for Irish constitutional nationalism: if the Protestant unionist opponents of law were made law's official advocates, what was the use of Irish nationalism within the law? Such feelings were not as yet widely articulated – Irish Catholics continued to volunteer for service despite the icy welcome from Kitchener and the army higher command, notably the former potential mutineers. But it made for dry tinder when the Easter Rising burst into flame, and the brutality of the Rising's suppression induced forest fires.

The most implacable army and navy supporters of the pre-war Tory rebellion were not necessarily the most vocal. Captain (afterwards Admiral Sir) Reginald Hall of Naval Intelligence was as convinced as Rudyard Kipling of the patriotic necessity of eradicating the political establishment which had sought to bring about Home Rule, and the war obligingly provided the possibility. Hall's underling Hugh Cleland Hoy recorded in his memoir *40 O.B.* that when a Zeppelin bombing raid narrowly missed the House of Commons, Hall's reaction was 'What a pity!' Professor Christopher Harvie has speculated that John Buchan's master-spy in *The Thirty-Nine Steps* (1914) was based on Hall: certainly that master counter-spy had eyes as hawkish as the bald archaeologist who threatened the United Kingdom and Richard Hannay. They also shared an utter lack of scruple, and both merited Hannay's obituary on his enemy:

> There was more in those eyes than any common triumph. They had been hooded like a bird of prey, and now they flamed with a hawk's pride. A white fanatic heat burned in them, and I realised for the first time the terrible thing I had been up against. This man was more than a spy: in his foul way he had been a patriot.

The foulness would show itself when Casement had been arrested and there was danger that his humanitarianism would lead great people to intercede for him so Hall arranged for the circulation of extracts from a diary in Casement's handwriting full of gross descriptions of homosexual encounters or imaginings. It did discourage many who had intended to speak for him, but Conan Doyle, who was contributing to Casement's defence, contemptuously replied that he thought his friend Roger Casement was guilty of treason although he knew Casement himself did not think he was, and did this diary contain proof of any crime worse than treason? The purveyor of pornography fled, but for a time Conan Doyle was denied further access to troops and records for his patriotic instalments of UK campaigns in France and Flanders. He redeemed himself in the public mind by publishing a story (*Strand*, April 1917) of Sherlock Holmes' war service as a UK spy pretending to be an Irish-American spy which necessitated his running into trouble with the Royal Irish Constabulary in Skibbereen, Co. Cork ('His Last Bow').

But Casement had been Hall's meat from the start, UK Naval Intelligence having tracked him to Germany, obtained details of his activities there, and awaited him at his point of arrival in Kerry where the submarine would land him while the German ship *Aud*, bearing its pitiful ration of arms, scuttled itself to avoid otherwise inevitable UK capture. Casement was taken to Dublin, searched, and promptly removed to London. Legally he was within the jurisdiction of the Irish Viceroy, Ivor Churchill Guest Lord Wimborne, and of Chief Secretary Augustine Birrell, but they were Liberal party appointments whom Hall wished to undermine, not to vindicate. In London Casement asked to see Sir William Tyrrell, secretary to Foreign Secretary Sir Edward Grey: that was denied, clearly for the same reason. The Liberal administration in Dublin was given the minimum information with the desired result that the insurrection broke out and the administration was ruined. James Connolly for one had taken up arms in the belief that the war would turn the UK back on a far more reactionary course eradicating all Labour's gains in recent years. That certainly was what Hall intended, but by the use of the insurrection with which Connolly had provided him. Its first fruits were to solidify the demand of the House of Commons to impose conscription, although Ireland was exempted for the moment. The implication was that the war was likely to become so unpopular that men would be no longer ready to supply it with enough volunteers, not exactly a morale-boosting response. The Easter Rising was after all a statement adverse to the war policy of the UK, although its clear imitation of the war effort betokened folly rather than flattery. The doctrine somewhat questionably ascribed to Connolly, that the UK government would not bombard Dublin buildings because capitalism preserves property, meant nothing to hardline English Tories such as Hall, many of whom would happily have sunk Ireland beneath the waves he bestrode if such a thing were possible.

The USA duly went to war in April 1917 thanks to Hindenburg and Ludendorff disdaining the propaganda victories of their predecessors, and thanks also to Hall's decoding and (after pause for the ideal moment) releasing to the Americans the Zimmermann Telegram wherein Germany offered Mexico bribes of its former possessions now part of its insatiable northern neighbour. Most American intellectuals followed the example of the mind-leaders in the lands of the Triple Alliance and Triple Entente, flinging themselves into patriotic attitudes. Randolph Bourne's *The War and the Intellectuals* wrote his lonely indictment of his contemporaries, crying in his essay 'War is the Health of the State':

> Patriotism becomes the dominant feeling, and produces immediately that intense and hopeless confusion between the relations which the individual bears and should bear towards the society of which he forms a part.

Hall's wartime patriotism and Connolly's are equally questioned by Bourne's logic. In fact, the one set off the other, with very little time separating their responses to the outbreak of war. Many a good English, Welsh or Scottish socialist wrapped the Union Jack around their persons. The Easter Rising found a different flag, the tricolour, but its votaries were as intoxicated by war as those by whom they were revolted. Their self-sacrifice offers no alibi, any more than do the unintended sacrifices of the 450 civilian non-combatant Dubliners slain and over 2,000 wounded. And the obvious ideological indictment of the Easter Rising Proclamation signatories is that they aborted their own best work. To the Tory critic of the Rising or to the IRA enthusiast for it, the works of James Connolly or Thomas MacDonagh make admirable fuel for their sacrificial bodies in the cause of a separate Ireland. To the reader who loves their writings, their sacrifice should be unforgiveable. It is as cruel a deprivation as they could have forced on us. Tom Clarke in 1915 wrote possibly the best Fenian memoir of imprisonment in *Glimpses of an Irish Felon's Prison Life* ('He alone never whines', commented Kingsley M Hancock CBE, former Superintendent of Scottish Prisons, after examining all Irish political prison recollections to have been published), Patrick Pearse was an educationist of originality, idealism and profundity, Joseph Mary Plunkett was a promising literary critic and a poet of aesthetic possibilities if as yet without finish, but we can argue they had gone as far as they could. Plunkett in particular was doomed, and would probably have been dead of tuberculosis at the end of May if General Sir John Maxwell had not shot him on behalf of the UK at the beginning of it. Clarke hardly had another book to write, and saw the Rising as his life's fulfilment. Pearse's life seems driven by the hope of that self-sacrifice. Even so, the Rising is left looking like Ireland's Revolution of the Intellectuals. And the most revolutionary part of it was that when it was over they seemed dead without heirs for their cultural beliefs.

They expected the deaths that the warfare state (which the UK had become) would visit upon them, whether they wanted those deaths or not. The new Ireland which came into being because of them aborted the intellectual freedom in which their different convictions had flourished. Pearse may have died for the Gaelic revival but it would be done to death by being beaten into children according to the worst Victorian educational principles which he abominated. Connolly's Labour movement seemed to have survived in apparent terror of being linked to the socialism he had preached.

III

A Long Way From Tipperary

> *Was it needless death after all?*
> *For England may keep faith*
> *For all that is done and said.*
> *We know their dream; enough*
> *To know they dreamed and are dead;*
> *And what if excess of love*
> *Bewildered them till they died?*
> *I write it out in a verse –*
> *MacDonagh and MacBride*
> *And Connolly and Pearse*
> *Now and in time to be,*
> *Wherever green is worn,*
> *Are changed, changed utterly:*
> *A terrible beauty is born.*
>
> WB Yeats, 'Easter 1916'

IN THE LARGER island the suppression of intellect by the intellectuals' patriotism was more straightforward. Scotland's first Socialist MP in its history, Robert Bontine Cunninghame Graham, embraced the UK war, and after its close denounced the non-violence of a rival Parliamentary candidate, the anti-war socialist Tom Johnston (editor of Glasgow's *Forward* for which Connolly had frequently written). Ireland had been the cause of Cunninghame Graham's imprisonment for six months in 1887-8 when he had been batoned down by police at a protest in Trafalgar Square against the imprisonment of the Irish Parnellite William O'Brien, and was then charged and sentenced for assaulting them. He had also worked with

Connolly on socialist politics in mid-1890s Scotland, counselling fair play to opponents inside the movement. In 1910 Connolly's Socialist Party of Ireland reprinted his 'An Irish Industrial Revival' from his 1902 essay-and-story collection *Success* (with his permission) as a penny pamphlet along with William Morris' poem 'The Day is Coming', the Irish-American biographer of the Fenian John Boyle O'Reilly James Jeffrey Roche's verses visualising the working-class as metaphoric Samson recovering strength, and Connolly's own 'Socialism and Nationalism' from 1897. Pride of place and title of the whole was given to 'An Irish Industrial Revival', Cunninghame Graham's savage portrait of an Irish happy-go-lucky countryside being transformed by an industrialisation enslaving the inhabitants. But two days before war came he appeared at an anti-war meeting at the scene of his arrest a quarter-century earlier, Trafalgar Square, and said that 'England, the mother of freedom and the home of liberty, must throw her weight in the crisis into the scale of humanity' (A Tschiffely, *Don Roberto*, 1937). He reported at the War Office for duty, erupted in rage when told he was too old for service at 62, but was mollified by being sent to South America to get horses for the fray. His chief reason for going to war may have been expressed in his story 'Brought Forward' published in 1916 in an eponymous volume. It records a workshop at Parkhead over lunchtime in days of debate of the Third Home Rule Bill the rival party leaders being the Tory Andrew Bonar Law (Canadian-born but from age 12 Helensburgh-domiciled, a Glasgow MP 1900–06, defeated, and thereafter sitting for English seats) and the Liberal Prime Minister HH Asquith (MP for East Fife):

> 'Man, a gran' speech by Bonar Law aboot Home Rule. They Irish, set them up, what do they make siccan a din aboot? Ca' ye it Home Rule? I juist ca' it Rome Rule. A miserable, priest-ridden crew, the hale rick-ma-tick o' them.'
> …'Bonar Law, ou aye, I kent him when he was leader of the South Side Parliament. He always was a dreary body, sort o' dreich like; no that I'm saying the man is pairfectly illiterate, as some are on his side o' the Hoose there in Westminster. I read his speech – the body is na blate, sort o' quick at figures, but does na take the pains to verify. Verification is the soul of mathematics. Bonar Law, eh! Did ye see how Maister Asquith trippit him handily in his tabulated figures on the jute business under Free Trade, showing that all he had advanced about protective tariffs and the drawback system was fair redeeklous… as well as several errors in the total sum?'
> Then others would cut in and words be bandied to and fro, impugning the good faith and honour of every section of the House of Commons, who, by the showing of their own speeches, were held to be dishonourable

rogues aiming at power and place, without a thought for anything but their own ends...

Jimmy and Geordie, hammering away in one end of the room, took little part in the debate...

One morning, after a reverse, Jimmy did not appear, and Geordie sat alone working away as usual, but if possible more dourly and more silently.

Towards midday it began to be whispered in the shop that Jimmy had enlisted, and men turned to Geordie to ask if he knew anything about it, and the silent Workman, brushing the sweat off his brow with his coat-sleeve rejoined: 'Aye, ou aye, I went wi' him yestreen to the headquarters o' the Camerons; he's joined the kilties richt enough. Ye mind he was a sergeant in South Africa.' Then he bent over to his work and did not join in the general conversation that ensued.

Days passed, and weeks, and his fellow-workmen, in the way men will, occasionally bantered Geordie, asking him if he was going to enlist, and whether he did not think shame to let his friend go off alone to fight. Geordie was silent under abuse and banter, as he had always been under the injustices of life, and by degrees withdrew into himself, and when he read his newspaper during the dinner-hour made no remark, but folded it and put it quietly into the pocket of his coat...

The workmen in the brassfitters' shop came to their work as usual on the day of the good news, and at the dinner-hour read the accounts of the great battle, clustering upon each other's shoulders in their eagerness. At last one turned to scan the list of casualties. Cameron, Campbell. McAllister, Jardine, they read, as they ran down the list, checking the names off with a match. The reader stopped, and looked towards the corner where Geordie still sat working silently.

All eyes were turned towards him, for the rest seemed to divine even before they heard the name. 'Geordie man, Jimmy's killed', the reader said, and as he spoke Geordie laid down his hammer, and, reaching for his coat, said, 'Jimmy's killed, is he? Well, some one's got to account for it.'

Then, opening the door, he walked out dourly, as if he felt the knapsack on his back and the avenging rifle in his hand.

Cunninghame Grahame's perception in the story is that of the Donegal playwright Frank McGuinness in his great play about Ulster Protestant soldiers in the Great War *Observe the Sons of Ulster Marching to the Somme* – in the end men died for one another.

But the former Irish Nationalist MP Professor Tom Kettle wrote from the front 'in the field before Guillemont, Somme, on 4 September 1916':

To My Daughter Betty, the Gift of God

In wiser days, my darling rosebud, blown
To beauty proud as was your mother's prime,
In that desired, delayed, incredible time,
You'll ask why I abandoned you, my own,
And the dear heart that was your baby throne,
To dice with death. And, oh! They'll give you rhyme
And reason: some will call the thing sublime,
And some decry it in a knowing tone.

So here, while the mad guns curse overhead,
And tired men sigh, with mud for couch and floor,
Know that we fools, now with the foolish dead,
Died not for flag, nor King, nor Emperor,
But for a dream, born in a herdsman's shed,
And for the sacred Scripture of the poor.

Tom Kettle was killed on 9 September 1916. He was not a socialist but had given strong moral support to Connolly and his fellow-strikers of the Irish Transport and General Workers' Union, fellow-victims of the great Lock-out in 1913–14, and his last lines seem inspired by Connolly's wartime slogan bannered outside the Labour headquarters in Liberty Hall 'WE SERVE NEITHER KING NOR KAISER BUT IRELAND'. The Easter insurgents included several leaders attempting Christlike self-sacrifice (although curiously unaware of Christ's death having saved other souls without taking lives in contrast to the 450 their sacrifices would sacrifice, not to speak of Ceannt's Volunteers turning out on Easter Monday on what they thought were ordinary manoeuvres to discover themselves in mid-insurrection, just as the UK private soldiers sent to Ireland found themselves dying in battle on Mount Street Bridge with no previous warning from their officers). It played a vital if theologically questionable part in the posthumous cult of the Easter insurgent leaders, notably Pearse.

The real poetic discovery of Christ amid the human slaughter was made by Patrick MacGill an Irish navvy fresh from reservoir-building and artisan tramping in Scotland followed by his classic novels of male Irish migration to Scotland (*Children of the Dead End*) and female (*The Rat-Pit*). He was personally a good, vigorous anti-clerical, having been driven into migration in Scotland by the rapacity of the local parish priest wringing seemingly endless donations from his poverty-stricken congregation to give his own house self-gratifying luxuries. But MacGill distinguished even better than James Connolly between clerics and

Christ. His poem came from the winter campaign of 1914–15 when he witnessed the slaughter in Givenchy, east of Bethune and well to the west of Lille:

A Soldier's Prayer

Givenchy village lies a wreck, Givenchy Church is bare,
No more the peasant maidens come to say their vespers there.
The altar rails are wrenched apart, with rubble littered o'er
The sacred, broken sanctuary-lamp lies smashed upon the floor;
And mute upon the crucifix He looks upon it all –
The great white Christ, the shrapnel-scourged, upon the eastern wall.

He sees the churchyard delved by shells, the tombstones flung about,
And dead men's skulls, and white, white bones the shells have shovelled out;
The trenches running line by line through meadow fields of green,
And bayonets on the parapets, the wasting flesh between;
Around Givenchy's ruined church the levels, poppy-red,
Are set apart for silent hosts, the legions of the dead.

And when at night on sentry-go, with danger keeping tryst,
I see upon the crucifix the blood-stained form of Christ
Defiled and maimed, the merciful on vigil all the time,
Pitying his children's wrath, their passion and their crime.
Mute, mute he hangs upon His Cross, the symbol of his pain,
And as men scourged Him long ago, they scourge Him once again –
There in the lonely war-lit night to Christ the Lord I call,
'Forgive the ones who work Thee harm. O Lord, forgive us all'.

It was, in a different form, the spirit of the Christmas truce 1914 when Fritz and Tommy gave each other little gifts and a handful had a game of football, perhaps the most sacred form of it ever played.

WB Yeats wrote a war poem against war poems:

On Being Asked for a War Poem

I think it better that in times like these
A poet's mouth be silent, for in truth
We have no gift to set a statesman right;
He has had enough of meddling who can please

> A young girl in the indolence of her youth,
> Or an old man upon a winter's night.

Fair enough, I find it pleasing, and (to purloin from Tom Lehrer) it is a sobering thought that when Yeats was my age, he had been dead for two years. But like Walt Whitman, he was large, contained multitudes, and contradicted himself, and straddled the circus animals pulling in so many directions (Chesterton visiting Ireland in 1924 remarked he had never realised Yeats was so horsey, but Yeats' proud Protestant descent preened itself for its 'hard-riding country gentlemen'). And nominally in memory of his godlike collaborator Augusta Lady Gregory's son Robert killed in action on 23 January 1918 he made a war poem. He had written poems of the Easter Rising capturing the change in Irish public response to the leaders become martyrs, and he wrote elsewhere directly in memory of Robert Gregory, but here he who had so successfully pursued aethereal fairies now proved himself the poet who understood most profoundly the moral, political and cultural loneliness of air combat, and thus spoke for the ambiguities of all the combatants from Ireland to Australia:

An Irish Airman Foresees His Death

> I know that I shall meet my fate
> Somewhere among the clouds above;
> Those that I fight I do not hate,
> Those that I guard I do not love;
>
> My country is Kiltartan Cross,
> My countryman Kiltartan's poor,
> No likely end could bring them loss
> Or leave them happier than before.
>
> Nor law, nor duty bade me fight,
> Nor public men, nor cheering crowds,
> A lonely impulse of delight
> Drove to this tumult in the clouds;
>
> I balanced all, brought all to mind,
> The years to come seemed waste of breath,
> A waste of breath the years behind
> In balance with this life, this death.

Hugh MacDiarmid had served in the UK army in that war when he was Christopher Murray Grieve, and in retrospect this could have been the one of all Yeats poems to speak most urgently for him. Yeats' ideas of poets leading the culture of their countries reworked would be welcomed among his principles, and if Yeats mysteriously conquered air when condescending to the battlefield, MacDiarmid brought Scots verse to a second birth by humanising the planets and discovering Christ far across the universe. It was happily symbolised when Yeats and himself urinated together on a lonely Irish road long after midnight and made their streams cross triumphantly. The Easter Rising won its supreme verse from Yeats, in 'Easter 1916' all the more because he knew it meant this heedless self-sacrifice set so much of his work aside including the entitlement of his own Protestant inheritance, quite apart from ennobling Major John MacBride, estranged husband of Yeats' beloved Maud Gonne. Yeats, conscious of the traditional place of the poet in Gaelic society in Ireland or Scotland, knew that epitaphs for the slain insurgents must be for fighters rather than for non-combatants, and hence the names in his songs would not include the pacifist Francis Sheehy-Skeffington, murdered by a demented UK officer, Bowen-Colthurst, also of Irish Protestant hard-riding country gentlemen. But the future would canonise Sheehy-Skeffington, whose courageous feminism, agnosticism and socialism alienated countless fellow Irish from him, yet he had also been among those to denounce Yeats' first play *The Countess Cathleen* where a Protestant landlord (female) sells her soul to redeem her Catholic tenants, and also denounced Yeats' Abbey production of Synge's *The Playboy of the Western World* so faithfully refusing to prettify peasant conversational freedom. That latter part of Sheehy-Skeffington's legacy would thrive in post-Easter Ireland, as Sheehy-Skeffington's widow Hannah would show when in her turn denouncing the Abbey's first production of Sean O'Casey's *The Plough and the Stars* the supremely truthful artistic statement of the comedy and tragedy of the Rising, from the brave Orangewoman killed trying to save the life of the wife of one of Connolly's officers, to the magnificent chorus-figure of the drunken worker Fluther Good who spoke for all Ireland in bitterly asking English soldiers complaining of Irish cowardice, did they expect us to come out in our skins and throw stones? O'Casey showed how the Dublin slums revealed their humanity and their reality, and was called anti-patriotic for it. Connolly admired Sheehy-Skeffington, naming him to be his literary executor although knowing Sheehy-Skeffington as pacifist had opposed the Rising (only to be told that he was already dead) but he did not agree with him about *The Countess Cathleen*, Connolly mocking the pseudo-puritan journalists who threw up their hands in horror at the thought of an

Irishwoman selling her soul when, as Connolly said, their journey from the Abbey theatre to their own newspaper premises would have taken them past innumerable Irishwomen who had been forced by poverty to sell their bodies.

Scottish theatre learned many a lesson from O'Casey, as well as from Synge and Yeats, and, however involuntarily, would nourish Scottish nationalism (slouching towards its Bethlehem to be born) in *The Cheviot, the Stag, and the Black, Black Oil* staged by John McGrath and the 7:84 Company all over Scotland in the early 1970s, but it never won the Irish accolade of hostile riot in the theatre. And so, as we noticed, did Scottish poetry, but as at least two essayists in this book have shown, the Easter Rising under Yeats' auspices won an achievement in Scotland for which he had yearned without fulfilment in Ireland: impact on the supreme Gaelic poet, for Sorley MacLean or correctly Somhairle MacGill-Eain was acknowledged by all Irish Gaelic poets of value to be their master while he lived. Ewen Cameron's invaluable *Impaled upon a Thistle: Scotland since 1880* (2010) pointed out that:

> The war in the desert also produced some of the most notable Scottish poetry from the Second World War: in English, Sydney Goodsir Smith's sad 'El Alamein' from his 'Armageddon in Albyn'; and in Gaelic, Somhairle MacGill-Eain's 'Curaidhean', born out of his experience as an Eighth Army soldier.

There are other great names, most notably Hamish Henderson's *Elegies*. But the Second World War knew as a rule why it fought, much of the time. Yeats in 'Easter 1916' could show the ambiguities before and after the Rising, but his friend George Russell, writing as 'AE', faced the poetic hinge of the rival Irish battlefields, writing an immediate lament for the three Easter insurgent leaders he knew best, but then angrily realising that their apotheoses would deny the true heroes who had died for Ireland amidst their fellow soldiers in UK ranks:

Salutation

*To the Memory of Some I Knew Who
Are Dead and Who Loved Ireland*

Their dream had left me numb and cold,
    But yet my spirit rose in pride,
Refashioning in burnished gold
    The images of those who died,
Or were shut in the penal cell.

Here's to you, Pearse, your dream, not mine,
But yet the thought, for this you fell,
    Has turned life's waters into wine.

You who have died on Eastern hills
    Or fields of France as undismayed,
Who lit with interlinked wills
    The long heroic barricade,
You, too, in all the dreams you had,
    Thought of some thing for Ireland done.
Was it not so, Oh, shining lad,
    What lured you, Alan Anderson?

I listened to high talk from you,
    Thomas MacDonagh, and it seemed
The words were idle, but they grew
    To nobleness by death redeemed.
Life cannot utter words more great
    Than life may meet by sacrifice,
High words were equalled by high fate,
    You paid the price. You paid the price.

You who have fought on fields afar
    That other Ireland did you wrong
Who said you shadowed Ireland's star,
    Nor gave you laurel wreath nor song.
You proved by death, as true as they,
    In mightier conflicts played your part,
Equal, your sacrifice may weigh,
    Dear Kettle, of the generous heart.

The hope lives on age after age,
    Earth with its beauty might be won
For labour as a heritage,
    For this has Ireland lost a son.
This hope unto a flame to fan
    Men have put life by with a smile,
Here's to you, Connolly, *my* man,
    Who cast the last torch on the pile.

You, too, had Ireland in your care,
   Who watched o'er pits of blood and mire,
From iron roots leap up in air
   Wild forests, magical, of fire;
Yet while the Nuts of Death were shed
   Your memory would ever stray
To your own isle, Oh, gallant dead –
   This wreath, Will Redmond, on your clay.

Here's to you, men I never met,
   Yet hope to meet behind the veil,
Thronged on some starry parapet;
   That looks down upon Inishfail,
And sees the confluence of dreams
   That clashed together in our night,
One river, born from many streams,
   Roll in one blaze of blinding light.

Verses 2, 4, 6 are the children of anger in 1917 when the rising cult of the Easter martyrs began its dishonour of the other patriot dead, and so AE also remembered Alan Anderson, child of a colleague in the Irish Co-operative movement, and Tom Kettle, and Willie Redmond, another Home Ruler, still MP but killed at the front, beloved by almost all who knew him. Parnell himself in the witness-box charmingly testified to his own affection for Willie whose death 30 years later brought by-election victory for the newly-released surviving commandant of the Easter Rising, Eamon de Valera.

The first verses written, 1, 3, and 5, date from 1916 itself, sharp testimony asserting reality of memory, startlingly clear, Ulster-born precision in AE's speech, theosophy bristling from his beard, 'his wide eyes netting every shade and tint of hour, immortals nesting in his hair, statistics and seraphs locked behind his ample brow', thus captured in that generation's memoir of genius, Desmond Ryan's *Remembering Sion* (1934). Ryan as Pearse's pupil and later editor and hagiographer would have known AE's murals at Pearse's school, St Enda's, and their artist here conveyed the unreality of Pearse almost as though Pearse had become a painting, immortalising himself as a half-mythical half-miraculous Christ. MacDonagh teaching alongside Pearse recalled by Ryan:

with his neck-tie floating in the wind talking to any one for hours on anything... He respects Pearse too much to be quite at ease with him, for Thomas must argue or die. Thomas knows Pearse would not endure religious controversy, but Thomas must thrash out all such questions with those so inclined and he has a more robust humour than Pearse and wider interests. He is more a European, he says himself, and cannot get to the heart of Gaeldom so profoundly as Pearse. There are moments when the native speakers and the Gaelthacht bore him stiff and he returns to Elizabethan poetry and France and Greece and Rome, and rounds it all off with a night with the poets in his little lodge, and AE comes and smokes his pipe and drinks a modest glass with Thomas when Thomas has it, begad, and if not, begad, AE goes without, 'only an inch, in any case, like Emerson offered Whitman, saying: "Walt, we'll see the dawn"'.

AE's poem reads as though MacDonagh had gone out and got killed to clinch an argument. It would take little imagination to resurrect him, eighty years after, alongside his fellow-schoolmaster Norman MacCaig when his sublime Irish contemporary Seamus Heaney was visiting, MacDonagh the most rapid, most electric, of them all, with that perpetually intrusive 'begad!'

But of the Easter insurgents Connolly alone was AE's man, for whose cause in the cruel 1913 Lockout he had penned a ferocious polemic against Irish employers in the *Irish Times*. Yeats, more distant from them all, remembered Pearse heroically as equestrian with reviving Irish as his mount and MacDonagh as Yeats' fellow-poet of as yet unrealised full genius, murmuring in 'Easter 1916':

> This man had kept a school
> And rode our wingèd horse;
> This other his helper and friend
> Was coming into his force;
> He might have won face in the end,
> So sensitive his nature seemed,
> So daring and sweet his thought.

To do justice to all of that poem we would have to assimilate RF Foster's *Vivid Faces* (2015), the master history recreating that generation's mind and heart in its complexity. 'Easter 1916' in instructive contrast from AE's 'Salutation' wrote Connolly's name, but nothing about him, leaving him to come to life in Yeats' own prose memoir *The Trembling of the Veil* (1922) but as Yeats knew him in 1897 shortly after Connolly had come to Dublin from Edinburgh:

I find Maud Gonne at her hotel talking to a young working-man who looks very melancholy. She had offered to speak at one of the regular meetings of his Socialist society about Queen Victoria, and he has summoned what will be a great meeting in the open air. She has refused to speak, and he says that her refusal means his ruin, as nobody will ever believe that he had any promise at all. When he has left without complaint or anger, she gives me very cogent reasons against the open-air meeting, but I can think of nothing but the young man and his look of melancholy. He has left his address, and presently, at my persuasion, she drives to his tenement, where she finds him and his wife and children crowded into a very small space – perhaps there was only one room – and, moved by the sight, promises to speak. The young man is James Connolly...

IV

The Secret Scot

We are the Workers of Scotland
And we have not spoken yet.

The Worker (Glasgow) 29 January 1916
(Inspired by GK Chesterton, 'The Secret People':
'We are the people of England and we have not spoken yet', 1907)

AFTER THE WAR Cunninghame Graham denounced the new Irish politics with anti-Semitic sneers at de Valera. He recovered from the contagion of wartime chauvinism to become a father of modern Scottish nationalism, and thus of the most successful non-violent nationalist movement in the history of our islands – most successful because non-violent – but Tom Johnston, while retaining much of his earlier veneration for the old socialist during his own successful and beneficial political career to climax as Labour MP Secretary of State for Scotland in Churchill's coalition government of 1941–45, remained a life-long enemy of Scottish nationalism. It was prophetic of Scottish Labour's future antipathy, and Johnston was probably vital in fixing this card of identity. His *Memories* (1952) recalled his editorship of the Glasgow socialist weekly *Forward* featuring Connolly the critic of Irish nationalist politics:

In the brief 46 years of his life which was ended by a firing squad... after the abortive rising of Easter week in 1916, he had become a research scholar whose work on behalf of the working class in Ireland had become widely known in two continents.

...he, Connolly, was a cool level-headed analyst, precise, careful, and accustomed to weighing evidence and words, and to this hour it is a puzzle to me how he ever came to be a leader in an armed rebellion against the British Government, when his Citizen Army insurgents could only muster 118 rifles.

...[writing] for the *Forward*, mostly strictures on the Irish Home Rule Party nowhere did he ever give hint that he was developing into a military insurrectionist Sinn Féiner, and subsequent to his execution – he, though wounded, was taken from an hospital bed, and shot after drum-head court martial! – newspapers in America quoted lavishly from some of his writings in the USA where he had rather derided sentimental Irishism, and stressed instead the need for economic change.

Johnston had published his ground-breaking iconoclasm *Our Scottish Noble Families* in 1909, and in 1916 was working on his *History of the Working Classes in Scotland*. For him Connolly was a fellow-socialist, a fellow-journalist, a fellow-Scot, but above all a fellow-historian, each of them pioneering working-class history as attack and defence. Both of them sought to emancipate their fellow-workers by exposing them to historical realities and learning to overturn historical myths. Our current historiographical controversies between 'revisionists' and sentimentalists appear largely unaware that Connolly and Johnston would have been the most drastic 'revisionists' of their day, all the more since wartime UK professional historiography was toxically conscripted for the war effort, if less openly than the histories from the amateurs Conan Doyle and Buchan. Johnston recalled Connolly's quest for a historiography freeing itself from defensive devout apologetics in sectarian interests:

Once he sat in the *Forward* office, a thick-set man with a bulky black moustache, a soft musical voice, and shy retiring mannerisms, and elaborated his contention that it was necessary to upset the traditional adherences of both Catholic and Protestant workers in Ireland before any united labour effort was possible in that distracted country.

He had collected instances where, during the previous half century, the Catholic hierarchy had sided with landlordism and the English Government, and these he had produced in a pamphlet controversy with a learned Jesuit Father in Dublin. [*Labour, Nationality and Religion* (1910) – Johnston's note, indicating its rereading 40 years after.] His researches into the origins of the Battle of the Boyne must have been something of a shock to such Orangemen as saw the pamphlet. The Battle of the Boyne, he wrote: 'was the result of an alliance formed by pope Innocent XI with William, Prince of Orange against Louis King of France. King James of England joined with King Louis to obtain help to save his own throne, and the Pope joined in the league with William to curb the power of France. With the news of the defeat of the Irish at the Boyne reached Rome the Vatican was illuminated by order of the new Pope, Alexander VIII and special masses offered up in thanksgiving...'

Tom Johnston continued with quotation from Connolly's *Labour in Ireland* (the posthumous omnibus publication of the two separate historical works published by Connolly in his lifetime, *Labour in Irish History* and *The Reconquest of Ireland)*, which tells us he had nourished his place for Connolly in his small library after 1916. His sketch in his *Memories* concluded:

To Connolly the Irish question was a social question and to making it so he had devoted his adult life.

Johnston was quite ready to see the Irish migrants to Scotland as potential allies in working class liberation. In his *History of the Working Classes* he wrote of the late 18th century with 'law scorning Irish immigrants coming into the towns'. That the Irish scorned law as a matter of course was perceptive of him. He meant Irish Catholics aware 18th century law was imposed on them with the avowed intent to extirpate Roman Catholicism in Ireland. As Marx and Engels seem to have occasionally recognised, this gave a potential revolutionary quality to the Irish contribution to the British working class. Certainly it was basic to Connolly. *Forward* recognised from its weekly 'Catholic Socialist Notes' by John Wheatley that Glasgow was beginning to develop Catholics into assuming Catholicism and socialism could be seen as synonymous. Founded ten years after Connolly left Scotland in 1896, Wheatley's Catholic Socialism profited from some clerical sympathy but like Johnston Wheatley defied in war, even when Archbishop Maguire of Glasgow demanded that Catholics should flock to join the UK army. With a fine sarcasm which had evidently learned something from Connolly's published critiques of Irish clerics, Wheatley replied in *Forward*: 'We are assured that if Christ lived today he would don the patriotic khaki and place his services unreservedly at the disposal of Kitchener' leaving little doubt in anyone's mind how Kitchener would in fact dispose of them.

Johnston's own wartime journalism also harmonised with what Connolly was sending him from Ireland to print in *Forward*, the keynote on 15 August 1914 mourning war's destruction of working-class unity:

The whole working class movement stands committed to war upon war – stands so committed at the very height of its strength and influence.

And now, like the proverbial bolt from the blue, war is upon us, and war between the most important because the most socialist, nations of the earth. And we are helpless! What then becomes of all our resolutions, all our protests of fraternisation, all our threats of general strikes, all our carefully-built machinery of internationalism, all our hopes for the future? Were they all as sound and fury, signifying nothing?

Connolly here talked to Scotland appositely if ironically from the most beautiful and most inaccurate history play ever written (*Macbeth*, v.i.26-27), Macbeth suddenly widowed despairing that:

> all our yesterdays have lighted fools
> The way to dusty death. Out, out, brief candle!
> Life's but a walking shadow, a poor player,
> That struts and frets his hour upon the stage,
> And then is heard no more: it is a tale
> Told by an idiot, full of sound and fury,
> Signifying nothing.

Those Scottish workers who read *Forward* would probably have known the play and seen the context. And as Donal Nevin wrote in his magisterial *James Connolly: 'a Full Life'* (2005), quoting further, 'Connolly's fierce indictment of war, expressed in blunt, moving language, is worthy of a place in any anthology of anti-war literature':

When the German artilleryman, a socialist serving in the German Army of invasion, sends a shell into the ranks of the French Army, blowing off their heads, tearing out their bowels, and mangling the limbs of dozens of socialist comrades in that force, will the fact that he, before leaving for the front, 'demonstrated' against the war be of any value to the widows and orphans made by the shell he sent upon its mission of murder?

Or when the French rifleman pours his murderous rifle fire into the ranks of the German line of attack will he be able to derive any comfort from the probability that his bullets are murdering or maiming comrades who last year joined in thundering 'hochs' and cheers of greeting to the eloquent Jaurès when in Berlin he pleaded for international solidarity?

When the socialist pressed into the Army of the Austrian Kaiser, sticks a long cruel bayonet-knife into the stomach of the socialist conscript in the Army of the Russian Czar, and gives it a twist so that when pulled out it will pull the entrails along with it, will the terrible act lose any of its fiendish cruelty by the fact of their common theoretical adhesion to an anti-war propaganda in times of peace?

When the socialist soldier from the Baltic provinces of Russia is sent forward into Prussian Poland to bombard towns and villages until a red trail of blood and fire covers the homes of the unwilling Polish subjects of Prussia, as he gazes upon the corpses of those he has slaughtered and the homes he has destroyed, will he in his turn be comforted by the thought that the Czar whom he serves sent other soldiers a few years ago to carry the same devastation and murder into his own home by the Baltic Sea?

But why go on? Is it not clear as the fact of life itself that no insurrection of the working class, no general strike, no general uprising of the forces of Labour in Europe, could possibly carry with it or entail a greater slaughter of socialists than will their participation as soldiers in the campaigns of the armies of their respective countries?

Every shell which explodes in the midst of a German battalion will slaughter some socialists, every Austrian cavalry charge will leave the gashed and hacked bodies of Serbian or Russian socialists squirming and twisting in agony upon the ground, every Russian, Austrian, or German ship sent to the bottom or blown sky-high will mean sorrow and mourning in the homes of some socialist comrades of ours.

Tom Johnston would seem to have read and printed that in the conviction that Connolly was as implacably opposed to worker participation in war as he was himself. And his subsequent hatred of Scottish nationalism was probably intensified with anger against Irish nationalism for having seduced Connolly. Johnston, born in 1881, was the younger by over a dozen years, thus something of a pupil to Connolly during their few meetings. Connolly in Ireland kept very quiet about his years in the UK Army from 1882 to 1888 but he might have been a little more forthcoming in Scotland to trusted confidants. Whether or not Johnston and he had discussed it, this article leaves a deep impression that its author had seen bayonet combat in action. Much has been speculated as to Connolly's armed service in addition to his undoubted presence in Ireland in time of agrarian hostilities, his writings on India having suggested his presence there to some scholars. He may never have left our islands. But bayonets in 1882 suggest witness of the Battle of Tel-el-Kebir reached from Alexandria on 12 September, with its demands by the Irish General Sir Garnet Wolseley to make sure with bayonets that enemy soldiers lying prone were dead, for fear they might be shamming with a view to backstabbing. Elsewhere Connolly gave other evidence of having what one well-meaning writer called 'a bayonet fixation', which conveys all too horribly what memories may have oppressed his mind.

An ominous grace-note might have suggested what the collapse of international working-class solidarity might prompt Connolly to do:

> If these men must die, would it not be better to die in their own country fighting for freedom for their class, and for the abolition of war, than to go forth to strange countries and die slaughtering and slaughtered by their brothers that tyrants and profiteers might live?

That has an eerie ring of 'The Foggy Dew', a chaste post-Rising version of a ribald folk-song, authorship disputed between partisans of Brendan Behan's cousin Peadar Kearney (who certainly wrote some fine songs celebrating the Easter Rising, as well as the depressingly militaristic Irish national anthem), and proponents of Canon Charles O'Neill, Parish Priest of Kilcoo:

> Right proudly over Dublin town they hung out their flag of war
> It was better to die 'neath an Irish sky, than at Suvla or Sud-el-bar.

Whoever wrote it was well-informed with the corrosive resources of Irish satire. Suvla and Sud-el-bar (Sedd-el-bahir) were disastrous UK expeditions in early 1915 against Turkey with a hideous slaughter of Irish troops. As Ireland's contributions to UK service were blotted out of human memory by Irish and British alike, the corrupt text of another verse was rendered as 'lonely graves by Suvla's waves /On the fringe of the grey North Sea'. Those of sufficient maturity during the Great War would have made sense of it, as 'Suvla's waves /Or the fringe of the grey North Sea', which was fair enough – plenty of Irish kept up the death-toll in British as well as in Irish waters, although you were not limited to service in HM armed forces to be sure of death from German submarines. The sentiments themselves were mildly dotty. First, when you're dead, you're dead. Secondly, service whether for Cathleen Ni Houlihan or John Bull required your killing enemies before your death. Connolly's original version assumed working-class solidarity in Ireland yet it was quite likely that the enemy you shot in an Irish stramash would also be an Irish worker, and it is unlikely that Connolly would have shared the views later held by future IRA men that any Irish they killed deserved it for being on the other side, even if they were corpses of non-combatants. Curiously enough the song also has an echo of Tom Johnston, with its line how 'Britannia's Huns with their long-range guns sailed in through the foggy dew'. The popular version of the original

Huns' achievement was summed up in the words of *1066 And All That*: 'destroyed everything and everybody, including Goths, Ostrogoths, Vizigoths and even Vandals'. Their brutality rather than their comprehensiveness seems to have induced UK allusions to the Germans as 'Huns'. Johnston produced a pamphlet in 1918, which he probably anticipated by earlier instalments in *Forward* (whose suppression on various occasions frustrates the historian today having impoverished the public in its time): *The Huns at Home during Three Years of the Great War*. In fact the supposed Huns were the full war machine and its capitalist manipulators in Johnston's reading, where the song seems to limit them to the UK Navy. There was thus much common reason and rhetoric between Connolly at war's commencement and Johnston throughout its course. Johnston's courageous rejection of war was where he expected to find Connolly's continued comradeship. The views of editor and contributor continued in harmony for Connolly's essay for *Forward* on 15 August 1914, and regardless of his next two years it still speaks to us today:

> Civilisation is being destroyed before our eyes; the results of generations of propaganda and patient heroic plodding and self-sacrifice are being blown into annihilation from a hundred cannon mouths; thousands of comrades with whose souls we have lived in fraternal communion are about to be done to death; they whose one hope it was to be spared to co-operate in building the perfect society of the future are being driven to fratricidal slaughter in shambles where that hope will be buried under a sea of blood.
>
> I am not writing in captious criticism of my Continental comrades. We know too little about what is happening on the Continent, and events have moved too quickly for any of us to be in a position to criticise at all. But believing as I do that any action would be justified which would put a stop to this colossal crime now being perpetrated, I feel compelled to express the hope that ere long we may read of the paralysing of the internal transport service on the Continent, even should the act of paralysing necessitate the erection of Socialist barricades and acts of rioting by Socialist soldiers and sailors, as happened in Russia in 1905. Even an unsuccessful attempt at Social Revolution by force of arms, following the paralysis of the economic life of militarism, would be less disastrous to the Socialist cause than the act of Socialists allowing themselves to be used in the slaughter of their brothers in the cause. A great Continental uprising of the working class would stop the war; a universal protest at public meetings will not save a single life from being wantonly slaughtered.
>
> I make no war upon patriotism; never have done. But against the patriotism of capitalism – the patriotism which makes the interest of the

capitalist class the supreme test of duty and right – I place the patriotism of the working class, the patriotism which judges every public act by its effect upon the fortunes of those who toil. That which is good for the working class I esteem patriotic, but that party or movement is the most perfect embodiment of patriotism which most successfully works for the conquest by the working class of the control of the destinies of the land wherein they labour.

To me, therefore, the Socialist of another country is a fellow-patriot, as the capitalist of my own country is a natural enemy. I regard each nation as the possessor of a definite contribution to the common stock of civilisation, and I regard the capitalist class of each nation as being the logical and natural enemy of the national culture which constitutes that definite contribution.

Therefore, the stronger I am in my affection for national tradition, literature, language, and sympathies, the more firmly rooted I am in my opposition to that Capitalist class which in its soulless lust for power and gold would bray the nations as in a mortar.

Reasoning from such premises, therefore, this war appears to me as the most fearful crime of the centuries. In it the working class are to be sacrificed that a small clique of rulers and armament makers may sate their lust for power and their greed for wealth. Nations are to be obliterated, progress stopped, and international hatreds erected into deities to be worshipped.

James Connolly was a war casualty. He had denounced the Great War as 'the most fearful crime of the centuries' and when we look at the ultimate death-toll he proved a true prophet. He was not so much a Marxist as a Marxian, using Marx as a stimulus not as prison or a crutch, but however appropriate Marxian analysis may be, it need not be invoked to see the indictment which the masters of humanity drew up against themselves by their actions. No excuses will serve. It will not do to say the major responsibility lay with some other power: all those with any power were guilty. Unfortunately this also included those infected by the near-universal infection, even those such as Connolly who had courageously observed what was happening and yet failed to see how they themselves were breaking out with the same loathsome attraction to homicide.

Connolly's life and teaching up to 1914 had been a dedicated apostleship, seeking to evangelise the Irish by showing how their national identity should make them Socialists. In the end the cannibal devoured the missionary. But the missionary's originality was remarkable, and the more he studied and wrote the more he argued not only as Irish but also as Christian. Neither Irishness nor

Christianity need necessarily have been more than protective and convincing clothing, and Connolly's life forced him into strange disguises. It was no great compliment to Ireland that he felt it necessary to conceal his Scottish birth. He saw the longer he remained in Ireland (from 1896 to 1903, and from 1910 to 1916) that the ideological swirl growing more and more enthralling made for a new and vibrant journalism into which he played a great part, but the leading practitioners of new Irish journalism were often either xenophobes themselves or automatic utilisers of xenophobia. In common fellowship against the Boer War he found himself collaborating with Arthur Griffith, perhaps the most brilliant Irish journalist of his time, as concluded by Roy Foster in his fascinating intellectual history of the period, *Vivid Faces* – but Griffith's hatred of socialism and automatic rejection of freedom of speech for British-born persons meant Connolly felt forced to conceal his Scottish identity to permeate his Irish one. Griffith refused to allow my grandfather to speak during the discussion ensuing from a Griffith lecture, on the ground that he was English, though the family tradition is that Griffith feared proof that his capitalist economics were inferior to Grandfather's socialist economics. He would have used Scottish birth perpetually against Connolly rather than face his economics, especially in Griffith's own newspapers. Thus was born the legend of Connolly's birth in Clones, Co. Monaghan in 1870, which survived until 1961 when his biographer Desmond Greaves established reality of the Edinburgh birth in 1868.

In one letter home Connolly seems to have told a Scottish friend that his Catholicism no longer existed – 'no tincture of the faith' remained. But irrespective of the extent or absence of his 'cradle' Catholicism at any given time (and determining a man's beliefs for a lifetime on the basis of a single letter is pretty dubious), Connolly proved himself a great Catholic writer in thought processes irrespective of his actual views on specific questions. As for his religious beliefs, in his days as a prisoner dying of a gangrened leg and destined for execution, he received the sacrament of reconciliation and the union with God implicit in the Eucharist, asking his Protestant wife to convert to Catholicism. Those anxious to salute him as an atheist (which he never called himself) or denounce him as a hypocrite (which no contemporary seems to have called him) will no doubt stand bravely by their views or wallow in their invincible ignorance according to your preference. But he was asked on the eve of his execution to pray for the soldiers who would kill him, and instead of a simple affirmation, or an evasion, replied 'I will say a prayer for all brave men who do their duty according to their lights'. Much has been made of the Christlike character of Patrick Pearse, Sean Mac Diarmada and others of the executed leaders. But it was Connolly the Marxian who departed with prayers for his friends, his enemies, his mourners, and his killers, as Jesus Christ had done before him.

V

The Man from Everywhere

There was a beginning but you cannot see it.
There will be an end but you cannot see it.
They will not turn their faces to you though you call,
Who pace a logic merciless as light...
                    Robert Penn Warren, 'The Ballad of Billie Potts'

IF JAMES CONNOLLY had never existed, the Easter Rising could have taken place, and likely would have done. He was probably the only one of the seven signatories of the Rising Proclamation whose presence came from a serious failure in the existing state, that is to say the hideous living conditions of working-class Dublin and Belfast. If the historian looks for a Carlylean great man, a thing Connolly's Marxian perspective would have led him to deplore, his originality and zeal in applying his Catholic reasoning and Irish nationalist equipment to Marxian perspective distinguish him from the international identity parade of insurrection leaders, Anglophone social thinkers, trade union negotiators, socialist voices, and so forth. But he was not indispensable to the Rising; and apart from Jim Larkin in the USA since 1914 there were remarkable figures in Irish labour but none capable of pulling the weight he did. The metaphor comes easily. My father met him once when a boy, at a sports day in Pearse's school, St Enda's. Connolly was lying on the ground, exhausted after being one of a tug-of-war team. He was too breathless to talk, but my father seemed to like the look of him.

If Sean Mac Diarmada had never existed, the Easter Rising could not have taken place.

Connolly was so recognisable a name in 1916 that, once the immediate UK army censorship had been lifted and the first newspaper stories emerged, his death in action was quickly asserted, then his death from wounds, then his execution on 3 May, then his actual execution on 12 May. His unfortunate wife was told by a London paper while the insurrection was still continuing that she was a widow. Scots newspapers sometimes correctly claimed his birth in Scotland, but this seems to have been dismissed in Ireland if known, comparably to the legend in the *Catholic Herald* in some editions that he had a Liverpool upbringing, probably a conflation with Larkin. The Aberdeen press were able to justify his mention in their columns by the information that he had visited Aberdeen several times. His niece Mary was told by the man in her Edinburgh paper-shop that her uncle was in the paper. Fifty years later she recalled for TV interview what happened:

> He said 'Look who's in the paper, your uncle's in the paper. I said 'Never mind who's uncle's in the paper, just give me the paper' and I took the paper and I ran and I ran until I got home and my daddy said 'What's the matter with you?' And I said, 'Oh, Daddy, Daddy, Look what's happened to Uncle James!'

That would seem to have been a Catholic paper shop and a Catholic paper featuring a large picture of Connolly with the news that he had commanded the Easter insurrection and had been executed, the death at that point being false. Its logic was doubtless that pressmen assumed the commander would be the first to be shot, but Connolly's gangrened wound had brought him to separate hospitalization, ended when pressure was mounting to finish off the executions wherefore Maxwell finished him – and Mac Diarmada – first.

Sean Mac Diarmada was the only other signatory of the Easter Rising Proclamation to have lived in Scotland. His name has played no part in our book, and its absence has its own validity. He was the conspirator extraordinary, and if there are so few traces of his passage that was his intention.

Connolly was an ex-soldier who had been trained for such violence as the UK Government might deem necessary and whose mentality must always have seen violence as an option under extreme circumstances. It was never an option for his friend Francis Sheehy-Skeffington (murdered by a mad Irish officer in the UK forces in arms against the Rising). There was a logic in Connolly's conviction when war broke out that its repressive effect necessitated a revolt in arms to derail its prospects. If such things could be justified, the Dublin and Belfast slums were a ground of revolt for Connolly, such as his fellow-signatories lacked. Even so, the slaughter of civilians during the Rising called its justification on any grounds into question. It was a strange emancipation which condemned scores of Dubliners to death from the actions of those claiming to free them. Ironically, it recalls John Brown's raid at Harpers Ferry in 1859 seeking to free African-American slaves and finding its first casualty in a free African American. It was also a strange celebration that led Dubliners for the next century to hail the heroism of the

Easter insurgents with scarcely a mention of their victims.

There remains the contrast of Connolly's motivation from those of his colleagues. The UK might have failed in its duty to give an urban proletariat decent living conditions and adequate public health, but the long and tortured history of rural Ireland had lost its worst injustices by 1916. For Patrick Pearse, Thomas MacDonagh, Joseph Plunkett and Eamonn Ceannt, the Rising was art for art's sake. That was so in a very different sense for Mac Diarmada, and for his brave and terrible mentor, Tom Clarke, but there was nothing casual, aesthetic, or whimsical about their intent and its realisation. Connolly evidently decided on insurrection once war came, but the commitment of Pearse, MacDonagh, Plunkett and Ceannt were also the product of what in retrospect seems a global immersion in self-destruction. Thousands of young men across Europe flocked to enlist; the future Easter insurgents were prevented by their political beliefs from responding in like manner to the self-sacrificial climate, so they found another way of doing the same thing, however strange it seems to make war against the Great War as a method of participating in it. They were poets or musicians in arms who like their fellows in the UK forces in many cases went to war in defiance of reason, sometimes testifying against the slaughter in great lines but yet returning to the fight. WB Yeats may have distorted or mistaken the motivation of his friend Augusta Gregory's son Robert killed in air combat for the UK, but his great poem had a universally representative quality that reflected German, French, Russian and Austrian soldiers, and probably some of those who died as Easter soldiers, drawn in through the pre-war Irish Volunteers inspired as much as anything for defence against Carson's unionists who were arming themselves against Home Rule but whom Ulster Catholics feared might suddenly begin to slaughter them. The advent of the war removed that danger, but the Irish Volunteers continued military manoeuvres from August 1914 to Easter 1916 (apart from their majority who joined the UK forces at John Redmond's request). One of the ugliest methods of sending men out to be slaughtered was for women to shame them into enlistment. One motive for the Rising was to answer any hint that its participants were cowards in refusing to enlist for the UK.

The Great War convinced Connolly at its outbreak that it had to be answered by war to check its otherwise inevitable effects of setting back Labour's painful gains to date. The war supposedly began by Belgium's refusal to capitulate to Germany saving France from immediate destruction. The same logic would inspire the thought of an Irish revolt stopping the UK war machine in its tracks. Connolly spoke of a giant being killed by a pin stuck in its heart by a child. The cult of youth inflamed all sides in the

Great War inviting the postwar response 'war is the time when the old men come back into their own, and the young men who are pressing on their heels are miraculously removed'. (Leslie Charteris, 'The Noble Sportsman' *Boodle* (1933)). There was an old man in Mac Diarmada's story, an old man ready to die himself but determined to take as much youth with him as he could – the old Fenian Tom Clarke. Mac Diarmada would be his agent from 1908. Mac Diarmada himself was born in Kiltyclogher, co. Leitrim in 1883. It was grim and inhospitable farmland, and urban magnets drew brothers and compatriots forth, not so much to Dublin as to Belfast, Glasgow and Edinburgh. His first major biographer Gerard MacAtasney noted that in 1907:

> Emigration to Scotland was so common amongst the population of counties such as Leitrim and Fermanagh that the Fermanagh *Herald* carried a weekly diary of events entitled 'In and around Glasgow'.

He was from a large family of siblings some of whom made their way to North America, others to UK cities. John Joseph McDermott (as he still was then) came to Edinburgh in 1903 joining a cousin alongside whom he worked as a gardener. It offered an urban setting where rural background would be more useful than normally, but he later dismissed the experience with memories of dislike of 'raking paths'. Nothing else seems to remain to feed possible speculation about his Edinburgh identity. He had no overlap with Connolly, now beginning his longer American sojourn. He might, however, unknowingly have seen some of Connolly's elder brother John's family if he attended the main Irish ecclesiastical thoroughfare St Patrick's in the Cowgate, though he gave up Catholic practice for some years until shortly before his execution. But his younger brother Daniel (after trying his luck in Belfast) settled in Edinburgh at least for a time. By 1908, Mac Diarmada, fluent in tongue privately and publicly, was lecturing in the cause of the non-violent anti-Westminster Sinn Féin political party still devoted to Arthur Griffith and his idea of an Irish dual monarchy with Britain on the lines of Hungary's relationship to Austria, and Daniel became President of the new Sinn Féin John Mitchel Club in Edinburgh. So Edinburgh may have given him his earliest education in an alien environment where his fellow-Catholics from Ireland would often have previous commitment to John Redmond and the Home Rule party and may have looked suspiciously on this charming newcomer whose plausible manners would not necessarily alleviate anxiety that new politics could derail existing gravy-trains. He was Ireland-obsessed from the start, a natural product of exile, and being in the UK, the same country in which he had been born (however much he resented it) he could have found Edinburgh, and still more Glasgow and North Lanark, places where he could almost think of himself as still being in Ireland. The Irish in Victorian and Edwardian Scotland thought themselves Irish more than Scots until 1923 and in many cases long afterwards. Young John Joseph qualified for acceptability in Scotland in one respect. He loved the poetry of Burns, his one notable exception to his restriction to Ireland, and not much of one considering the Irish delight in Burns in recitation and song throughout the 19th and early 20th centuries. Survivors remembered his singing voice as musical and memorable in rendition of Moore's melodies as well as Burns. He does not seem to have been a pretentious performer, but his songs remained for many decades in the minds of some auditors. It was all part of his endless charm which wound its way around men and women alike.

He needed it. His biographer Brian Feeney estimated that by 1908 Mac Diarmada had become the 'only full-time paid revolutionary in Ireland'. For what exactly he was a revolutionary, might have puzzled close observers. He was building up Sinn Féin by managing a by-election in early 1908 in North Leitrim, the constituency of his birth, when an incumbent Redmondite nationalist defected to Sinn Féin, resigned and ran for office under his new colours, obtaining slightly more than one-third of his successful opponent's votes. Nevertheless as a good propagandist Arthur Griffith declared the result a moral victory which meant that Mac Diarmada had to be treated as a success. Financially it was also a success. Mac Diarmada was also a member of the Irish Republican Brotherhood as the Fenians in Ireland were called, and its American brethren had financed the election. Henceforth Mac Diarmada was actually organising for the IRB and came directly under the influence of Tom Clarke after both of them had settled in Dublin for the first time. From this Mac Diarmada made his way through the mass of new and rejuvenated Irish societies, the Gaelic Athletic Association, the Gaelic League, the Irish Volunteers, the Irish You-name-it-he-was-it. He was appointed manager of the IRB paper *Irish Freedom*, he made endless visits to each of the 32 counties, he covered his tracks so well that historians despair of following him through the omnipresence of his honeycombs. He was brave, and had to be, since the vigour of Irish politics led to ugly assaults and batterings all the worse after he had been disabled by polio, limping badly thereafter. He probably had his own agents in various hostile nationalist organisations. Ironically his perhaps temporary indifference to his cradle Catholicism was matched by his equal indifference to socialism, which would not have prevented his converting a few socialists to IRB aspirations for insurrection. Clarke was the crux of Mac Diarmada's pilgrimages, and Clarke's intransigence came from 15 years in

English prisons at their most punitive, for intent to dynamite UK institutions and any civilian populations in the way. Desmond Ryan likened him to the tragic, noble and implacable figure of Milton's Satan at his greatest in the first two books of *Paradise Lost*. As his widow testified so well, Clarke was lovable as well as implacable. But his great virtues were locked in an Anglophobia infinitely darker than the racism of Griffith. Mac Diarmada became his devotee, finding his ideal father. All things were turned towards the ultimate Irish insurrection for which Clarke had thirsted so long. It was a wonderful symphony in idealism and intrigue, courage and cruelty, lion-hearts and lies. The war provided the opportunity for all – and also for Captain Reginald Hall, who having broken the German codes knew what the future insurgents were doing well before they did.

Meanwhile we are left looking at a figure raking a path in some Edinburgh residence and wondering what might have expedited his decision to leave it.

As AE wrote, and Graham Greene quoted: 'In the lost boyhood of Judas, Christ was betrayed.'

VI

A Valediction, Forbidding Mourning

For Lycidas is dead, dead ere his prime,
Young Lycidas and hath not left his peer.
Who would not sing for Lycidas? He knew
Himself to sing and build the lofty rhyme.

Milton, 'Lycidas'

IS IT REALLY possible that the Easter Rising can retain its immediacy a century later?

In the wrong hands, certainly. Legend, and still more history with judicious admixtures of legend, can prove lethal regardless of having been laid down in the foul rag and bone shops of our hearts aeons earlier. The Easter Rising contained figures of gallantry, genius, grandeur, and so did the war which spawned them and against which they took their stand. The great writings of the participants are still there to inspire and engage us – Clarke, Pearse, MacDonagh, Plunkett, and above all Connolly – but they must be given their context or like the sorcerer's apprentice we destroy ourselves in summoning magic we cannot control.

As the contributors to this book show, Scotland's interaction with Dublin's Easter Rising takes various possible forms from then and now, above all in the genius of Connolly, child of our capital city who so long denied its paternity. And the recent history of Scotland tells another story. The Easter Rising was tragedy, comedy and poetry, games deadly serious and seriousness turned into game.

But from the viewpoint of all participants – German, English, Irish, Scottish – it was a game of death. It has so much to teach us, and so much for us to honour as well as mourn. But it remains a past event waiting to trap futures. And so however humdrum and even banal by comparison, Scotland was the wise sister, and the poisoned chalice presented to her lips was poured on the ground. Ireland won her freedom at a price Daniel O'Connell had said would be too great if it cost one drop of blood, and it was much more than one drop or one martyr. Scotland had the longer road, but the road of peace. The Irish past summons us provided we keep it as tutor not as jailer. The Scottish future can remain one of ideals provided we blunt their agency for hurt.

So much could be developed further, playing harps or pipes to our hearts' content, all the more with so varied a collection of documents (or essays) ranging from pedagogical analyses to very raw material, the whole dominated by the editorship of Kirsty Lusk, whose work celebrates the new Irishwomen of 1916, and Willy Maley, whose studies of Irish/Scottish cultural interaction are as far flung and as seminal as could be asked. It is a privilege for all of us to appear under their inspirational auspices.

But further congratulations must give way to commiserations. To my joy our contributors contained many great names including foremost critics and artists of our time, but all of us are dwarfed now that in the last 48 hours as I write comes the misery that we have lost Ian Bell, James Connolly's great-nephew, the most appropriate of all contributors to reflect on the interaction of Scotland's future and Ireland's Rising. His paper the Glasgow *Herald* mourned him in a mighty essay on 11 and 12 December 2015, but its headline cries for us all:

Man of Principle Who Waged War on Lies, Greed and Avarice.

Contributors

Allan Armstrong is the author of *From Davitt to Connolly, 'Internationalism from Below' and the challenge to the UK state and British Imperialism, 1889–95*, and *The Ghost of James Connolly: James Connolly and Edinburgh's New Trade Union. Labour and Socialist Movements (1890–96)*, and a contributor to *Unstated: Writers on Scottish Independence*, edited by Scott Hames. Allan is a member of RISE, Scotland's Left Alliance and the Radical Independence Campaign and a contributor to the Emancipation & Liberation blog. He is a retired teacher and conducts Radical Walks in Edinburgh.

Richard Barlow completed his PhD at Queen's University Belfast and he is now Assistant Professor of Modernism at Nanyang Technological University in Singapore. His research focuses on the influence of Scottish culture on Joyce's works, especially *Finnegans Wake*. He is a regular reviewer for the *Irish Studies Review* and *Notes and Queries* and his articles have appeared in publications such as *James Joyce Quarterly* and *Philosophy and Literature*.

Born and raised in Edinburgh, **Ian Bell** is a former holder of the Orwell Prize and has twice been named Scottish Journalist of the Year. He has published a two-volume biographical study of Bob Dylan, *Once Upon a Time/ Time Out of Mind*. A regular columnist for *The Herald* and *The Sunday Herald*, he died after a short illness as this book was going to press.

Alan Bissett is a novelist, playwright and performer from Falkirk, who now lives in Renfrewshire. He was Glenfiddich Scottish Writer of the Year in 2012. His novels include *Pack Men*, about the 2008 UEFA Cup Final, in which Rangers played in Manchester. It was shortlisted for the Scottish Arts Council/Scottish Mortgage Investment Trust Fiction of the Year Prize 2012. He is also co-editor of the collection of essays *Under a Union Flag: Rangers, Britain and Scottish Independence*. He is currently working on a play about Graeme Souness.

Joseph M Bradley is senior lecturer at the University of Stirling with a background in political science, sociology and modern history. He has written and edited several books, published widely in national and international academic journals on religion, culture, sport, identity and the media, and presented papers at conferences in Australia, Cuba, USA, Holland, Canada, Ireland, Germany and France. He has also published numerous newspaper articles on a diverse range of subjects. Born and raised in Scotland, his family roots are Irish, with family emigrating to Scotland from counties Offaly, Westmeath, Longford, Donegal, Derry, Tyrone, Down and Antrim.

Ray Burnett, currently living on Benbecula, is from Edinburgh, with family roots in Connolly's Old Town and has had an active engagement with Irish/Scottish cultural, social and political affairs since the early 1960s. He has a particular interest in the significance of James Connolly's writings for the building of a distinct Scottish left, organically rooted in the history and culture of Scotland.

Stuart Christie is a Glaswegian anarchist writer and publisher probably best known for being arrested in 1964 as an 18-year-old carrying explosives to assassinate the Spanish dictator General Franco. In 1971 he was arrested, tried and acquitted of membership of the 'Angry Brigade'. Founder of various publishing imprints, the latest being ChristieBooks, he has written on anarchism, the Spanish Revolution and the anarchist resistance to Franco, including a three-volume memoir: *My Granny Made Me An Anarchist*, *General Franco Made Me A Terrorist*, and *Edward Heath Made Me Angry*. He is also the author of *¡Pistoleros! The Chronicles of Farquhar McHarg*, a (lightly fictionalised) trilogy on the Spanish anarchist movement after the war of 1914–18.

Helen Clark, until her retirement in 2012, was the Special Projects Manager at City of Edinburgh Museums and Galleries. In 1986, Helen organised an exhibition in the City Arts Centre, *Sing A Rebel Song – the Story of James Connolly*, and wrote the accompanying pamphlet. Helen ensured that this exhibition was stored. The James Connolly Foundation, in conjunction with Edinburgh City Council, displayed it again in 2010. Helen has also written *Raise the Banners High*, about the Scottish trade union movement; *She Was Aye Working: Memories of Tenement Women in Edinburgh and Glasgow* (along with Elizabeth Carnegie); and most recently helped to produce the oral history, *Rainbow City – Stories from Gay, Lesbian, Bisexual and Transgender Edinburgh*.

Maria-Daniella Dick is Lecturer in Irish and Scottish Literature post-1900 at the University of Glasgow. With Julian Wolfreys, she is the co-author of *The Derrida Wordbook*. Her work is on the interrelation of literature post-1900 and the thinking of modernity, concentrating particularly on continental philosophy and French poststructuralism. She is currently working on a new monograph on Jacques Derrida, James Joyce and the linguistic turn; centred on the recent movement towards ethics and speculative realism, it is entitled *The Linguistic Return*. She has research interests in the areas of modernism and modernity; the literature and culture of the Irish and Scottish modern and contemporary periods, with a focus on James Joyce; and the city of Glasgow.

Des Dillon is an award-winning writer, born in Coatbridge. Studied English Literature. Taught English. Writer-in-Residence at Castlemilk 1998–2000. Poet, short story writer, novelist, dramatist, screenwriter and scriptwriter for stage and radio. Published in the USA, Russia, Sweden, in Catalan, French and Spanish. His novel *Me and Ma Gal* (1995) was included in *The List Guide to the 100 Best Scottish Books of All Time* (2005). Anthologised internationally. His latest award was The Lion and Unicorn Prize for the best of Irish and British literature in the Russian language (2007).

Owen Dudley Edwards, FRSE, FRHists, FSA (Scot.) was born in Dublin in 1938, studied at Belvedere College (for reference to which, see James Joyce's *A Portrait of the Artist as a Young Man*) and University College, Dublin, then at the Johns Hopkins University in Baltimore, Maryland, subsequently teaching in the University of Oregon. He then worked as a journalist for a year in Dublin. He taught in the

University of Aberdeen for two years (1966–68), and since then at the University of Edinburgh whence he retired in 2005 but where he still gives occasional lectures. His subject is History and he has written extensively about Ireland.

Peter Geoghegan is an Irish journalist and writer living in Glasgow. His latest book, *The People's Referendum: Why Scotland Will Never Be the Same Again*, was published in January 2015 by Luath Press.

Pearse Hutchinson (1927–2012) was a Glasgow-born poet. Both parents had Irish connections. He moved to Dublin in 1932, and died there in 2012, after a life of travel and translation. He described himself as 'a man of languages rather than nations', and was well versed in Irish and Catalan. This essay first appeared in Dermot Bolger (ed.), *16 on 16 – Irish Writers on the Easter Rising – Letters from a New Island* (Dublin: Raven *Arts Press, 1988*), pp. 23-25. Vincent Woods holds the copyright for Pearse's work and has kindly granted permission to reproduce this essay.

Shaun Kavanagh was born and raised in Greenock. He graduated from Glasgow Caledonian University in 2010 in History and Politics, and is currently a PhD Student in History at the University of Glasgow, where he works as a graduate teaching assistant. He also works as a Scottish parliamentary researcher, and still holds a season ticket for Greenock Morton FC.

Billy Kay is a writer and broadcaster specialising in Scottish cultural history. His books include *Scots: The Mither Tongue, Knee Deep in Claret* and *The Scottish World*. The latter has a chapter on Scottish/Irish history entitled 'Thistle and Shamrock Entwined'. His radio series include *Odyssey, The Scots of Ulster* and *The Cause: A History of Scottish Nationalism*. He also contributed to the books, *Scotland and Ulster* edited by Ian S Wood and *Varieties of Scottishness*, proceedings of the Cultural Traditions Group conference 1996, edited by John Erskine and Gordon Lucy.

Aaron Kelly is originally from Belfast and teaches at Edinburgh University. He is author of *The Thriller and Northern Ireland* (2005), *Irvine Welsh* (2005), *Twentieth-Century Irish Literature* (2008) and *James Kelman: Politics and Aesthetics* (2013). He has guest edited two special issues of *The Irish Review*: *Contemporary Northern Irish Culture* (2009) and *Cultures of Class* (2013).

Phil Kelly grew up in Belfast and lives there with his wife and daughters. He studied politics at Queen's University Belfast. His working life was spent in shops and retail. He is currently unemployed.

James Kelman's recent fiction includes short story collections *The Good Times, If it is your life* and *A Lean Third*. His novel *How late it was, how* late won the 1994 Booker Prize. Other novels include *Translated Accounts, You Have to be Careful in the Land of the Free, Kieron Smith, Boy*, and *Mo said she was quirky*, which was the Saltire Society Book of the Year for 2012. Kelman is also a dramatist whose work includes *Hardie and Baird and Other Plays*. Some of his essays are available in *And the Judges Said...*

Kirsty Lusk is a doctoral candidate at the University of Glasgow. She received her MPhil in Irish Writing from Trinity College Dublin and holds an MA (Hons) in English Literature from the University of Glasgow. She is currently researching Scottish-Irish connections in the late 19th and early 20th century from a literary perspective in order to explore the legacy of independence, equality and commemoration within a comparative Irish-Scottish framework.

Richard B McCready is a graduate of the University of Dundee and has a PhD for a study of the social and political impact of the Irish in Dundee in the 19th and 20th centuries. He has worked in further and higher education, as well as the House of Commons and the Scottish Parliament. He has also worked promoting co-operatives in the Scottish economy. He is currently an elected member of Dundee City Council. He is an honorary Associate Researcher at the Centre for the Study of Religion and Politics, University of St Andrews.

Kevin McKenna is a columnist for *The Observer* whose work also appears in *The Herald, The Daily Mail, The Times, The National* and the *Scottish Catholic Observer*. He is also a regular contributor to BBC television and radio. He is a former Deputy Editor of *The Herald* and *Scotland on Sunday* and was Sports Editor in Chief of The Scotsman Publications. He does not climb Munros in his spare time.

Willy Maley is Professor of English Literature at the University of Glasgow. Recent work includes two essay collections: *Celtic Connections: Irish-Scottish Relations and the Politics of Culture*, co-edited with Alison O'Malley-Younger (Oxford and Frankfurt am Main: Peter Lang, 2013), and *Romantic Ireland: From Tone to Gonne; Fresh Perspectives on Nineteenth-Century Ireland* (Newcastle: Cambridge Scholars Publishing, 2013), co-edited with Paddy Lyons and John Miller.

Niall O'Gallagher is a Gaelic poet. His first collection, *Beatha Ùr* (2013), was described by critics as 'eloquent', 'erotic' and 'iconoclastic'. A second, *Suain nan Trì Latha*, will be published in 2016. He lives in Glasgow.

Dr Alison O'Malley-Younger is a Senior Lecturer in English at the University of Sunderland. With Professor John Strachan (Bath Spa University), she is co-director of NEICN (The North East Irish Culture Network). She has published in the fields of Contemporary Critical Theory, Irish Cultural History, Women's Writing in Ireland, Advertising and Commodity Culture, Music Hall and Commodity Culture in 19th-century Ireland, Blackwood's Magazine, Celtic Gothic, Irish Literature and Irish Drama (from the 18th century to the present). She has edited and contributed to: *Representing Ireland: Past, Present and Future* (2005) with Frank Beardow; *Essays on Modern Irish Literature* (2007) and *Ireland at War and Peace* (2011), both with John Strachan; *No Country for Old Men: Fresh Perspectives on Irish Literature* (2008), with Paddy Lyons; and *Celtic Connections: Irish-Scottish Relations and the Politics of Culture* (2012), with Willy Maley.

Alan Riach is the Professor of Scottish Literature at Glasgow University and the author of *Hugh MacDiarmid's Epic Poetry* (1991), *The Poetry of Hugh MacDiarmid* (1999), *Representing Scotland in Literature, Popular Culture and Iconography*

(2005) and co-author with Alexander Moffat of both *Arts of Resistance: Poets, Portraits and Landscapes of Modern Scotland* (2009), described by the *Times Literary Supplement* as 'a landmark book' and *Arts of Independence: The Cultural Argument and Why It Matters Most* (2014). His fifth book of poems, *Homecoming* (2009), follows *Clearances* (2001), *First & Last Songs* (1995), *An Open Return* (1991) and *This Folding Map* (1990).

Kevin Rooney originates from Belfast and now lives in London. He is a writer and teacher. He has written on a range of topics including Irish politics, Irish republicanism, education, civil liberties and football. He has contributed to books on a variety of issues including the peace process in the six counties, Education for Mutual Understanding in post-conflict societies and Education for Citizenship in England. He is a civil liberties campaigner and devotes much of his time actively campaigning against the Offensive Behaviour Football and Threatening Communication Act (OBA). He is currently undertaking a part time PhD into the regulation of Celtic and Rangers fans under the OBA. He is co-author with James Heartfield of *Who's Afraid of the Easter Rising? 1916–2016* (Zero Books, 2015). Apart from politics and education the other great passion in his life is Celtic Football Club.

Michael Shaw completed his PhD at the University of Glasgow in 2015. This project examined how the styles and ideas of the late Victorian 'yellow '90s' supported the Scottish national revival at the *fin de siècle*. His current research interests include: Scottish orientalism, Patrick Geddes' education theories, and eugenics in the 1890s. Michael has contributed a chapter on the interaction between national and queer identities in William Sharp's work to Duc Dau and Shale Preston's *Queer Victorian Families: Curious Relations in Literature* (Routledge, 2015). He has also published political journalism in the *Sunday Herald*.

Irvine Welsh is the author of 11 novels and four books of shorter fiction. He currently lives in Chicago.

Endnotes

The shirt that was on Connolly: Sorley MacLean and the Easter Rising

1   This could also be translated as 'tormented, wounded'.

2   The poem's slightly odd descriptions of 'tanks' and 'cavalry' perhaps also point to MacLean's own experience of war creeping into the text here. As Christopher Whyte points out, war service had a 'dramatic effect' on MacLean's work (Whyte, 64). However, reserve cavalry were transported to Dublin during the Rising and some improvised armoured trucks were used by the British. Thanks to Niall Whelehan for help with historical details.

3   See his comments in the 5 February 1916 issue of *Worker's Republic*: 'no agency less potent than the red tide of war on Irish soil will ever be able to enable the Irish race to recover its self-respect... without the slightest trace of irreverence, but in all due humility and awe, we recognise that of us, as of mankind before Calvary, it may truly be said: "Without the shedding of Blood there is no Redemption"' (Connolly, qtd in Foster, 479).

4   See also: ...an fhèile/ Nach do reub an cuan,/ Nach do mhill mìle bliadhna:/ Buaidh a' Ghàidheil buan.

    ...the humanity/ that the sea did not tear,/ that a thousand years did not spoil: the quality of the Gael permanent (MacLean, 280-1).

5   For a recording of MacLean reading 'National Museum of Ireland', see the 1974 film 'Sorley MacLean's Island', produced by Ogam Films, http://ssa.nls.uk/film/3141

6   The chair is a recurring symbol in MacLean's work on Connolly: 'tightly bound to the chair you would be executed in' / 'ceangailte gu dlùth ri cathair air feadh do thìre' (MacLean, 442-3). The seat in which Connolly is executed becomes elevated to the position of a throne or ceremonial chair in 'Àrd-Mhusaeum na h-Éireann' through a connection to the Lia Fail.

7   Similarly, Terry Eagleton has written of an Irish 'time warping' in which '[a]nti-historicist consciousness blends the archaic with the absolutely contemporary, squeezing out the dreary continuum between them' (Eagleton, 278-9).

Who Fears to Speak?

8   *The Daily Record*, 'Millennium Life: How two tribes lit sectarian fire', 22/5/99, p. 37.

9   ATQ Stewart, *The Narrow Ground: Aspects of Ulster, 1609–1969* (London: Faber and Faber, 1977).

10 Graham Walker, *Intimate Strangers: Political and Cultural Interaction between Scotland and Ulster in Modern Times* (Edinburgh: John Donald, 1995).

11 Ronald Kowalski, '"Cry for us, Argentina": Sport and national identity in late twenti-

eth-century Scotland', in *Sport and National Identity in the Post-War World*, edited by Adrian Smith and Dilwyn Porter (London: Routledge, 2004), pp. 69-87.

12   *The Herald*, 15/8/15, p. 3.

13   David Archibald, '"We're just big bullies...": Gregory Burke's *Black Watch*', *The Drouth*, 26 (2012), pp. 8-13.

14   Tom Peterkin in *The Scotsman*, 14/1/2012, 'Scottish independence referendum: Salmond claims links to Irish freedom struggle', http://www.scotsman.com/news/politics/top-stories/scottish-independence-referendum-salmond-claims-links-to-irish-freedom-struggle-1-2055994, accessed 21/8/15.

15   Ewen MacAskill & Ian Cobain, http://www.theguardian.com/uk-news/2014/feb/11/british-forces-century-warfare-end, accessed 12/8/15.

'They will never understand why I am here': The Irony of Connolly's Scottish Connections

16   C Desmond Greaves, *The Life and Times of James Connolly* (London: Lawrence & Wishart, 1961), p. 338. Greaves cites as his source *Voice of Labour*, May 10, 1919, adding: 'This is the earliest account of this conversation, which was subsequently given an entirely different cast.' It was Greaves' opinion that this earliest version was 'perfectly comprehensible' and therefore the most accurate, a view with which I would concur.

17   The only leader within the socialist and labour movement to openly express his support for Connolly at the time of the Rising was John Maclean – but this was as a prisoner in Edinburgh Castle to his captors, following his imprisonment for 'sedition' in April 1916. His daughter, Nan Milton, gave an interesting account of this as told to her by Seamus Reader who had been arrested in May, after the Rising, and also taken to Edinburgh Castle as a prisoner of war where, Reader told her, 'one of the Argyll and Sutherland Highlanders told me that John Maclean had been a prisoner there. Some of the soldiers had admiration for your father and James Connolly'. Nan Milton, *John Maclean* (London: Pluto Press, 1973), p.129. In late May Maclean had been transferred from Edinburgh to Peterhead. A degree of muted sympathy and support amongst pockets of ordinary workers was also confirmed to me by Nan Milton and Harry McCone, Maclean's associate at the time, in personal conversations in the early 1970s. See also Harry McShane, *No Mean Fighter* (London: Pluto Press, 1978), p.117. A similar degree of rank-and-file support is also alluded to in the Fife mining communities; see the recollections of John McArthur in Ian MacDougall, *Militant Miners* (Edinburgh: Polygon, 1981), p. 18. For Seamus Reader see Máirtín S Ó Catháin, *Irish Republicanism in Scotland 1858–1916* (Dublin: Irish Academic Press, 2007).

18   Ray Burnett, 'In the shadow of Calton Hill', in E Bort (ed.), *Commemorating Ireland: History, Politics, Culture* (Dublin: Irish Academic Press, 2004), pp. 133-166, at p. 152.

19   *The Scotsman*, 29 July 1848, quoted in *ibid.*, p. 154.

20   Ray Burnett, *op. cit.*, p 152

21 'Ray Burnett, '*Viva la Gillie More*: Hamish Henderson, Gramsci and subaltern Scotland' in E Bort (ed.), *Anent Hamish* Henderson (Ochtertyre: Grace Notes Publications, 2015), pp. 219-259; For the variant forms of the Jacobite tradition, including its national subaltern, see William Donaldson, *The Jacobite Song, Political Myth and National Identity* (Aberdeen: Aberdeen University Press, 1988), pp. 72-89.

22 See EP Thompson, *William Morris: Romantic to Revolutionary* (New York: Pantheon Books, 1955), pp. 350-357.

23 For the notion of 'britification' as it subsequently developed within the late 20th century left in Scotland, see Ray Burnett, 'When the Finger Points at the Moon', in James D Young (ed.), *Scotland at the Crossroads* (Glasgow: Clydeside Press, 1990), pp. 90-110.

24 For the prevailing Englishness within 'British' political culture see Philip Dodd, 'Englishness and the national culture' and Robert Colls, 'Englishness and the political culture' in Robert Colls and Philip Dodd (eds.), *Englishness, Politics and Culture 1880–1920* (London: Croom Helm, 1986; 2nd ed. 2014), pp. 25-52 and 53-84; Paul Ward, *Red Flag and Union Jack, Englishness, Patriotism and the British Left, 1881–1924* (Woodbridge, Suffolk: Boydell and Brewer, 1998).

25 R Ascal [James Connolly], 'Plain Talk', *The Labour Chronicle* (1 February, 1895), p. 2.

26 James Connolly, *Erin's Hope…. the End and the Means,* in Owen Dudley Edwards and Bernard Ransom (eds.), *James Connolly Selected Political Writings* (London: Jonathan Cape, 1973), pp. 165-191 at pp. 187-8. The *Shan Van Vocht* and the two *Labour Leader* articles were subsequently put together and published as a pamphlet of this name, first published 1897 and in several editions, reprints and collected works at various times since.

27 James Connolly to John C Matheson, 8 Apr 1903, in Donal Nevin (ed.), *Between Comrades, James Connolly Letters and Correspondence, 1889-1916* (Dublin: Gill and Macmillan, 2007), pp. 223-4.

28 John C Matheson to James Connolly, 16 Feb 1908, in *ibid.*, pp. 344-347.

29 *Ibid.*

30 *Ibid.*

31 John C Matheson to James Connolly, 2 Oct 1910, in *ibid.*, pp. 436-42; quotation at p. 438.

32 Ray Burnett, 'Land Raids and the Scottish Left', *Cencrastus* 18 (1984), pp. 2-6.

33 John C Matheson to James Connolly, 11 Dec 1910, in D Nevin, *op. cit.*, pp. 447-9.

34 *The Workers' Republic*, 13 November 1915.

35 *Scottish Review*, 39, 1916.

36 Brian Behan and Kathleen Behan, *Mother of All the Behans: The Story of Kathleen Behan as told to Brian Behan* (London: Hutchinson, 1984), p. 78.

The Behans: Rebels of a Century

37 *Mother of All the Behans*, p. 93.

38 *Mother of All the Behans*, p. 39.

39 After Jack Furlong's death, Kathleen was helped financially by Michael Collins, in whose memory Brendan would later write 'The Laughing Boy'.

40 *Mother of All the Behans*, p. 39.

41 *Mother of All the Behans*, p. 47.

42 Ulick O'Connor, *Brendan Behan* (London: Hamish Hamilton, 1970), p. 25.

43 Dominic Behan, *My Brother Brendan* (London: Leslie Frewin (Publishers) Ltd, 1965), p. 49.

44 *Mother of All the Behans*, pp. 105-106.

45 *Mother of All the Behans*, p. 75.

46 Behan, *My Brother Brendan*, p. 7.

47 O'Connor, *Brendan Behan*, p. 27.

48 *The Letters of Brendan Behan*, edited by EH Mikhail (Montreal and Kingston: McGill-Queen's University Press, 1992), p. 13.

49 Mikhail (ed.), *Letters*, p. 82.

50 Behan, *My Brother Brendan*, p. 130.

51 Behan, *My Brother Brendan*, p. 7.

52 O'Connor, *Brendan Behan*, p. 245.

53 For the history of this volume, see James Kelman's Introduction to Hugh Savage, *Born Up a Close: Memoirs of a Brigton Boy* (Argyll: Argyll Publishing, 2006).

54 In 1958, Henderson and Behan had produced a programme for the BBC with Sean O'Boyle entitled 'The Scots and Irish Balladmakers'. For 'Call Me Comrade', see the digital version of Farquhar McLay (ed.), *Workers City: The Real Glasgow Stands Up* (Glasgow: Clydeside Press, 1988) at http://www.workerscity.org/.

55 *Mother of All the Behans*, p. 43.

56 *Mother of All the Behans*, p. 43.

A Beautiful Thing Wronged

57 Irish who imitate English.

Home Rule, Sinn Féin and the Irish Republican Movement in Greenock

58   I am indebted to Stephen Coyle who provided much of the background of the republican movement in Greenock and Port Glasgow in a talk given to the Inverclyde branch of Cairde na hÉireann in the Ancient Order of Hibernians Hall in Port Glasgow, 2 May 2012, and to Mártín O'Catháin's work *Irish Republicanism in Scotland 1858–1916: Fenians in Exile* (Dublin: Irish Academic Press, 2007)

59   *Greenock Advertiser,* 19 September; 26 September 1865.

60   *Greenock Advertiser,* 26 September 1865.

61   See Elaine W McFarland, 'A Reality and Yet Impalpable: The Fenian Panic in Mid-Victorian Scotland' *Scottish Historical Review,* 77, 204 (1998), pp. 199-223.

62   *Greenock Telegraph,* 29 June 1892.

63   Statement by James Nolan, *Bureau of Military History,* 1913–21, Document No. WS 1,369.

64   *Ibid.*

65   NAS, HH/55/62 (IV), 16-17 October, 1920

66   It is unclear if whether 'Mr McGivern' was actually John McGivern of the John Dillon branch of the Land League mentioned previously. However, the gap in time would make this unlikely.

67   Statement by Witness Maurice J Collins, Document No. WS 550, *Bureau of Military History,* 1913.

68   David Fitzpatrick, 'A curious middle place: The Irish in Britain, 1871–1921' in Roger Swift and Sheridan Gilley, eds., *The Irish in Britain, 1815–1939* (Savage, Maryland: Barnes and Noble, 1989).

69   See Mártín O'Catháin, 'A Winnowing Spirit: Sinn Féin in Scotland, 1905–38', in Martin J Mitchell, ed., *New Perspectives on the Irish in Scotland* (Edinburgh: Birlinn, 2008).

James Connolly's Stations

70   Bruton's speech can be found: http://www.reform.org/site/2014/09/18/reform-group-seminar_18-sep-2014/ Sections are also reported in the *Irish Times* 18 September 2014 as 'Scotland Shows 1916 Rising Was A Mistake': www.irishtimes.com/news/politics/scotland-shows-1916-rising-a-mistake-says-john-bruton-1.1932540

71   Kearney, Richard. 'Myth and Terror', *The Crane Bag* 2.1-2 (1977), pp. 125-39.

72   David Lloyd, *Irish Culture and Colonial Modernity: The Transformation of Oral Space* (Cambridge: Cambridge UP, 2011), 119.

73   TW Adorno, *Negative Dialektik* (Frankfurt: Surkamp Verlag, 1966), p. 311. Our translation.

74   *Socialism Made Easy* in *James Connolly: Selected Writings*, ed. Peter Berresford Ellis (London: Pluto, 1997), pp. 136-7.

75   *Intercontinental Press* (Vol. 3 Jan-April 1965).

76   Margaret Skinnider quoted in *Irish Independent* (21 April 1964).

A Slant on Connolly and the Scotch Ideas

77   *Born up a Close: Memoirs of a Brigton Boy* (Glendaruel: Argyll Publishing, 2007).

78   In 1951–52 he and others resigned the Party alongside McShane. This was some years before the Hungarian revolution.

79   Bruce Glasier's reminiscences of William Morris check out <http://www.archive.org/stream/williammorrisandooglasuoft/williammorrisandooglasuoft_djvu.txt>

80   See the Meek essay cited below, pp. 1, 2.

81   See 'KARL MARX' by Chris Matthew Sciabarra for an introduction, http://www.nyu.edu/projects/sciabarra/essays/ieesmarx.htm. Sciabarra takes this reference directly from a brilliant little essay by Ronald L Meek: *The Scottish Contribution to Marxist Sociology* [reprinted from *Democracy and the Labour Movement*, Lawrence & Wishart 1955].

82   *Labour, Nationality and Religion*, The Harp Library, Dublin 1910.

83   See p. 32 *James Connolly: Selected Writings*, edited by Peter Berresford Ellis.

84   Available generally, published originally in 1910.

85   http://www.gla.ac.uk/services/specialcollections/collectionsa-z/hilladamson/disruptionpicture/

86   See Thomas Brown in his preface to the *Annals of the Disruption* (Edinburgh: MacNiven & Wallace, 1893).

87   For example, the first Scottish branch of the Social Democrat Federation, branches of the Labour Church; the Scottish Land Restoration League; the Scottish Labour Party itself.

88   See p91 Donald E Meek's essay 'Preaching the Land Gospel, The Reverend Donald MacCallum [1849-1929] in Skye, Tiree and Lochs, Lewis' which is in the *Recovering from the Clearances* collection, edited by Ewan A Cameron (The Islands Book Trust, 2013).

89   See pamphlet *The Radical Revolt: A Description of the Glasgow Rising in 1820, the March and Battle of Bonnymuir*: written by Andrew Hardie (secretly) in Prison and Smuggled out (Published by P Walsh, Rutherglen).

90   She was the first translator into English of the philosophical work of Hegel, which 'historians of philosophy have ignored.' For further information on Helen Macfarlane begin from https://en.wikipedia.org/wiki/Helen_Macfarlane#cite_note-7].

91   p. 210 George Buchanan: Glasgow Quartercentenary Studies 1906 [James Maclehose & Sons, Glasgow 1907] see TD Robb's essay, 'Sixteenth-Century Humanism as illustrated by the Life and Work of George Buchanan'. Although the obelisk to

Buchanan's memory is situated in Killearn, he is thought to have 'first saw the light of day' a couple of miles distant, in a cottage 'near the bank of the little winding river Blane,'. See pxi-xii of the Introduction. The cottage was close to the home of Sir Alexander Lawrie, known as The Moss, Dumgoyne; and it is possible Rennie Mackintosh had a hand in an extension to the building. The place was knocked down in the 1960s. Beyond Dumgoyne Hill the road forks left to Aberfoyle and the traveller passes, almost immediately, through the tiny village of Dumgoyne.

92 p. 204.

93 He also tutored both Mary Queen of Scots and her son James VI [1st of the United Kingdom].

94 On Thomas Reid, see http://plato.stanford.edu/entries/reid/ for a good introduction to this major Scottish philosopher. In Germany Immanuel Kant led the challenge; others thought that through Hume the existence of an unknowable God might exist, one utterly remote from humanity.

95 See James Connolly's opening lines of his Foreword.

96 See http://plato.stanford.edu/entries/reid/

97 See http://plato.stanford.edu/entries/goedel/

98 http://www.clerkmaxwellfoundation.org/html/who_was_maxwell-.html

99 See http://www.newble.co.uk/chalmers/biography.html

100 See https://en.wikipedia.org/wiki/Hugh_Miller for an entry into the difficulties faced by such as Hugh Miller.

101 For some idea of his work in this see http://www.newble.co.uk/chalmers/literature.html

102 For a contemporary account of his funeral go to <http://www.newble.co.uk/chalmers/biography.html>

103 See *The Manifesto of the Socialist League* by William Morris <https://www.marxists.org/archive/morris/works/1885/manifst1.htm>

104 Pp. 30-31 for more detail on this in *All for the Cause: Willie Nairn 1856–1902, Stonebreaker Philosopher Marxist*, by Hugh Savage and Les Forster.

105 See p. 11 *All for the Cause: Willie Nairn 1856-1902 Stonebreaker, Philosopher, Marxist written* by Hugh Savage and Les Forster (Glasgow: Clydeside Press, 1993).

106 Organised by David Lowe, see p98 of his *Souvenirs of Scottish Labour* (W & R Holmes, Glasgow 1919).

107 P. 27 *James Larkin: Lion of the Fold*, edited by Donal Nevin (Gill & Macmillan 1998).

Short Skirts, Strong Boots and a Revolver: Scotland and the Women of 1916

108 Countess Constance Markievicz, 'Buy a Revolver' (1915) in *In Their Own Voice: Women and Irish Nationalism (1995)*, ed. Margaret Ward (Cork: Attic Press, 2001),

pp. 51-53

109   Countess Constance Markievicz, 'Buy a Revolver' (1915)

110   Countess Constance Markievicz, 'Buy a Revolver' (1915)

111   Thomas Bartlett, *Ireland: A History* (Cambridge: Cambridge University Press, 2010), p. 388.

112   Margaret Skinnider, *Doing My Bit For Ireland* (New York: Century Press, 1917).

113   Margaret Skinnider, *Doing My Bit For Ireland*

114   Margaret Skinnider, *Doing My Bit For Ireland*

115   'NORA CONNOLLY O'BRIEN', *Glasnevintrust.ie* (2015) http://www.glasnevintrust.ie/visit-glasnevin/interactive-map/nora-connolly-obrien-1/

116   Margaret Skinnider, *Doing My Bit For Ireland* (New York: Century Press, 1917).

117   Nora Connolly O'Brien, interviewed by Uinseaan O'Neill, *Survivors (1980)* (Dublin: Argenta Publications, 1987), pp. 183-215

118   Margaret Ward, 'Introduction' to *In Their Own Voices: Women and Irish Nationalism (1995)*, ed. Margaret Ward (Cork: Attic Press, 2001), pp. 1-2, p.1.

119   Margaret Skinnider, *Doing My Bit For Ireland* (New York: Century Press, 1917).

120   Kathleen Clarke, *Kathleen Clarke: Revolutionary Woman*, ed. Helen Litton (Dublin: O'Brien Press, 1991), p.71

121   Margaret Skinnider, in *Military Service Pensions Collection* at *Military Archives*, http://mspcsearch.militaryarchives.ie/docs/files//PDF_Pensions/RI/IP724MARGARETSKINNIDER/WIP724MARGARETSKINNIDER.pdf

122   Nicola Sturgeon, 'Scottish Women's Convention' (Scottish Parliament: 14 March 2015) http://news.scotland.gov.uk/Speeches-Briefings/Scottish-Women-s-Convention-1744.aspx

123   Nicola Sturgeon, 'Scottish Women's Convention'.

124   Nicola Sturgeon, 'Scottish Women's Convention'.

'Pure James Connolly': From Cowgate to Clydeside

125   Nicola Sturgeon, 'Scottish Women's Convention'.

126   An earlier version of this essay was published as 'James Connolly, Colonialism, and 'Celtic Communism'', in *Perspectives* (Magazine of Scotland's Democratic Left) 28 (Winter 2010–11), pp. 15-18. See also Willy Maley and Niall O'Gallagher, 'Coming Clean about the Red and the Green: Celtic Communism in Maclean, MacDiarmid and MacLean Again', in Willy Maley and Alison O'Malley-Younger (eds.), *Celtic Connections: Irish-Scottish Relations and the Politics of Culture* (Oxford and Frankfurt am Main: Peter Lang, 2013), pp. 133-151.

127   Paul Routledge, *John Hume: A Biography* (London: HarperCollins, 1997), p. 20.

128   Murray Pittock, *Celtic Identity and the British Image* (Manchester: Manchester

University Press, 1999), p. 77.

129   Owen Dudley Edwards, 'Connolly and Irish Tradition', *The Furrow* 30, 7 (1979), p. 411.

130   Edwards, 'Connolly and Irish Tradition', p. 411.

131   Edwards, 'Connolly and Irish Tradition', p. 412.

132   Edwards, 'Connolly and Irish Tradition', p. 424.

133   Joan Smith, 'Labour Tradition in Glasgow and Liverpool', *History Workshop Journal* 17, 1 (1984), p. 37.

134   Cathal O'Shannon, 'Labour Day', *Voice of Labour*, 30 March 1918, cited in Young, 'John Maclean, Socialism and the Easter Rising', p. 30.

135   James Hunter, 'The Gaelic Connection: The Highlands, Ireland and Nationalism, 1873–1922', *The Scottish Historical Review* 54, 158 (1975), p. 198.

136   John Maclean, 'Reflections on Belfast', *Justice* (24 August 1907), p. 4, https://www.marxists.org/archive/maclean/works/1907-belfast.htm

137   James D Young, 'John Maclean, Socialism and the Easter Rising', *Saothar* 16 (1990), p. 26.

138   Alasdair Gray, *Why Scots Should Rule Scotland 1997: A Carnaptious History of Britain from Roman Times until now* (Edinburgh: Canongate, 1997), p. 35.

139   Jonathan Githens-Mazer, 'Ancient Erin, Modern Socialism: Myths, Memories and Symbols of the Irish Nation in the Writings of James Connolly', *Interventions* 10, 1 (2008), p. 98.

140   James Connolly, 'July the 12th', *Forward* (12 July 1913)

      https://www.marxists.org/archive/connolly/1913/07/july12.htm

141   James Connolly, 'Labour and the Proposed Partition of Ireland', *Irish Worker* (14 March 1914), https://www.marxists.org/archive/connolly/1914/03/laborpar.htm

142   'John Maclean, Socialism and the Easter Rising', pp. 26-7.

143   Gavin Foster, "Scotsmen, Stand by Ireland': John Maclean and the Irish Revolution', *History Ireland* 16, 1 (2008), p. 34.

144   Young, 'John Maclean, Socialism and the Easter Rising', p. 31.

145   John Maclean, *The Irish Tragedy: Scotland's Disgrace* (1920), http://www.marxists.org/archive/maclean/works/1920-tit.htm, accessed 17 August 2015.

146   John Maclean, General Election Address, November 1922, http://www.marxists.org/archive/maclean/works/1922-election.htm, accessed 17 August 2015.

147   David Lloyd, 'Rethinking National Marxism: James Connolly and "Celtic Communism"', *Interventions* 5, 3 (2003), p. 351.

148   Christopher Harvie, 'Ballads of a Nation', *History Today* 49, 9 (1999), p. 14.

149   Irvine Welsh, *Bedroom Secrets of the Master Chefs* (London: Jonathan Cape, 2006), pp. 104-5.

150 Irvine Welsh, *If You Liked School, You'll Love Work* (London: Jonathan Cape, 2007), pp. 371-2.

151 Tom Toremans, 'An Interview with Alasdair Gray and James Kelman', *Contemporary Literature* 44, 4 (2003), pp. 576-7.

152 Roxy Harris, 'An Interview with James Kelman', *Wasafiri* 24, 2 (2009), p. 23.

153 For a discussion of James Connolly's army career, about which there is still some doubt and debate, see John Callow, *James Connolly & The Re-Conquest of Ireland* (London: Evans Mitchell Books, 2013), p. 28. I am grateful to Stephen Coyle for this reference.

154 Austen Morgan, *James Connolly: A Political Biography* (Manchester: Manchester University Press, 1988), p. 13.

'Mad, Motiveless and Meaningless'? The Dundee Irish and the Easter Rising

155 National Library of Ireland (NLI), Ms 13,911, James Connolly in Dundee to Lillie Reynolds in Perth, 17 April 1888, James Connolly Papers.

156 John F McCaffrey, 'Roman Catholics in Scotland in the 19th and 20th Centuries' *Records of the Scottish Church History Society*, XXI, (1983), p. 276.

157 Roger Swift (ed.), *Irish Migrants in Britain 1815–1914* (Cork: Cork University Press, 2002).

158 *Dundee Advertiser* 8 May 1908.

159 *Dundee Advertiser* 25 April 1916.

160 *Dundee Advertiser* 28 April 1916.

161 *Dundee Advertiser* 28 April 1916.

162 *Dundee Advertiser* 28 April 1916.

163 *Dundee Advertiser* 1 May 1916.

164 *Dundee Catholic Herald* 29 April 1916.

165 *Dundee Advertiser* 1 May 1916.

166 *Dundee Advertiser* 1 May 1916.

167 *Dundee Advertiser* 2 May 1916.

168 *Dundee Catholic Herald* 13 May 1916.

169 *Dundee Advertiser* 3 May 1916.

170 *Dundee Advertiser* 4 May 1916.

171 *Dundee Advertiser* 2 May 1916.

172 *Dundee Advertiser* 6 May 1916.

173 *Dundee Advertiser* 30 June 1916.

174   MLR Smith, *Fighting for Ireland? The Military Strategy of the Irish Republican Movement* (Routledge, London, 1995), p. 31.

175   Leon Ó Broin, *Michael Collins* (Gill & MacMillan, Dublin, 1980), p. 26.

176   Paul Bew, 'Moderate Nationalism and the Irish Revolution, 1916–1923', *Historical Journal* 42, 3 (1999), p. 73.

177   *Dundee Catholic Herald* 17 June 1916; *Dundee Catholic Herald* 24 June 1916.

178   *Dundee Advertiser* 30 October 1920.

Scotland is my home, but Ireland my country: The Border Crossing Women of 1916

179   Seamus Heaney, 'The Trance and the Translation', *The Guardian* (30 November 2002), http://www.theguardian.com/books/2002/nov/30/featuresreviews.guardianreview20, accessed 27 August 2015.

180   Sean O'Casey, *The Story of the Irish Citizen Army* (Dublin: Maunsel & Co, 1919), p. 56.

181   FX Martin (ed.), *The Irish Volunteers, 1913–15* (Dublin: James Duffy & Co., 1963), p. 72.

182   Most notably Margaret Ward's *Unmanageable Revolutionaries: Women and Irish Nationalism* (London: Pluto Press, 1995), Sinead McCoole's *No Ordinary Women: Irish Female Activists in the Revolutionary Years, 1900–23* (Dublin: The O'Brien Press, 2004), Ruth Taillon's *When History Was Made: The Women of 1916* (Belfast: Beyond the Pale Press, 1996), and Ann Matthews' *Renegades: Irish Republican Women 1900–1922* (Cork: Mercier Press, 2010).

183   Susan Kingsley Kent, *Gender and Power in Britain 1640–1990* (London: Routledge, 1999), p. 263.

184   Ward, *Unmanageable Revolutionaries*, p. 88.

185   Margaret Ward, 'Irish Women and Nationalism', *Irish Studies Review*, 5, 17 (1996/7), p.8

186   Taillon, *When History was Made*, p. xvi. See the excellent review of Taillon's pioneering book by Sally Trueman-Dicken in *Irish Studies Review* 5, 17 (1996/7), pp. 47-49.

187   Anne Marecco, *The Rebel Countess: The Life and Times of Constance Markievicz* (London: Weidenfeld and Nicholson, 1967), p. 2.

188   Marecco, *The Rebel Countess*, p. 2.

189   Sean O'Faoláin, *Constance Markievicz* (London: Cresset Library, 1987), p. 120.

190   Louise Ryan, 'Furies and Die-hards: Women in Irish Republicanism in the Early Twentieth Century', *Gender and History* 11: 2 (1999), pp. 256-275.

191   Diana Norman, *Terrible Beauty: A Life of Constance Markievicz, 1868–1927* (London: Hodder and Stoughton, 1987), p. 13.

192   Joshua Wanhope, 'A Romance of Easter Week in Dublin', a review of Margaret

Skinnider, *Doing my Bit for Ireland* (New York, 1917) in the *New York Call* (1 July 1917), p. 14, cited in Lisa Weihman, '*Doing my Bit for Ireland*: Transgressing Gender in the Easter Rising', Éire-Ireland 39: 3&4 (2004), p. 236.

193 Weihman, '*Doing my Bit for Ireland*: Transgressing Gender in the Easter Rising', p. 238.

194 Sikata Banerjee, *Muscular Nationalism: Gender, Violence and Empire in India and Ireland, 1914–2004* (New York: New York University Press, 2012), p. 90.

195 Margaret Skinnider, *Doing my Bit for Ireland* (New York: The Century Co., 1917), p. 6.

196 Skinnider, *Doing my Bit for Ireland*, p. 3.

197 Skinnider, *Doing my Bit for Ireland*, p. 9.

198 Skinnider, *Doing my Bit for Ireland*, pp. 9-10.

199 Skinnider, *Doing my Bit for Ireland*, p. 63.

200 Skinnider, *Doing my Bit for Ireland*, p. 64.

201 Skinnider, *Doing my Bit for Ireland*, p. 64.

202 Skinnider, *Doing my Bit for Ireland*, p. 20.

203 Cited in Karen Steele, *Women, Press, and Politics During the Irish Revival* (Syracuse: Syracuse University Press, 2007), p. 112.

204 Lauren Arrington, *Revolutionary Lives: Constance and Casimir Markievicz* (Princeton, New Jersey: Princeton University Press, 2016), p. 44.

205 Arrington, *Revolutionary Lives*, p. 44.

206 Arrington, *Revolutionary Lives* p. 232.

207 Arrington, *Revolutionary Lives* p. 231.

208 Cited in Jacqueline Van Voris, *Constance De Markievicz in the Cause of Ireland* (Amherst: University of Massachusetts Press, 1967), p. 303.

209 Willy Maley and Niall O'Gallagher, 'Coming Clean about the Red and the Green: Celtic Communism in Maclean, MacDiarmid and MacLean Again', in Willy Maley and Alison O'Malley-Younger (eds.), *Celtic Connections: Irish-Scottish Relations and the Politics of Culture* (Oxford: Peter Lang, 2012), p. 135.

210 Maley and O'Gallagher, 'Coming Clean about the Red and the Green', p. 148.

To Rise for a Life Worth Having

211 See Scott Lyall, *Hugh MacDiarmid's Poetry and Politics of Place: Imagining a Scottish Republic* (Edinburgh University Press, 2006), pp. 32-33.

212 See Alan Riach's 'WB Yeats and Hugh MacDiarmid: Kingly Cousins' in Emma Dymock and Margery Palmer McCulloch, eds., *Scottish and International Modernisms: Relationships and Reconfigurations* (Glasgow: Association for Scottish Literary Studies, 2011), pp. 87-100, and Patrick Crotty's 'Swordsmen: WB Yeats and Hugh MacDiarmid' in Mackay, Longley and Brearton, eds., *Modern Irish and Scottish*

Poetry (Cambridge University Press, 2011), pp. 20-38. Further work on MacDiarmid's relations with Ireland are in Edwin Morgan's essay, 'Hugh MacDiarmid and James Joyce', in *Crossing the Border* (Manchester: Carcanet, 1990) and in Alan Bold's essay *Hugh MacDiarmid and Ireland* (Edinburgh: Edinburgh College of Art, 1985) and Alan Riach's *Hugh MacDiarmid's Epic Poetry* (Edinburgh: Edinburgh University Press, 1991).

213   JD Fergusson, *Modern Scottish Painting* (1943), edited and introduced by Alexander Moffat and Alan Riach (Edinburgh: Luath Press, 2015), p.75.

214   See Hugh MacDiarmid, *Lucky Poet: A Self-Study in Literature and Political Ideas* (1943), ed. Alan Riach (Manchester: Carcanet, 1994), p.382. MacDiarmid glosses a 'Hjokfinnie body' as 'a buried Finn up again'. It's worth noting that *Lucky Poet* was published in the same year, in the middle of the Second World War, as JD Fergusson's *Modern Scottish Painting* and Sorley MacLean's breakthrough first full volume of poetry in Gaelic, *Dain do Eimhir*, three key texts confirming a regeneration of the arts in Scotland arising from a deep sense of the value of the Celtic world. The previous year, MacDiarmid contributed an essay to *The New Scotland: 17 Chapters on Scottish Reconstruction, Highlands and Industrial* (Glasgow: Civic Press, 1942), collected in MacDiarmid, *Selected Prose*, ed. Alan Riach (Manchester: Carcanet, 1992), pp.150-70, in which he argues for the prospective value of a new generation of Scottish poets, pre-eminently MacLean, and says that 'there is about to be an effervescence of high and varied talent, running through all the departments of Scottish art and affairs [...] as characterised (and constituted) the conditions in Ireland at and after 1916'.

215   See John Purser, *Erik Chisholm, Scottish Modernist 1904–1965: Chasing a Restless Muse* (Woodbridge: Boydell & Brewer, 2009), pp.111-21.

'Let the People Sing': Rebel Songs, the Rising, and Remembrance

216   The song was published in *The Socialist* (May 1903) and can be found online at https://www.marxists.org/archive/connolly/1903/05/rebelsng.htm.

217   *Songs of Freedom by Irish Authors* (Dublin 1907), republished in Owen Dudley Edwards & Bernard Ransom (eds), *James Connolly: Selected Political Writings* (New York 1974), and available online at https://www.marxists.org/archive/connolly/1907/xx/revsong.htm

218   Clair Wills, *Dublin 1916: The Siege of the GPO* (London: Profile Books Ltd, 2010), pp. 138-9.

219   D George Boyce, 'Craig, James, first Viscount Craigavon (1871–1940)', *Oxford Dictionary of National Biography*, Oxford University Press, 2004; online edition, January 2011 [http://www.oxforddnb.com/view/article/32609, accessed 18 Aug 2015]

Before the Rising: Home Rule and the Celtic Revival

220   'The Court', *The Scotsman*, 18 July 1889, p. 4.

221   EW McFarland, *John Ferguson 1836–1906: Irish Issues in Scottish Politics* (East Linton: Tuckwell Press, 2003), p. 211.

222   *Ibid.*

223 For a detailed discussion of the Scottish Land Leagues and their relationship to Ireland's, see Andrew Newby, *Ireland, Radicalism and the Scottish Highlands, c 1870–1912* (Edinburgh: Edinburgh University Press, 2007).

224 *Ibid.*, p. 50.

225 Donald M MacRaild, *Irish Migrants in Modern Britain, 1750–1922* (Houndmills: Macmillan Press Ltd, 1999), p. 146.

226 Sir Reginald Coupland, *Welsh and Scottish Nationalism: A Study* (London: Collins, 1954), p. 303.

227 James Hunter, 'The Gaelic Connection: The Highlands, Ireland and Nationalism, 1873–1922', *The Scottish Historical Review*, 54: 158 (1975), pp. 178-204 (p. 182).

228 *Ibid.*, p. 183.

229 Ruaraidh Erskine, 'Gaelic Confederation', *Guth na Bliadhna*, III (1906), pp. 11-25.

230 PH Pearse, '"Education" in the West of Ireland', *Guth na Bliadhna*, II (1905), pp. 375-380.

231 Richard Ellmann, *Yeats: The Man and the Masks* (London: Penguin, 1988), p. 132.

232 William F Halloran, 'WB Yeats, William Sharp and Fiona Macleod: A Celtic Drama, 1897', *Yeats Annual*, 14 (2001), 159-208 (pp. 187-198).

233 Patrick Geddes, 'Keltic Art', 26 July 1899, p. 8 [Archives and Special Collections, University of Strathclyde: T-GED 5/2/7].

Some other books published by **Luath Press**

Homage to Caledonia
Daniel Gray
ISBN 978-1-906817-16-9 PBK £9.99

Small Nations in a Big World
Michael Keating and Malcolm Harvey
ISBN: 978-1-910021-77-4 PBK £9.99

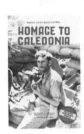

'If I don't go and fight fascism, I'll just have to wait and fight it here.'
JOHN 'PATSY' MCEWAN, DUNDEE

What drove so many ordinary Scots to volunteer for a foreign war? The war in Spain gripped the entire nation, from the men and women who went to serve in the war to the people back home who dug into their limited resources to send huge amounts of aid to the republican army.

Their stories are simply and honestly told, often in their own words: the soldiers who made their own way to Spain over the Pyrenees when the UK government banned anyone from going to support either side; the nurses and ambulance personnel who discovered for themselves the horrors of modern warfare that struck down women and children as well as their men. Yet for every tale of distress and loss, there is a tale of a drunken Scottish volunteer urinating in his general's boots, the dark comedy of learning to shoot with sticks as rifles were so scarce, or lying about their age to get into the training camps.

Small northern European nations have been a major point of reference in the Scottish independence debate. For nationalists, they have been an 'arc of prosperity' while in the aftermath of the financial crash, unionists lampooned the 'arc of insolvency'. Both characterisations are equally misleading. Small nations can do well in the global marketplace, yet they face the world in very different ways. Some accept market logic and take the 'low road' of low wages, low taxes and light regulation, with a correspondingly low level of public services. Others take the 'high road' of social investment, which entails a larger public sector and higher taxes. Such a strategy requires innovative government, flexibility and social partnership.

Keating and Harvey compare the experience of the Nordic and Baltic states and Ireland, which have taken very different roads and ask what lessons can be learnt for Scotland. They conclude that an independent nation is possible but that hard choices would need to be taken.

Details of books published by Luath Press can be found at:
www.luath.co.uk

Luath Press Limited

committed to publishing well written books worth reading

LUATH PRESS takes its name from Robert Burns, whose little collie Luath (*Gael.*, swift or nimble) tripped up Jean Armour at a wedding and gave him the chance to speak to the woman who was to be his wife and the abiding love of his life. Burns called one of the 'Twa Dogs' Luath after Cuchullin's hunting dog in Ossian's *Fingal*.

Luath Press was established in 1981 in the heart of Burns country, and is now based a few steps up the road from Burns' first lodgings on Edinburgh's Royal Mile. Luath offers you distinctive writing with a hint of unexpected pleasures.

Most bookshops in the UK, the US, Canada, Australia, New Zealand and parts of Europe, either carry our books in stock or can order them for you. To order direct from us, please send a £sterling cheque, postal order, international money order or your credit card details (number, address of cardholder and expiry date) to us at the address below. Please add post and packing as follows: UK – £1.00 per delivery address; overseas surface mail – £2.50 per delivery address; overseas airmail – £3.50 for the first book to each delivery address, plus £1.00 for each additional book by airmail to the same address. If your order is a gift, we will happily enclose your card or message at no extra charge.

Luath Press Limited
543/2 Castlehill
The Royal Mile
Edinburgh EH1 2ND
Scotland
Telephone: +44 (0)131 225 4326 (24 hours)
email: sales@luath. co.uk
Website: www. luath.co.uk